AN ILLUSTRATED WORLD
HISTORY

III

REVOLUTION AND EMPIRE

Also available in this series:

REVOLUTION AND EMPIRE
was created and produced by
McRae Publishing Ltd, London
www.mcraepublishing.co.uk

Publishers: Anne McRae, Marco Nardi
Series Editor: Anne McRae
Authors: Neil Morris, Neil Grant, John Malam
Art Director: Marco Nardi
Layouts: Rebecca Milner
Project Editor: Loredana Agosta
Research: Valerie Meek, Claire Moore,
Loredana Agosta
Repro: Litocolor, Florence

DISCLAIMER:

An Illustrated World History has previously been
published in 24 volumes by McRae Books, now
an imprint of McRae Publishing Ltd.

The Publishers of *An Illustrated World History* would like
to thank all the authors and consultants who have
participated in the elaboration of the text and the
supervision of the illustrations created for this work.

Chapter I - **Settling the Americas**
Author: NEIL MORRIS
Consultant: DR. RONALD H. FRITZE, Dean of Arts
and Sciences and Professor of History, Athens
State University, Alabama.

Chapter II - **Asian and African Empires**
Authors: NEIL MORRIS
Consultant: DR. GREGORY POSSEHL, Professor
of Archeology, Department of Anthropology,
University of Pennsylvania, and Curator of the
Asian Section, University of Pennsylvania
Museum of Archeology and Anthropology.

Chapter III - **The Industrial Revolution**
Author: NEIL MORRIS
Consultant: PAT HUDSON, Professor of History,
Cardiff University.

Chapter IV - **Enlightenment and Revolution**
Author: NEIL GRANT
Consultant: DR. RONALD H. FRITZE, Dean of Arts
and Sciences and Professor of History, Athens
State University, Alabama.

Chapter V - **Voyages of Discovery**
Author: NEIL MORRIS
Consultant: DR. JOSEPH BERGIN, DR. JOSEPH
BERGIN, Professor of Modern History at
Manchester University, Fellow of the British
Academy.

Chapter VI - **The Age of Empire**
Author: ANNE MCRAE
Consultant: BARBARA JEAN BUSH, Professor of
Imperial History at University of Sheffield
Hallam, Sheffield.

An Imprint of Sterling Publishing
387 Park Avenue South
New York, NY 10016

ISBN 978-1-4351-5437-7

Manufactured in Hong Kong
Lot #:
2 4 6 8 10 9 7 5 3 1
02/14

AN ILLUSTRATED WORLD
HISTORY

REVOLUTION
EMPIRE

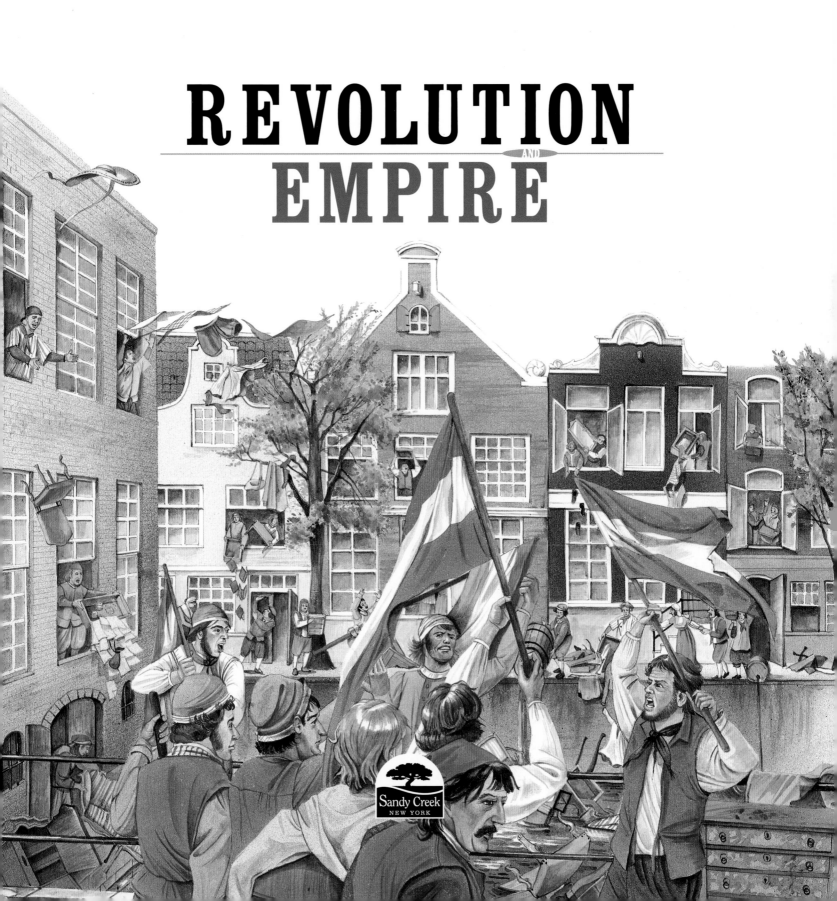

Sandy Creek
NEW YORK

Contents

Following the great voyages of exploration made by Columbus and others, Europeans sailed across the Atlantic to colonize the two American continents that the explorers had discovered. They found that this "New World" offered many treasures, from silver and brazilwood in the south, to valuable furs in the north.

The Spanish dominated Central and South America and by the 18th century they had established four viceroyalties. The Portuguese took coastal Brazil and quickly expanded inland. In the north, the British and French vied for control of Canada. The thirteen British colonies of North America came together, created a constitution, and by 1783 had won a revolutionary war to gain full independence. This chapter tells the story of European settlement in the Americas, from the beginning of the 16th to the end of the 18th century. During that time many of the colonies became self-governing provinces of their mother country, while the United States became a separate nation.

A European portrait of the Native American princess Pocahontas, who sailed from Virginia to England in 1616.

Native American slaves working on a Spanish sugar plantation in Latin America.

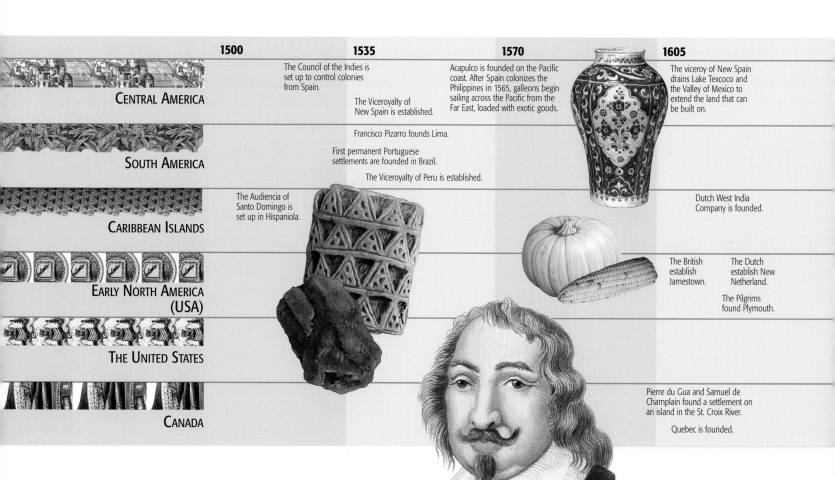

	1500	**1535**	**1570**	**1605**
CENTRAL AMERICA		The Council of the Indies is set up to control colonies from Spain.	Acapulco is founded on the Pacific coast. After Spain colonizes the Philippines in 1565, galleons begin sailing across the Pacific from the Far East, loaded with exotic goods.	The viceroy of New Spain drains Lake Texcoco and the Valley of Mexico to extend the land that can be built on.
		The Viceroyalty of New Spain is established.		
SOUTH AMERICA		Francisco Pizarro founds Lima.		
		First permanent Portuguese settlements are founded in Brazil.		
		The Viceroyalty of Peru is established.		
CARIBBEAN ISLANDS	The Audiencia of Santo Domingo is set up in Hispaniola.			Dutch West India Company is founded.
EARLY NORTH AMERICA (USA)				The British establish Jamestown. / The Dutch establish New Netherland. / The Pilgrims found Plymouth.
THE UNITED STATES				
CANADA				Pierre du Gua and Samuel de Champlain found a settlement on an island in the St. Croix River. Quebec is founded.

Settling the Americas

The Sanctuary of Bom Jesus in Congonhas, Brazil, was built in the colonial Baroque style in the 18th century. The church was designed by Aleijadinho (see page 36).

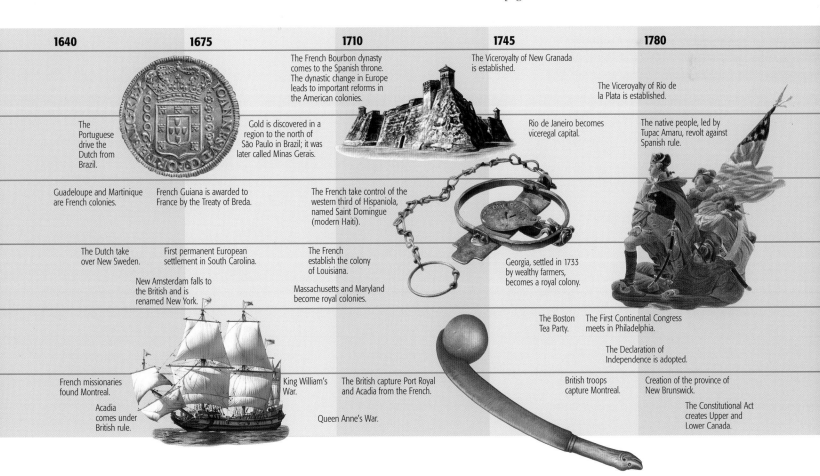

1640	1675	1710	1745	1780

The French Bourbon dynasty comes to the Spanish throne. The dynastic change in Europe leads to important reforms in the American colonies.

The Viceroyalty of New Granada is established.

The Viceroyalty of Rio de la Plata is established.

The Portuguese drive the Dutch from Brazil.

Gold is discovered in a region to the north of São Paulo in Brazil; it was later called Minas Gerais.

Rio de Janeiro becomes viceregal capital.

The native people, led by Tupac Amaru, revolt against Spanish rule.

Guadeloupe and Martinique are French colonies.

French Guiana is awarded to France by the Treaty of Breda.

The French take control of the western third of Hispaniola, named Saint Domingue (modern Haiti).

The Dutch take over New Sweden.

First permanent European settlement in South Carolina.

The French establish the colony of Louisiana.

Georgia, settled in 1733 by wealthy farmers, becomes a royal colony.

New Amsterdam falls to the British and is renamed New York.

Massachusetts and Maryland become royal colonies.

The Boston Tea Party.

The First Continental Congress meets in Philadelphia.

The Declaration of Independence is adopted.

French missionaries found Montreal.

King William's War.

The British capture Port Royal and Acadia from the French.

British troops capture Montreal.

Creation of the province of New Brunswick.

Acadia comes under British rule.

Queen Anne's War.

The Constitutional Act creates Upper and Lower Canada.

Colonization

European colonists sailed to the Americas for a variety of reasons. Once there, they reacted and developed in different ways, according to local conditions and the cooperation or opposition they encountered from the local peoples. Colonization was devastating for native peoples, many of whom died of diseases carried by the Europeans. The newcomers set up forms of government and trade that benefited themselves and their European homelands.

Left: This vase shows the three peoples of colonial Latin America—Native Americans, Europeans, and Africans.

European Powers

The major European powers—Spain, Portugal, England, France, and the Netherlands—saw the Americas as an opportunity to maintain or even increase their individual share of growing world trade. There was inevitably great rivalry between ambitious merchants and colonists on the American continents, as they fought for control over goods and trade routes. This reflected the political and religious struggles that were going on between the nations in Europe.

Above: Like many other European monarchs, George III of Great Britain and Ireland (reigned 1760–1820), encouraged tough policies toward the American colonies.

Native Peoples

The Spanish conquest of Central and South America destroyed the native cultures, including the magnificent Aztec and Inca civilizations. The colonists who followed the conquerors ruled by a system of forced labor. The situation was different in North America, where smaller tribes of Native Americans had to learn quickly to adapt to the ways of the new settlers. Some fought each other as well as the European invaders, as their lands disappeared and their ways of life changed.

Right: A Spanish colonial portrait of Manco Cupac, the legendary first Inca emperor. Descendants of the Inca in Peru were forced to work for Spanish colonists.

In Search of Freedom

People emigrated to the American colonies for many different reasons. Some, such as the Puritan Pilgrims, went in search of religious freedom. European merchants were more interested in the economic benefits of trade, and many did not stay in the colonies for long. They needed workers, some of whom were happy to accept free passage for the prospect of a new life.

Growing Colonies

Throughout the Americas, local conditions shaped the way in which colonies developed and European colonists adapted to their new way of life there. Climate, geography, and natural resources varied enormously between the tropics of Central America and South America and the colder regions of the northern British colonies and Canada. European settlers had to adapt quickly to these local conditions in order to survive.

Left: This is how Plymouth colony looked seven years after it was founded in 1620 (see page 23).

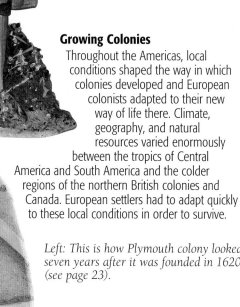

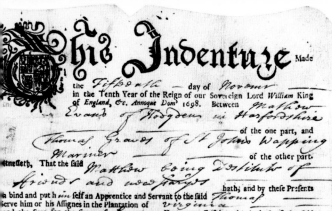

Left: This 1698 certificate of indenture promises free passage and maintenance to a 15-year-old Englishman in return for four years' work and servitude on a Virginia plantation.

Below: Pennsylvania Quakers. Many left Europe to avoid religious persecution.

The Mayflower Compact

Colonists decided on their own forms of government. In 1620, before coming ashore on the American coast, the Pilgrims aboard the Mayflower drew up and signed an agreement. They decided to join together as a "civil body politic" and obey the laws to be drawn up for their colony by those chosen by common consent.

Below: Forty-one men signed the Mayflower Compact off Cape Cod on November 11, 1620.

The Spanish in North and Central America

A 1649 map of the Spanish walled city of Santo Domingo, on the coast of Hispaniola.

Spanish colonial territories in the Americas grew during the 15-year rule of the first viceroy of New Spain. This expansion led to the successful exploitation of the gold and silver that the Spanish had been so keen to find. The colonies were run under a system called *encomienda*, by which the Spanish crown granted colonists the right to demand tribute in gold or labor from native inhabitants. At the same time colonists were responsible for protecting native peoples and instructing them in Christianity, though many did not take this responsibility seriously.

Portrait of Antonio de Mendoza (c.1490–1552), first viceroy of New Spain and third viceroy of Peru.

Pacific Trade

Acapulco was founded on a deep natural harbor on the Pacific coast of New Spain in 1550. After Spain colonized the Philippines in 1565, so-called Manila galleons began sailing across the Pacific from the Far East, loaded with Chinese silk, porcelain, precious stones, and other exotic goods. The ships unloaded at Acapulco, and goods were taken overland to the Gulf of Mexico for further shipment to Europe. The Manila galleons loaded up with Mexican silver for the return voyage.

This enameled earthenware jar from Mexico shows a Chinese influence.

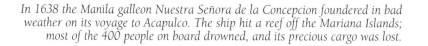

In 1638 the Manila galleon Nuestra Señora de la Concepcion foundered in bad weather on its voyage to Acapulco. The ship hit a reef off the Mariana Islands; most of the 400 people on board drowned, and its precious cargo was lost.

Treasure Fleets

From the 1560s, fleets of galleons sailed from Spain to the American colonies. They loaded up with gold, silver, copper, tobacco, and other precious goods, before leaving the Mexican port of Veracruz for the return voyage across the Atlantic, protected by warships. They often faced terrible storms, as well as danger from pirates, and many ships were lost.

Spanish Colonial Government

Each of the Spanish viceroyalties, or colonial provinces, was run on behalf of the king of Spain by a viceroy. This senior official acted as governor, supervisor of the colonial treasury, captain-general of the military, and vice-patron of the Church. The viceroy was also president of the audiencias, regional courts and administrative centers. As a third tier of the hierarchy, each region had a number of local parishes and mayors.

The Council of the Indies

The Council of the Indies, which was resident in Spain, was made up of six to ten councillors appointed by the king. The Council ran the American viceroyalties on behalf of the monarch, preparing and issuing all laws relating to the colonies, approving expenditure by officials, and acting as an appeal court. Among the councillors were lawyers, clergymen, geographers, mathematicians, and secretaries.

This illustration of San José del Cabo, on the Pacific coast of Baja California, Mexico, dates from 1762. A Spanish galleon is seen arriving from the Philippines.

THE VICEROYALTY OF NEW SPAIN C. 1650

- Audiencia of Santo Domingo, 1511
- Audiencia of Mexico, 1529
- Audiencia of Guatemala, 1544
- Audiencia of Nueva Galicia, 1549

ATLANTIC OCEAN

Gulf of Mexico

GUADALAJARA

MEXICO

SANTO DOMINGO

Caribbean Sea

GUATEMALA

PACIFIC OCEAN

New Spain and its Regions

The Viceroyalty of New Spain was divided into four audiencias (judicial districts), shown on the map with their founding dates and capitals. The courts of the audiencias had authority to hear complaints against captains general or even the viceroy. They were also supposed to safeguard the rights of local native people, setting aside two days a week to hear cases involving locals.

The Spanish in South America

Portrait of Diego de Almagro (1475–1538).

The early colonial period in South America was complicated by disagreements between the conquistadors. Ten years after the Spaniards occupied the former Inca capital of Cuzco, the viceroyalty of Peru was established as the second such colony in the Americas. Disputes continued, and the first viceroy, Blasco Núñez Vela, was killed in battle by supporters of Gonzalo Pizarro, brother of Francisco. By 1600 the region had seen 14 viceroys, but by that time Peru was considered the most valuable Spanish possession in the Americas.

SOUTH AMERICA

1535
Francisco Pizarro founds Lima.

1536
Unsuccessful Native American rebellion led by Manco Capac.

1539
La Plata (modern Sucre, in Bolivia) is founded on the site of a Charcas Native American village.

1543
The Viceroyalty of Peru is established.

1568
A Spanish mint (for silver coins) is established in Lima.

1569–81
Francisco de Toledo is one of the most able viceroys of Peru.

1578
The port of Callao, near Lima, is pillaged by Sir Francis Drake.

From Conquistadors to Rulers

The Spanish conquistador Diego de Almagro had helped Francisco Pizarro conquer the Inca empire, and the two friends became joint captains general in the new colony. After they fell out over the running of the city of Cuzco, Pizarro's forces won the day and executed Almagro. In 1541, Pizarro was killed by followers of Almagro's son, who was then defeated in battle by soldiers of the Spanish king. Two years later, the first official viceroy took office.

This silver-gilt enameled monstrance (a container for the consecrated Host) was made in 1646 by a Spanish craftsman in Lima.

The silver mine was dug into Cerro Rico ("rich hill"), above Potosí.

Silver City

The discovery of silver in the Andes Mountains of present-day Bolivia in 1545 led to the foundation of the city of Potosí. Large-scale excavation began at a mine near the city, which lay to the southwest of La Plata. Silver bullion was soon being sent to Spain, and people flocked to Potosí. By 1650 the population of the city, which lies at 13,000 feet (3,976 m) above sea level, had reached about 160,000.

Lima

The city of Lima was founded in 1535 by Francisco Pizarro. It was built on the banks of the Rio Rimac, just 8 miles (13 km) inland from the Pacific coast. Two years later Pizarro established the port of Callao on the coast, and the port and city formed a major distribution point for gold and silver. Lima became a focal point for Spanish expansion, and by the 17th century it was the center of Spanish government in South America. It is the capital and largest city of modern Peru.

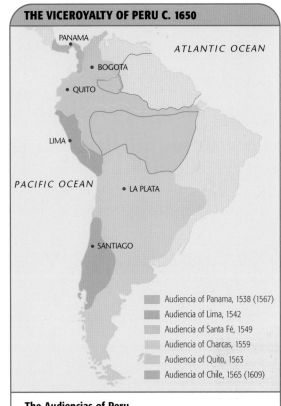

THE VICEROYALTY OF PERU C. 1650

PANAMA

ATLANTIC OCEAN

• BOGOTA

• QUITO

LIMA •

PACIFIC OCEAN

• LA PLATA

• SANTIAGO

■	Audiencia of Panama, 1538 (1567)
■	Audiencia of Lima, 1542
■	Audiencia of Santa Fé, 1549
■	Audiencia of Charcas, 1559
■	Audiencia of Quito, 1563
■	Audiencia of Chile, 1565 (1609)

The Audiencias of Peru

The Viceroyalty of Peru was divided into six audiencias, shown on the map with their founding dates and capitals. The territory bordered New Spain to the northwest of the Panamá region and to the northeast of Santa Fé. From 1559 the huge territory of Charcas covered modern Bolivia and included parts of present-day Argentina, Chile, Peru, and Paraguay.

Native American workers and llamas carried silver-rich ore down from the mine to the growing city of Potosí.

Slaving Expeditions

From the 1620s, colonial entrepreneurs began organizing slave-hunting expeditions into the Brazilian interior. The journeys were undertaken by adventurers called *bandeirantes*, who raided native villages and Jesuit missions. Most *bandeirantes* were from the São Paulo region, and many were part Native American. In one early expedition, a group raided 21 villages and captured about 2,500 slaves.

Bandeirantes cut their way through the rainforest, with slaves literally in tow.

The Captaincy System

In 1533, a year after the first colonies had been established by the Portuguese admiral Martim Afonso de Sousa, King João III divided the Brazilian coastline into 15 parallel strips. These strips of land, some of which were larger than Portugal itself, were hereditary fiefs known as captaincies. They were granted to individuals, who were allowed to develop their land economically, to charge taxes to colonists, and to enslave native people. The captaincy system lasted for more than 200 years.

Portrait of Martim Afonso de Sousa (c.1500–64).

The Portuguese in Brazil

The Portuguese settlement of Brazil was based on trade and commercial interests (see pages 20–21). Settlers exploited the colony's brazilwood, then grew sugar cane and mined the gold and diamonds that were plentiful in the region. The coastal area was divided by the Portuguese king into captaincies, where individuals were encouraged to use their entrepreneurial skills to exploit the natural resources—including the native population—to the full. Slave-hunters led the drive to explore and conquer the interior of Brazil.

Expanding Boundaries

São Paulo bandeirantes *headed north toward the Amazon River, west into present-day Paraguay, and south toward the Plate River. In the process they expanded the boundaries of the Portuguese colony. Jesuit missionaries protested, but were forced to move ahead of the slave hunters. The map shows the expansion of Portuguese territory.*

- Portuguese lands by 1600
- Portuguese lands by 1750
- Portuguese frontier lands
- Gold
- Diamonds
- → Slaving expeditions

THE EXPANSION OF BRAZIL

ATLANTIC OCEAN

- MANAUS
- BAHIA
- RIO DE JANEIRO
- SAO VICENTE
- SAO PAULO

Mining for Gold

In 1690 *bandeirantes* discovered gold to the north of São Paulo, in a region that was later called Minas Gerais ("general mines"). The discovery led to an enormous gold rush, as more people emigrated from Portugal and existing colonists swarmed down from the northeast of Brazil. Most prospectors used slaves to pan for gold in streams; pits and excavations were less common. In 1729 diamonds were also discovered in the region, adding to its importance.

These gold coins were minted at Minas Gerais in 1726.

Peoples of Brazil

From about 1550, the owners of sugar plantations began to use more black slave labor imported from Africa. They replaced native slave workers on many large estates. A mixture of Europeans, Native Americans, and Africans made up the Brazilian population, and many children were born to a combination of the three groups. In the 18th century, foreign minister Marques de Pombal (1699–1782), encouraged the social mingling of native peoples and Portuguese.

Above: A Portuguese nobleman is carried in luxury, illustrating the master-servant relationship.

BRAZIL

1532
First permanent Portuguese settlements are founded in Brazil.

1554
São Paulo is founded by Portuguese Jesuit priests.

1580–1640
Portugal is under Spanish rule.

1660
Amazonian settlement of Manaus is founded.

1700
A royal despatch denounces the barbarous treatment of slaves.

1709
Minas Gerais becomes a separate captaincy.

1759
Jesuits are expelled from Portugal and Brazil.

1763
Rio de Janeiro becomes viceregal capital.

This astronomical compendium, made by the English instrument-maker Humphrey Cole in 1569, included a sundial and an engraved list of latitudes. It may have belonged to Drake.

Buccaneers

The term buccaneer comes from the French *boucan*, a grill for smoking dried meat for sailors to eat at sea. The first buccaneers were a group of French outlaws in Hispaniola who began raiding passing ships in the early 17th century. They were later joined by English and Dutch sea adventurers, who terrorized Spanish ships from bases in Tortuga and Jamaica.

Anne Bonny and Mary Read dressed as men to sail as pirates with Jack Rackham.

Blackbeard's larger ship tries to chase down a sloop. Queen Anne's Revenge captured 18 ships in 7 months.

The Age of Piracy

Large treasure fleets regularly left Cartagena and other ports along the Spanish Main (the Central and South American coast of the Caribbean Sea). Along with less protected Spanish galleons and the ports themselves, the ships were vulnerable to attack by pirates. Many of these sea adventurers operated outside any law, while others were privateers, authorized by their monarch to attack ships of an enemy country. Gold and silver from the Spanish colonies formed their greatest prize.

The Golden Age

The period from about 1690 to 1730 has been called the "golden age" of piracy. As well as terrorizing the Spanish Main, pirates set up in the Bahamas to attack the Atlantic seaboard. Among the causes for this dramatic increase in piracy were the large number of seamen who were unemployed or very poorly paid for their work. Naval action, especially by the British royal fleet, finally put an end to the period.

Portrait of Christopher Myngs by Sir Peter Lely (1618–80).

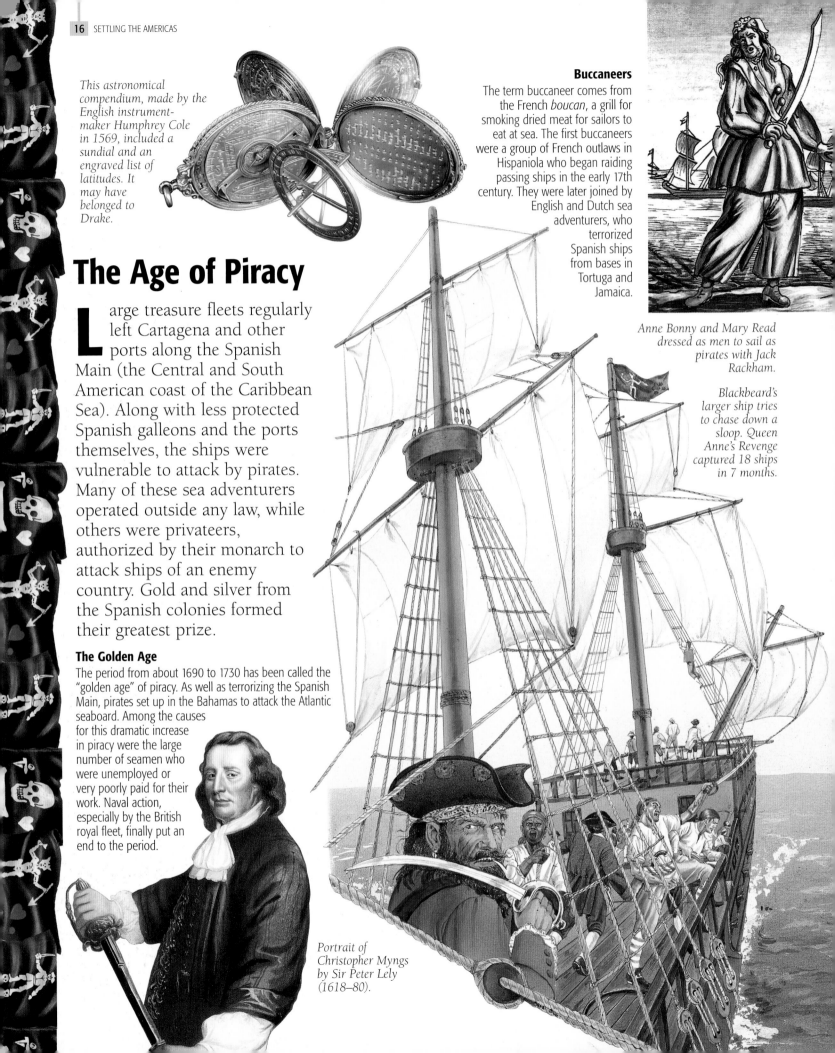

Flintlock pistols were popular pirate weapons.

The Pirate Ship

Though pirates such as Blackbeard and Bartholomew Roberts liked to sail in big, well-armed ships, most preferred smaller craft. One of the most popular pirate ships was the sloop, which normally had a mainsail and a foresail and could carry up to 75 men. It was a highly maneuvrable craft with a shallow draught, which made it easy to sail and hide in creeks and lagoons.

The Queen's Sea Dogs

Seeing Catholic Spain as an enemy, Elizabeth I of England (reigned 1558–1603) gave Protestant Dutch privateers safe harbour. She then encouraged English captains, who were sometimes known as "sea rovers" or "sea dogs," to raid Spanish ships. The queen sponsored her privateers, who were given licences called "letters of marque," and she shared in their spoils.

Blackbeard

Blackbeard was the nickname of Edward Teach, an English seaman who sailed first as a privateer. In 1717 he captured a French transport ship, which he armed with 40 guns and renamed *Queen Anne's Revenge*. Blackbeard terrorized the Virginia and Carolina coasts of North America, until he was killed by a lieutenant of the Royal Navy. Divers discovered the remains of his ship off the coast of North Carolina in 1996.

Above: Early 19th-century painting of an English captain capturing a French privateer.

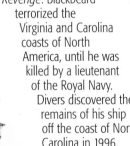

Blackbeard's pirate flag, or Jolly Roger, showed a horned skeleton holding an hourglass.

Bartholomew Roberts' flag. ABH stood for "A Barbadian's Head" and AMH for "A Martiniquan's Head" (both Caribbean islanders).

Stede Bonnet's flag had a dagger and heart flanking a skull and bone.

The British, Dutch, and French in Latin America

In addition to Portugal, other European nations were not happy simply to allow Spain to dominate the Central and South American region. British and French privateers began carrying out raids on parts of the Spanish-controled West Indies in the 16th century. Both countries then founded colonies on the small Lesser Antilles islands. They were followed by the Dutch. The three nations tried to keep their colonies from trading with other countries. This and the wish for territory led to disagreements between all the major European powers.

This stamp was used with red ocher pigment to make tattoos by native people of the Caribbean islands before the arrival of the Europeans.

Dutch naturalists were amazed at the animals and plants they found in Brazil, including the anteater.

The Dutch in the Caribbean
The Dutch occupied a group of small islands off the Caribbean coast of the Spanish viceroyalty of Peru (modern Venezuela). In 1643 they settled Curaçao, which had been first visited by the Spanish more than 140 years earlier, and made it a trading island for the region. In the following century, Curaçao became the center of the Caribbean slave trade. It was later part of the Netherlands Antilles, which included Bonaire and Aruba.

The British
Beginning in the 1620s, the British claimed many islands of the Lesser Antilles. Early possessions included Saint Kitts, Barbados, Nevis, Antigua, Montserrat, and Jamaica. Later in the century, slaves were brought from Africa to work on sugar plantations, but the owners often returned to Britain once they had made their fortune. The British also founded settlements on the Caribbean coast of Belize, where they found and cut logwood trees to produce useful dyes.

The French
The French had tried to establish a settlement at Rio de Janeiro in the mid-16th century, but were driven out by the Portuguese. They were more successful further north, and they drove the Dutch out of what became French Guiana in 1667. By then the islands of Guadeloupe and Martinique had passed to the French crown. All three territories remain departments of France to this day. Toward the end of the 17th century the French gained the western part of Hispaniola and began taking African slaves there to work on coffee plantations.

An 18th-century painting of a West Indian Creole woman with her African servant.

BRITISH, DUTCH, AND FRENCH PRESENCE IN THE REGION

Caribbean Sea

	British by 1655
	British by 1750
	Dutch by 1655
	Dutch by 1750
	French by 1655
	French by 1750

ATLANTIC OCEAN

SOUTH AMERICA

The Three Powers' Control and Settlement
The map shows the extent of British, Dutch, and French settlement throughout the region of coastal South America, the larger Caribbean islands of the Greater Antilles, and the much smaller islands of the Lesser Antilles. The total land areas settled were very small compared with the enormous Spanish colonies and Portuguese Brazil, but they gave the three other powers a colonial foothold in the region.

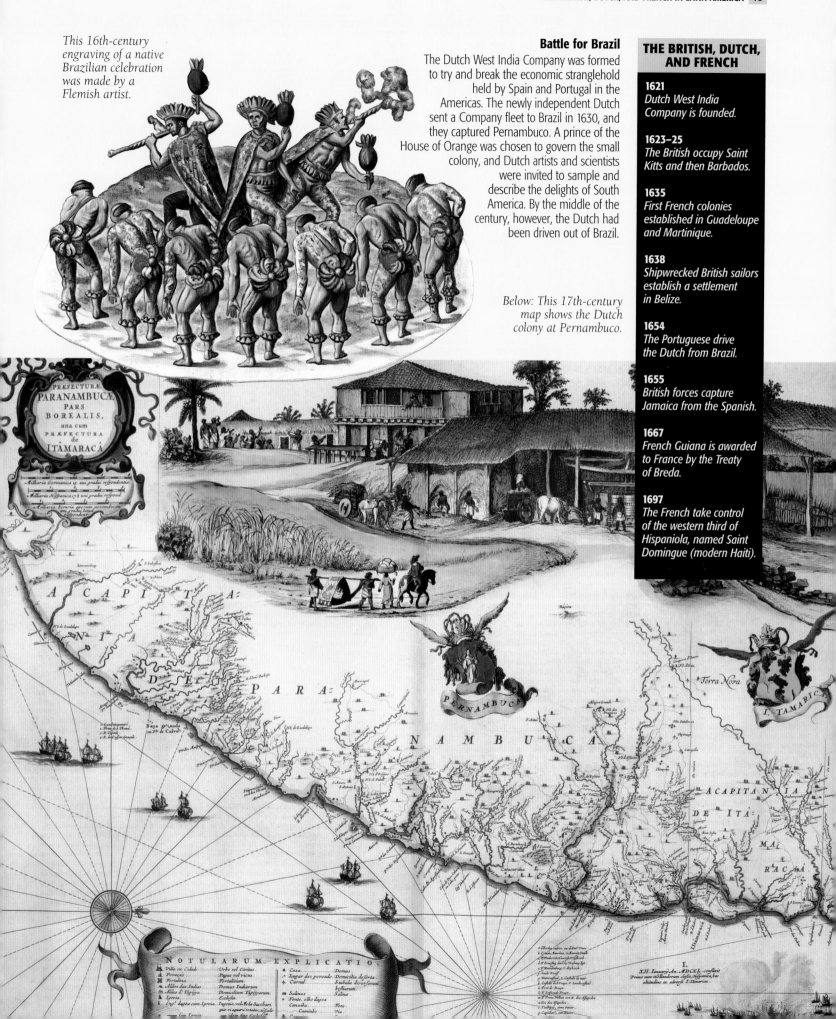

This 16th-century engraving of a native Brazilian celebration was made by a Flemish artist.

Battle for Brazil

The Dutch West India Company was formed to try and break the economic stranglehold held by Spain and Portugal in the Americas. The newly independent Dutch sent a Company fleet to Brazil in 1630, and they captured Pernambuco. A prince of the House of Orange was chosen to govern the small colony, and Dutch artists and scientists were invited to sample and describe the delights of South America. By the middle of the century, however, the Dutch had been driven out of Brazil.

Below: This 17th-century map shows the Dutch colony at Pernambuco.

THE BRITISH, DUTCH, AND FRENCH

1621
Dutch West India Company is founded.

1623–25
The British occupy Saint Kitts and then Barbados.

1635
First French colonies established in Guadeloupe and Martinique.

1638
Shipwrecked British sailors establish a settlement in Belize.

1654
The Portuguese drive the Dutch from Brazil.

1655
British forces capture Jamaica from the Spanish.

1667
French Guiana is awarded to France by the Treaty of Breda.

1697
The French take control of the western third of Hispaniola, named Saint Domingue (modern Haiti).

Trade and Industry

Transatlantic trade was based on produce from the Americas, manufactured goods from Europe, and slaves from Africa. The American produce began with brazilwood and sugar, to which were added tobacco and furs from the north. Along with imported slaves, Native Americans provided the labor in many colonial industries. In the fur trade (see page 27), Europeans found it useful to make alliances with native tribes. The colonists were constantly on the lookout for new opportunities, such as coffee, which was introduced to Brazil in the early 18th century.

Cattle were used as draft animals as well as for milk, meat, and leather.

Brazilwood and Cattle

The attraction of brazilwood (also known as dyewood) to the colonists was that the core of this tropical hardwood gave a red pigment that was found to be ideal for dyeing cloth. This was very useful to the European textile industry, and the Portuguese colony was eventually named after its vital resource and first export. During the 1530s cattle were introduced to the colony to meet the demand for meat. As cattlemen needed more land for grazing, they moved to the interior of the region.

Leaves and flowers of the brazilwood tree.

Sugar Cane

Sugar cane was not native to the Americas, but it quickly became a most important resource. The Portuguese had experience of growing it on their Atlantic islands, and cane was first planted in Brazil around 1516. Soon large plantations were producing quantities of a substance that gradually replaced honey as a sweetener in European food. Around the middle of the 17th century the focus of sugar production and export shifted to the Caribbean islands.

Below: In the early days sugar cane was harvested by Native American workers. They were later replaced by slaves brought for the purpose from Africa.

1 The harvested cane stalks were taken to a mill, where they were crushed and produced a sugary juice.

2 The juice was treated with lime and then boiled in kettles over a brick furnace.

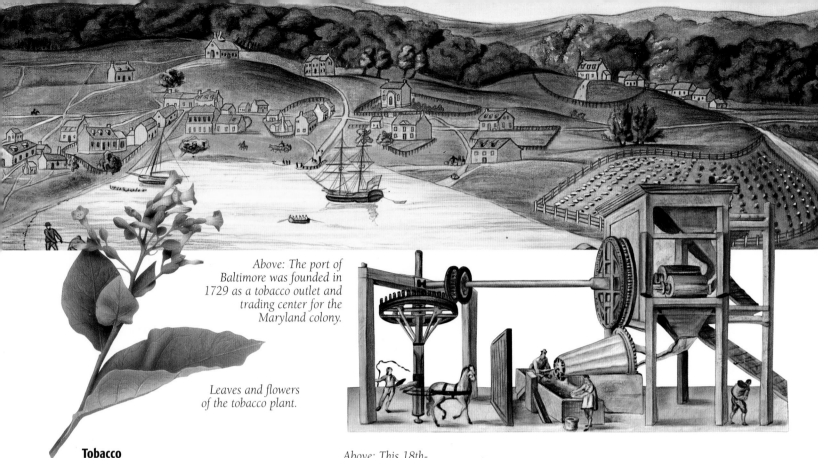

Above: The port of Baltimore was founded in 1729 as a tobacco outlet and trading center for the Maryland colony.

Leaves and flowers of the tobacco plant.

Tobacco

Native Americans had long been smoking dried leaves from the tobacco plant when the Europeans arrived. Colonists were cultivating tobacco in Hispaniola by 1531, in Brazil by 1600 (by which time it had been exported and introduced throughout Europe), and in Virginia by 1612. Demand for tobacco quickly grew in Europe, where it was exchanged for manufactured goods.

Above: This 18th-century engraving shows dried tobacco leaves being sieved by machine at the Royal Tobacco Factory in Mexico.

3 The boiled juice was then skimmed with long-handled dippers as it crystallized and produced sugar.

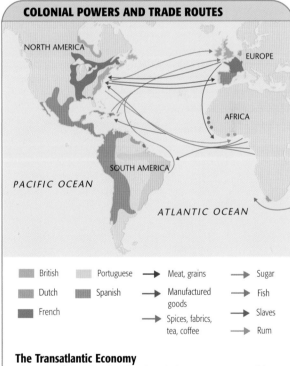

COLONIAL POWERS AND TRADE ROUTES

NORTH AMERICA

EUROPE

AFRICA

SOUTH AMERICA

PACIFIC OCEAN

ATLANTIC OCEAN

■ British	■ Portuguese	→ Meat, grains
■ Dutch	■ Spanish	→ Manufactured goods
■ French		→ Spices, fabrics, tea, coffee
→ Sugar	→ Fish	→ Slaves
→ Rum		

The Transatlantic Economy

The map shows the triangle of trade between Europe, Africa, and the Americas in the mid-18th century. Spain, Portugal, and the other colonial powers were driven by a firm belief that all trade generated wealth, which meant it had to be encouraged and protected to the full. They also believed that the colonies existed only to benefit the mother country, so exploitation was seen in a positive light.

The British in North America

The first British colony in North America, established on Roanoke Island in the 1580s, was doomed to fail. It was not until twenty years later that the British succeeded in establishing their first permanent colony. Life in this and successive settlements was hard, but the Puritan colonists were well suited to the difficulties. Many battles were fought and some treaties made with the Native Americans whose homelands the settlers invaded. By 1670 the British had established twelve of the original Thirteen Colonies (see pages 28–29), and the settlements were growing fast.

Right: This Native American buckskin cloak is known as Powhatan's Mantle. It was named after the chief of the tribe that attacked Jamestown.

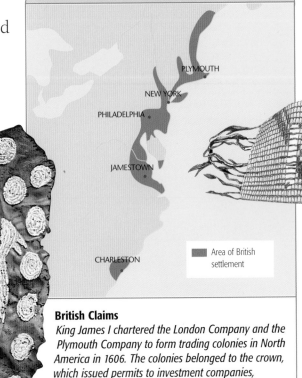

EARLY BRITISH SETTLEMENTS

PLYMOUTH
NEW YORK
PHILADELPHIA
JAMESTOWN
CHARLESTON

Area of British settlement

British Claims

King James I chartered the London Company and the Plymouth Company to form trading colonies in North America in 1606. The colonies belonged to the crown, which issued permits to investment companies, groups, and individuals. Colonies then offered cheap land to encourage settlers, and in some cases reserved some land for public use. This map shows the extent of British settlement about 100 years after the original charter.

Jamestown

The first permanent colony was formed by 104 men and boys, who arrived in America in three ships. They named their settlement Jamestown, after the English king. They were soon followed by more settlers, including women, but the first years of the colony were very hard. The land was swampy, safe drinking water was scarce, and the settlers faced starvation, disease, and attacks by native inhabitants. Nevertheless, by 1619 the colony's population numbered about a thousand.

Below: In January 1608 all the houses in Jamestown were destroyed by fire. The fortified settlement had to be completely rebuilt.

Thanksgiving

The Puritans who founded Plymouth colony in December 1620 had a harsh first winter in America. About half their number of 102 men, women, and children died. But by the following summer, despite poor crops of peas and wheat, the settlers' maize was growing well. In the early autumn of 1621, the governor of the colony called for a festival to thank God for the harvest. The Thanksgiving feast included goose, turkey, and fish, as well as fruit, vegetables, and cornbread. Some Native Americans also took part in the outdoor festival.

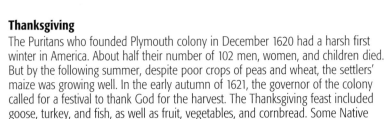

Craftworkers of the Delaware tribe wove wampum belts (made of shell beads) to commemorate their treaty with Penn.

Colonists soon came to appreciate native foods such as squash, corn, and beans.

Pennsylvania

In 1681 Charles II granted territory to the west of the Delaware River to William Penn (1644–1718). The grant was in settlement of a debt to Penn's father, who had been a distinguished admiral, and the region was named Pennsylvania in the admiral's honor. William Penn was a Quaker, and he saw the new colony as a refuge for those who shared his beliefs. In 1683 Penn signed a peace treaty and land-purchase agreement with local Native Americans. As governor, Penn introduced the colony's first constitution.

BRITISH SETTLEMENTS

1607
First permanent British settlement in America is established at Jamestown.

1614
Native American chief's daughter Pocahontas marries settler and tobacco-grower John Rolfe.

1620
The Puritan Pilgrim Fathers arrive in the Mayflower and found Plymouth settlement.

1624
King James I makes Virginia (including Jamestown) a royal colony.

1664
The British take control of the future Pennsylvania region from the Dutch.

1670
First permanent European settlement in South Carolina (near Charleston).

1676
Colonists rebel against the government in Virginia.

1691
Massachusetts (including Plymouth) and Maryland become royal colonies.

The Dutch and the Swedish in North America

S ettlements and ownership of land in the colony of New Netherland were encouraged and funded by the Dutch West India Company, which was granted a charter to develop trade with the Americas. For 17 years the Dutch were joined by Swedish and Finnish colonists sent by the rival New Sweden Company. Competition between the two colonies ended in Dutch victory, though the Swedes and other nationalities were allowed to stay and continue their own customs. In its turn, New Netherland eventually fell to the British.

Peter Stuyvesant lost a leg fighting for the Dutch in 1644. In this illustration he rebukes a cobbler who dared criticize his autocratic methods.

Peter Stuyvesant

Peter Stuyvesant (c.1592–1672) was director general of all the Dutch possessions in North America and the Caribbean. He was a tough, autocratic leader, disliked by many of the New Amsterdam colonists, who saw him as too devoted to the interests of the West India Company. Stuyvesant responded by establishing a municipal government for the city, which he still dominated. After being ousted by the British, Stuyvesant settled on his *bouwerij* (farm) in New York, after which the Bowery district is named.

The official seal of New Netherland.

The skyline of New Amsterdam included a windmill, Reformed church, weighing beam, and gallows.

The Dutch Buy Manhattan

In 1625, a group of Dutch colonists built a fort on Manhattan island and named their settlement New Amsterdam. A year later, the Dutch governor Peter Minuit bought the island from native Manates tribesmen for beads and trinkets worth 60 Dutch guilders. Over the next few years Breuckelen (now Brooklyn) and other settlements were established. In 1629, the Dutch brought in the patroon system by which any West India Company member who settled 50 colonists within four years became a land owner (patroon) who effectively controled the settlers' lives.

NIEUW AMSTERDAM
op t Eylant Manhattans.

NEW AMSTERDAM

1621
*Dutch West India
Company is founded.*

1624
*Dutch West India
Company establishes New
Netherland at Fort Orange
(now Albany, New York).*

1638
*First Swedish settlement
is founded on the River
Delaware.*

1646
*Peter Stuyvesant is
appointed director general
of New Netherland.*

1655
*The Dutch take over
New Sweden.*

1664
*New Amsterdam falls to
a British fleet and is
renamed New York (after
the Duke of York, later
King James II).*

1673–74
*The Dutch briefly retake
New York, before it
becomes British again
under the Treaty of
Westminster.*

British New York

The fierce trading rivalry between the British and the Dutch led to a fleet of British warships attacking New Netherland in 1664. Many of the Dutch colonists refused to fight for their despotic governor, and the British captured the colony. It came under the control of the Duke of York, for which he paid 40 beaver skins a year to his brother, King Charles II.

The Old Swedes Church, in present-day Wilmington, was built by Lutheran colonists in 1698.

The Kalmar Nyckel was one of the two ships that sailed from Sweden in 1638. This sturdy ship made four return crossings of the Atlantic.

New Sweden

The only Swedish colony in America was founded at Fort Christina (named after the Swedish queen), now Wilmington, Delaware. The first expedition was led by Dutchman Peter Minuit (see opposite) and included Swedish, Finnish, Dutch, and German settlers, who became farmers and fur traders. Unfortunately for the Scandinavians, the colony lay within the territory of New Netherland, and Peter Stuyvesant eventually forced them to surrender.

The French and Louisiana

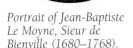

n 1674, just eleven years after the establishment of New France as a royal province further north, French explorers were canoeing down the Mississippi River. This allowed them to expand their fur-trading activities further south. The provincial governor had hoped that this waterway would lead to the west and Asia, but by 1682 the explorers had reached the Gulf of Mexico and claimed the entire region drained by the river for France. This led to the establishment of the colony of Louisiana.

Portrait of Jean-Baptiste Le Moyne, Sieur de Bienville (1680–1768).

FRENCH SETTLEMENT

1674
Jolliet and Marquette explore the Mississippi basin.

1682
La Salle leads a canoeing expedition down the Mississippi River.

1688
La Salle's settlement at Fort St. Louis (near Victoria, Texas) is destroyed by Karankawa tribesmen.

1699
French Jesuits found a mission at the fur-trading post of Cahokia, Illinois; Le Moyne establishes the colony of Louisiana.

1701–12
Sieur de Bienville is governor of Louisiana.

1702
Fort Louis de la Mobile (near Mobile, Alabama) becomes capital of Louisiana colony.

1718
Sieur de Bienville founds the city of New Orleans.

Louisiana

In 1682 La Salle claimed the entire Mississippi valley for France, naming it Louisiana in honor of his king, Louis XIV. Seventeen years later, Pierre Le Moyne established the colony of Louisiana at Biloxi Bay (now Ocean Springs, Mississippi). Pierre and his brother Jean-Baptiste were sons of the French colonist and fur trader Charles Le Moyne. The brothers built forts near the mouth of the great river, which helped persuade their king to colonize the region.

Down the Mississippi

The French first explored the Mississippi when the governor of New France sent explorer Louis Jolliet and Jesuit missionary Jacques Marquette from Lake Michigan to see whether the great river flowed west to the Pacific. They reached the confluence of the Arkansas River. Eight years later, René-Robert Cavelier (Sieur de La Salle) canoed the entire length of the river and reached its mouth at the Gulf of Mexico.

This flint cross, made by native Illinois tribesmen, was given to Father Marquette.

THE FRENCH IN NORTH AMERICA

FORT ST PIERRE

FORT ST CROIX

FORT BEAUHARNAIS

FORT CHARTRES

FORT PRUDHOMME

FORT PICKAWILLANY

FORT PRESQU'ISLE

FORT CREVECOEUR

ATLANTIC OCEAN

FORT ROSALIE

FORT CONDÉ

NEW ORLEANS

FORT ST LOUIS

Gulf of Mexico

→ Route of La Salle 1679–1682

→ Route of Jolliet 1672–1673

French 1713

French 1750

● French fort

French Territory

The map shows the extent of French settlement by 1713, including the growing number of trading posts. La Salle's Mississippi exploration opened up new territory all the way to the Gulf of Mexico. The French then set about building protective forts to link the colony of Louisiana with the rest of New France to the north.

French fur-trappers used iron beaver traps like these.

There was a great demand for beaver fur in Europe, especially to make hats.

French traders and Native American trappers exchanged knives, kettles, and other goods for pelts.

The Fur Trade

French policy was to establish fur-trading posts and small colonies over wide areas. In order to develop their fur-trade interests, the French realized that a good relationship with local Native Americans was important. After building Fort St. Louis on the Illinois River, La Salle wanted to found a colony at the mouth of the Mississippi and returned to France to pick up colonists. But his ships missed their destination and eventually set up a colony at Matagorda Bay, Texas.

The Thirteen Colonies

The Liberty Bell was ordered from England in 1751 to celebrate the 50th anniversary of Penn's Charter of Privileges. Today it hangs in a pavilion near Independence Hall in Philadelphia.

Title page of a book published in 1812.

During the 17th century small American settlements grew into larger colonies. By the mid-1700s, they formed 13 British colonies that stretched down the coast from New England to Georgia (the last of the 13). Each colony had its own governor and laws, but all were subject to British control. French territorial claims ended in 1763, but by this time restrictive British trade laws and taxes were causing unrest among the colonists.

Colonial Government

Powerful governors introduced different "frames of government" to their territories, some more liberal than others. In Pennsylvania, William Penn created a council that proposed laws and an assembly that approved them. Then, in 1701, he granted a new constitution, called the Charter of Privileges, which gave all lawmaking power to the lower house of the assembly. The charter was a great step forward toward liberal self-government.

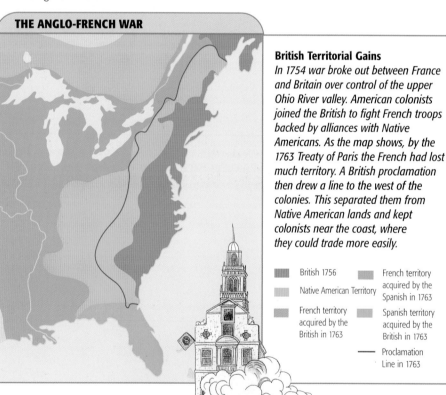

THE ANGLO-FRENCH WAR

British Territorial Gains
In 1754 war broke out between France and Britain over control of the upper Ohio River valley. American colonists joined the British to fight French troops backed by alliances with Native Americans. As the map shows, by the 1763 Treaty of Paris the French had lost much territory. A British proclamation then drew a line to the west of the colonies. This separated them from Native American lands and kept colonists near the coast, where they could trade more easily.

- British 1756
- Native American Territory
- French territory acquired by the British in 1763
- French territory acquired by the Spanish in 1763
- Spanish territory acquired by the British in 1763
- Proclamation Line in 1763

This engraving of the Boston Massacre was made by the famous patriot Paul Revere.

The Boson Tea Party

On December 16, 1773, anti-British rebels disguised as Native Americans got onto British ships in Boston harbor. The rebels protested against taxes and the power of the British East India Company by throwing more than 300 chests of tea overboard. This act of defiance, which became known as the "Boston Tea Party," led to tough countermeasures that further united the colonists.

The Boston Massacre

On March 5, 1770, British troops reacted to street protests against new colonial taxes. Soldiers fired into an angry crowd outside the Customs House in Boston, killing three people and injuring others. American revolutionaries called the incident the "Boston Massacre" and used it to provoke further opposition to British colonial policies.

Right: This cartoon of 1774 shows protestors forcing tea down the throat of a tax collector.

Above: During the Boston Tea Party a group of about 60 American patriots attacked the tea chests of three ships in Boston harbor.

Navigation Acts

Beginning in 1651, Navigation Acts were passed by the English parliament to protect its trade and shipping. Some were aimed at the American colonies and the Dutch, to stop them profiting from trade between the West Indies and Europe. Goods such as sugar, cotton, and tobacco had to be shipped on English vessels, and from 1663 all European goods bound for the American colonies had to pass through an English port and were subject to duty.

Portrait of Thomas Hancock (1702–64), a wealthy Bostonian merchant who flouted regulations in shipping goods to and from the colonies.

THIRTEEN COLONIES

Virginia
(first permanent settlement 1607), began at Jamestown, became a royal colony in 1624.

Massachusetts
(settled 1620), started by Pilgrims at Plymouth, which became part of the larger colony in 1691.

New Hampshire
(settled 1623), ruled by the government of Massachusetts Bay, became a colony in 1679.

New York
(settled 1624), became a royal colony in 1685.

Connecticut
(settled 1633), became a colony in 1636.

Maryland
(settled 1634), founded by a family of wealthy Roman Catholics.

Rhode Island
(settled 1636), granted a charter in 1644, became a colony in 1647.

Delaware
(settled 1638), part of Pennsylvania until 1704, when it gained its own assembly.

Pennsylvania
(settled 1643), under liberal policies of William Penn became the most prosperous colony.

North Carolina
(settled 1653), constitution first drafted in 1669.

New Jersey
(settled 1660), first government in 1665, made a royal colony in 1702.

South Carolina
(settled 1670), separated from North Carolina in 1729.

Georgia
(settled 1733), founded by wealthy settlers as colony of small farms, became a royal colony in 1752.

The American Revolution

American colonists' resentment at British authoritarian rule led to the Thirteen Colonies forming a Continental Congress in 1774. The following year, as anti-British feeling grew, the first hostile skirmishes took place between American militiamen and British troops. These battles marked the beginning of the American Revolution (1775–83), also known as the Revolutionary War in America or (in Britain) the War of American Independence. The French, Spanish, and Dutch took the opportunity to help reduce British control of America.

Commander in Chief

George Washington (1732–99) came from a wealthy Virginian family and fought for the British in the Anglo-French War. In 1775 Congress unanimously elected him commander in chief of the American forces, though he had not sought the position. He won ordinary American people over to the cause, and they saw him as a symbol of independence. Washington played a major role in the colonies' struggle for independence.

Detail of a painting showing Washington crossing the Delaware River in December, 1776. This led to an inspirational victory at Trenton, New Jersey.

A surveying compass owned by George Washington, who was a professional surveyor in civilian life.

Conflicting Armies

The American forces were first made up of militiamen, who fought for their separate colonies. They expected to fight for a short time and then return home. In 1775 Congress established the Continental Army, with an overall commander and a series of generals. They brought training and discipline to their troops, much needed to combat the British soldiers (known as "redcoats" because of their uniforms). The British army was a professional force, including foreign mercenaries hired from German princes.

Revolutionary Hero

Benjamin Franklin was born in Boston and at first wanted the American Colonies to stay in the British Empire. But he also wanted just rights for the colonists, and these were not granted. Franklin tried unsuccessfully to get French Canadians to join the war, and in 1776 was sent by Congress to France as a commissioner. There he was seen as a hero, leading his people to freedom from its feudal past.

Portrait of Benjamin Franklin (1706–90), famous scientist, author, and diplomat.

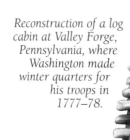

Reconstruction of a log cabin at Valley Forge, Pennsylvania, where Washington made winter quarters for his troops in 1777–78.

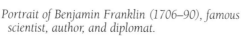

Left: The original Declaration of Independence was written and signed on parchment.

The Declaration of Independence

In June 1776, Congress set up a committee to draft a declaration, and Thomas Jefferson of Virginia was appointed to complete this. Delegates debated the draft, which was formally adopted on July 4. The Declaration was printed and read out to a large crowd in Philadelphia days later. It famously stated: "We hold these truths to be self-evident, that all men are created equal, that they are endowed by their Creator with certain unalienable rights, that among these are life, liberty, and the pursuit of happiness."

Below: Thomas Jefferson and his committee present the Declaration to the president of Congress, John Hancock.

Foreign Allies

When the Americans beat the British at Saratoga in 1777, France realized that Britain might be defeated and decided to join the war. French troops played a decisive part in land battles, and the French navy supported the Americans by holding the British off at sea. The Spanish and Dutch navies also helped by keeping British ships occupied in Europe.

The young French nobleman, Marquis de Lafayette, arrived in America in 1777 to fight for the colonists.

Legend says that a Philadelphia seamstress named Betsy Ross sewed the first Stars and Stripes flag in 1776.

The United States

Even after they had established a Congress, declared independence, and won the Revolutionary War, the 13 former colonies were still separate states. However, their representatives soon took steps to complete unification by agreeing a Constitution and setting up a federal government. Objections by individual states were overcome by allowing them to retain certain powers and making sure the new government represented all of them fairly, irrespective of their size. By 1789 the United States had their first president, George Washington.

Drawing of the Great Seal of the United States by Charles Thomson, Secretary of Congress. The seal was adopted in 1782.

New Government

In 1787 state delegates met in Philadelphia to discuss a new constitution. Agreement was finally reached, and by 1790 all thirteen states had ratified the new system. The federal government was to have three branches: an executive, headed by a president; a legislature, with two parts (a House of Representatives and a Senate); and a judiciary. The Constitution referred to citizens as "We the people of the United States."

James Madison of Virginia formulated many of the federal agreements and is often called the "Father of the Constitution." He became the fourth US president in 1809.

THE UNITED STATES IN 1803

The Louisiana Purchase
In 1803 the Senate approved the wish of President Thomas Jefferson to accept an offer from Napoleon to buy the French territory of Louisiana (see page 26). The United States paid $15 million for a vast tract of land between the Mississippi River and the Rocky Mountains, stretching from the Gulf of Mexico to Canada. As the map shows, the new territory doubled the size of the new nation.

Gulf of Mexico

▦ States by 1803	▦ Northwest Territory	▦ Other territory in present-day United States
▦ Louisiana Purchase 1803	▦ Other territories	

Women vote in New Jersey. This was the only state to give women this right (and only from 1790 to 1807).

The British Surrender

George Washington and his American army were helped by French land and sea forces at Yorktown. A joint army besieged the British under General Lord Cornwallis at the tobacco port in Virginia. Any potential help from the British navy was stopped by a French fleet of 24 ships that closed off Chesapeake Bay. Cornwallis was left with no alternative but to surrender, and about 8,000 British troops were taken prisoner.

Left: In this painting, Siege of Yorktown, French general Comte de Rochambeau (pointing) and George Washington (to his left) discuss strategy.

Independent States

The original colonies made up the first 13 states, but they formed a loose confederation. Each state had its own constitution and retained the right to regulate trade and collect taxes. Despite the fact that the 1781 Articles of Confederation had created a "perpetual union" between the states, people at first considered themselves citizens of their state rather than of a unified nation.

Robert R. Livingston was US minister to France from 1801 to 1804. He helped negotiate the Louisiana Purchase in Paris.

This English cartoon of 1782 shows Britannia making it up with her daughter America.

Dear Mama say no more about it

Be a good Girl and give me a Bufs

Liberty

George for Ever.

The Treaty of Paris

Benjamin Franklin and others negotiated the final peace treaty between the British and Americans, which was signed in Paris in 1783. The treaty recognized the independence of the United States, with boundaries extending west to the Mississippi River, north to Canada, and south to Florida (which Britain lost to Spain). The treaty also granted the Americans fishing rights off the coast of Newfoundland.

THE UNITED STATES

1781
October 19, British forces surrender at Yorktown, Virginia.

1783
September 3, peace treaty is signed between the British and Americans in Paris; separate peace treaties are signed between Britain and France, and Britain and Spain.

1784
Peace treaty between Britain and the Netherlands.

1787
State delegates agree a Constitution.

1789
George Washington is elected 1st president.

1791
10 amendments (known as the Bill of Rights) are added to the Constitution.

1791–96
Three new states added —Vermont, Kentucky, and Tennessee.

1797
John Adams becomes 2nd president.

1800
Congress moves from Philadelphia to Washington (the new capital).

1801
Thomas Jefferson becomes 3rd president.

1803
The Louisiana Purchase; Ohio becomes 17th state.

The Church in Latin America

From early in the 16th century the king of Spain was authorized by the Pope to found Roman Catholic churches and appoint all religious officials in Spanish America. The main aim was to convert the local population. It is said that in 1531 two visions of the Virgin Mary appeared to a native convert to the north of Mexico City and commanded that a church be built there. Today, the original church has been replaced with a new basilica.

Above: Painted image of the Virgin of Guadalupe. In 1754 the Pope made the Virgin of Guadalupe patroness of New Spain.

Above: The Truro Synagogue, at Newport, Rhode Island, is the oldest standing synagogue in the United States.

Witch Hunt

In the 17th century there was great fear of witchcraft and possession by the devil. The most famous witch hunt took place in Salem, Massachusetts, in 1692. When a group of teenage girls began having strange fits, parents and grandparents were arrested on suspicion of witchcraft. Nineteen men and women were convicted and hanged, and another male "witch" was pressed to death with stones. Many more were imprisoned, but released the following year.

The Inquisition

From the earliest times of European settlement, the Roman Catholic clergy held great power in the Spanish colonies. They saw it as their duty to convert Native Americans to Christianity. In 1569 King Philip II of Spain strengthened Catholic control by establishing tribunals of the Inquisition in both New Spain and Peru. Their main purpose was to seek out and punish heretics, who were burned at the stake if they refused to repent.

Native Americans were seen as savages by early Spanish conquerors. This victim was blessed by a clergyman as he was burned at the stake.

Religion in the New World

Religion played an important role in the colonization of the Americas. Roman Catholicism dominated Latin America, which did not escape the harsh attentions of the Inquisition. In the North American colonies, Protestants outnumbered other groups, though there were also Catholics and Jews. Many colonists had left Europe to escape persecution, and religious freedom was made law in the Bill of Rights of 1791. In the new United States, no religious group received official recognition as a state church.

Jewish Settlements

Many early American colonists were Jewish or *conversos* (Jews who had converted to Christianity). Some found their way illegally to the New World, since even "New Christians" were officially not allowed to emigrate. Many converted Portuguese merchants went to Brazil, and inquisitors in the colonies referred to all Jewish people as "Portuguese Jews." The Dutch offered more religious freedom, and the first Jewish community in North America was in New Amsterdam.

Right: In 1660, Mary Dyer was hanged for spreading Quaker beliefs in the colony of Massachusetts.

Toward Toleration

Religious tolerance was certainly not practiced in all the American colonies. Puritans in New England wanted fellow colonists to worship in the same way, and those who failed to conform were sometimes fined, beaten, or imprisoned. The situation changed as groups with different religious views arrived. In New York and New Jersey there was no established church. In Pennsylvania and Delaware, all churches had freedom of worship. In 1649, Maryland's leaders passed a religious toleration act.

This Bible, printed in 1665, belonged to William Penn's daughter-in-law.

Below: This 19th-century painting shows the chaotic scene at the Salem witch trials.

Colonial Art and Architecture

The art and architecture of the American colonies naturally developed from European methods and styles. In Spanish and Portuguese South America, the Baroque style was most evident in architecture and sculpture. In North America, a naive form of painting was gradually replaced by more formal, refined techniques. Similar developments were seen in architecture, as colonists tried to match the sophistication of their mother country.

A limner's portrait of 1664.

North American painters

Early colonial painters had no formal training. They created the simple, bold compositions that made up the folk art of the 17th century. Known as limners, folk artists earned a living by traveling around painting faithful, natural portraits of local residents. By the following century, American portrait painters were more influenced by the sophisticated styles of European art. Many had studied in Europe.

Left: A painted and gilded wooden image of the Virgin of Quito. It was made around 1750 in New Granada (modern Ecuador), from a model by Bernardo Legarda.

Latin American artists

From the late 16th century, colonial painters, sculptors, and craftworkers belonged to European-style guilds. Indigenous artists learned European methods from engravings and prints. Many guilds did not allow non-Spaniards to reach the highest ranks, but some artists (such as the mestizo painter and sculptor Bernardo Legarda), produced brilliant work. Artists were dependent on commissions from patrons, and especially from the Roman Catholic Church.

Below: Portrait of silversmith and patriot Paul Revere painted in 1770 by John Singleton Copley of Boston.

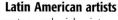

Left: The Church of São Francisco de Assis in Ouro Preto, Brazil, was designed in 1766 by Antonio Francisco Lisboa (known as Aleijadinho, meaning "little cripple").

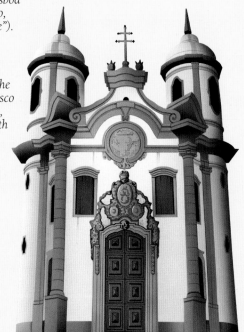

Right: The façade of the Church of San Francisco Acatepec near Puebla, Mexico, is covered with glazed tiles. The church was built around 1760.

Spanish-American Architecture

Colonial architects followed Spanish styles, which native craftsmen learned to put into effect. The earliest public buildings were in the decorative Plateresque (or "silverwork") style. During the 17th century Baroque ornamentation became dominant, since this was the style supported by the Catholic Church and Spanish monarchy. The elaborate late-Baroque style known as Churrigueresque (after the Churriguera family of architects) was also evident in Spanish America.

Above: The Penha Building in Willemstad, Curaçao, was built in the Dutch style in 1708. The Netherlands took control of this Caribbean island in 1634.

The Peale Family painted about 1770 by Charles Willson Peale of Maryland. The artist's sons (named Raphaelle, Rembrandt, Rubens, and Titian) also became painters.

The Caribbean

The colonial powers of Spain, Britain, France, and the Netherlands took their own architectural styles and building methods to the islands of the West Indies. Public buildings were a way of showing national identity, which made colonial architecture all the more important.

Above: Destrehan Plantation, on the banks of the Mississippi in Louisiana, was built as a planter's family home in 1787. It shows the French Creole colonial style.

North America

Colonial architecture reflected European styles and varied according to national influences on individual colonies and, later, states. In the southern colonies, wealthy planters built large, comfortable homes. During the 18th century, the British colonies adopted a Georgian style that was formal, elegant, and well proportioned. Some early Georgian houses were built in Williamsburg, Virginia.

Left: Thomas Jefferson (who was US president from 1801 to 1809) designed this house, called Monticello, in the Neoclassical style. It was built near Charlottesville, Virginia, between 1769 and 1808, and it became the Jefferson family home.

Hudson's Bay Company

The company had sole trading rights in the region that formed the drainage basin of the Hudson Bay, where they soon built trading posts. The region was named Rupert's Land, after Prince Rupert, the company's first governor. Company agents got furs from Native American hunters, offering guns, knives, and kettles in exchange. They beat off competition from others to remain the biggest, most powerful fur-trading company.

A Hudson's Bay Company brass trading token. Furs were sold for tokens, which could be exchanged for European goods.

Early Canadian Settlements

French explorers established the first permanent settlements in what was to become Canada in the early 17th century. They founded the colony of New France and attracted many fur-trappers and traders to the region. Migration from Europe was slow, however. Conditions were harsh, relations with local Native American tribes were difficult, and the British were also keen to exploit the fur trade. This rivalry led to war between French and British colonists before the end of the century.

New France

The first permanent European settlement was founded in 1605 by Sieur de Monts and Champlain at Port Royal (near present-day Annapolis Royal, Nova Scotia). The region around the settlement became known as Acadia. Three years later, the two Frenchmen built a fur-trading fort on the St. Lawrence River at a place called Quebec, where they befriended the local Algonquin people. The wider region controlled by the French was soon called New France, and a company was set up to settle the colony.

Below: Drawing by Champlain of the settlement at Port Royal.

Right: Samuel de Champlain (1567–1635), who was appointed commander of New France in 1613.

The King's Daughters

Before New France became a royal province, colonization was not successful. Almost all French settlers were men, and few took their wives and families. King Louis XIV decided to put this right by giving free passage and small dowries to healthy women of childbearing age. Known as the *Filles du Roi* (King's Daughters), more than 800 young women arrived in the colony between 1663 and 1673. Most found husbands, and the policy resulted in the population growing to about 8,500 by 1676.

The Iroquois

The fur trade in much of the New France region was controlled by a confederacy of Iroquois tribes whose lands covered the routes west. The French made enemies of the Iroquois by siding with rival tribes, which led to native warriors making many attacks on French settlements. In the late 1660s some Iroquois tribes were forced to make peace with the French.

This notched staff lists the five tribal groups of the Iroquois Great Council.

Anglo-French Rivalry

The success of the Hudson's Bay Company meant that New France was caught between the British in northern Rupert's Land and the Iroquois—who were supported by the British and Dutch—in the south. The French also wanted to dominate the fur trade, while many British colonists were pushing for more land for farming. In 1689 hostilities broke out at the start of the so-called King William's War, during which the British captured Fort Royal but failed to take Quebec.

Above: William of Orange, who ruled Britain as William III (1689–1702) together with his wife Mary II. He opposed France in Europe and North America.

Below: Some of the "King's Daughters" arriving in Quebec in 1667. They were presented first to Bishop François Laballe and Jean-Baptiste Talon, respectively bishop and royal agent of New France.

WAR IN CANADA

1702–13
Queen Anne's War.

1710
The British capture Port Royal and Acadia from the French.

1711
Unsuccessful British and Iroquois attack on Quebec and Montreal.

1713
Treaty of Utrecht confirms loss of French territory.

1744–48
King George's War.

1748
Treaty of Aix-la-Chapelle gives captured territory back to Britain and France.

1749
A British naval base is established at Halifax, Nova Scotia.

1755
Beginning of deportation and exile of Acadians.

The Fight for Canada

There were two more Anglo-British wars in the first half of the 18th century, during which there were many skirmishes and some major battles, as the nations continued to dispute Canadian territory. Both wars involved the Native Americans whose original lands were being disputed by European settlers, and both sides were happy to seek the help of native allies. But the conflicts between the two nations were also linked to the wider issues fought over in the Wars of the Spanish and Austrian Succession.

During Queen Anne's War, the British made an unsuccessful naval attack on Quebec.

Queen Anne's War

This war, named after Britain's Queen Anne (ruled 1702–14), broke out when French forces and their Algonquian allies raided British settlements. The British then made several attacks on Port Royal in Acadia, which they finally captured in 1710. The war ended with the signing of the Treaty of Utrecht, by which the French had to give up Nova Scotia, Newfoundland, and territory around Hudson Bay. But the treaty did not define the boundaries between the two nations' colonies clearly, so peace was not secured.

Portrait of Sir William Johnson, who encouraged and organized Iroquois war parties against the French.

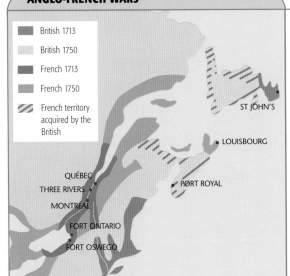

ANGLO-FRENCH WARS

- ▇ British 1713
- ▨ British 1750
- ▇ French 1713
- ▨ French 1750
- ▨ French territory acquired by the British

ST JOHN'S

LOUISBOURG

QUÉBEC
THREE RIVERS
MONTREAL
PORT ROYAL
FORT ONTARIO
FORT OSWEGO

Territorial Changes

Territory was taken and retaken by both sides in the series of wars, and the periods between the wars were never entirely peaceful. The 1713 peace treaty gave important coastal territory to Britain, as shown on this map. By 1750 large stretches of territory had been acquired by both colonial nations, but New France had been squeezed into a narrow strip.

King George's War

The third Anglo-French colonial conflict was named after King George II, who ruled Britain from 1727 to 1760. It began when French forces tried and failed to retake Nova Scotia. The biggest victory went to the British in 1745, when naval ships and New England troops captured the important French fortress of Louisbourg on Cape Breton Island.

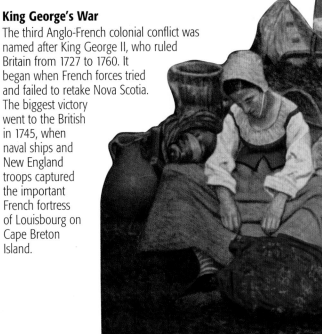

The city of Quebec.

Expulsion of the Acadians

In 1755, the British tried to force the French Acadians to swear an oath of allegiance to King George II. When the Acadians refused, the British decided to expel them. Some escaped to Quebec, but over the next few years many thousands were transported by ship to British colonies further south. Some made their way to French-ruled Louisiana, while others were eventually able to return to Nova Scotia and New Brunswick.

Left: Scalps were sometimes stretched on a wooden hoop, as in this 18th-century example.

Native Raids

Warfare was brutal among the British, French, and Native Americans. Many European settlers were killed by roaming bands of Native Americans. Some native warriors scalped dead victims to gain war trophies or even to exchange for the bounty that was offered as an incentive by the Europeans. Other settlers were taken prisoner, and some white captives adapted to tribal life and made little attempt to return to their colony.

An Algonquian war club.

Right: The Acadians were rounded up, ready to be put on board ship and transported south.

Under British Rule

The fourth and final Anglo-French War broke out over control of the upper Ohio River valley (see page 28). It led to the famous capture of Quebec by General Wolfe's British troops, and finally resulted in the surrender of New France to Britain in 1763. Twenty-eight years later, Britain divided the former colony of Quebec into the provinces of Upper and Lower Canada (the name coming from Iroquoian *kanata*, meaning "village"). By that time the British had lost control of their Thirteen American Colonies, adding importance to their Canadian possessions.

Chief Pontiac rallies his allied warriors to fight the British.

The Death of General Wolfe was painted about 1771 by the famous American artist Benjamin West.

After the Treaty of Paris

With the decline of French power, Native American tribes were concerned at the loss of their lands to British troops and colonists. Chief Pontiac of the Ottawa tribe, whose homelands were to the north of Lake Huron, set about uniting neighboring tribes to try to oust the invaders. Pontiac's warriors took many British fortified posts, but after some of his allies deserted him, the native leader was forced to make peace in 1766.

This print of the Battle of the Plains of Abraham shows all the action in one scene.

The Fall of New France to the British

In 1759 General James Wolfe led a British attack on Quebec, which was held by French troops under the Marquis de Montcalm. At first Wolfe's attacks failed, but then he audaciously ordered 5,000 troops to scale a steep cliff to the Plains of Abraham, near Quebec. The plan worked, but Wolfe was killed in the attack. The French general also died a few hours later. The loss of Quebec was decisive in the fall of New France to the British.

Portrait of Sir Guy Carleton (1724–1808).

The Quebec Act

The British general and governor Sir Guy Carleton and others realized that for peace and stability in Quebec they needed to gain the support of the French colonists who outnumbered their own people. The Quebec Act of 1774 gave French settlers greater freedom, granting the use of French civil law and religious freedom to Roman Catholics. Protestants in the American colonies were very unhappy at this.

Engraving of Benedict Arnold (1741–1801). He went over to the British side in 1780 and was branded a traitor by the Americans.

Invasion of Canada

In the autumn of 1775 (the first year of the American Revolution), American colonial armies invaded Canada. Their aim was to stop British forces rushing south to fight the Thirteen Colonies. Colonel Benedict Arnold led one American force, and General Richard Montgomery another. When they failed to capture Quebec, Montgomery was killed and Arnold wounded. The Americans then retreated to New York.

Structure of the government in 1791.

KING

Parliament in London

Governor General

Upper Canada — Lower Canada

Lieutenant Governor — Representative of the Governor

Executive Council — Legislative Council — Executive Council — Legislative Council

Assembly — Assembly

People of Upper Canada — People of Lower Canada

The Constitutional Act

After the American Revolution some American colonists loyal to Britain moved to Quebec. They were, however, unhappy at the form of government there, leading to the passing of a new Constitutional Act. This divided the colony of Quebec into two provinces—Upper Canada (later Ontario) and Lower Canada (later Quebec)—each with its own elected assembly and British-appointed council. Many of the rights granted in the Quebec Act, including religious freedom, were retained for the Lower province, which had mainly French-speaking inhabitants.

BRITISH RULE

1754–63
Anglo-French War, the American front of the Seven Years' War (1756–63) in Europe.

1760
British troops capture Montreal.

1763
The Treaty of Paris gives French land in Canada to Britain.

1763–66
Pontiac's War (also called Pontiac's Conspiracy).

1775–76
Canadian colonists refuse to join the revolution of the Thirteen American Colonies.

1784
Creation of the province of New Brunswick out of western Nova Scotia (New Acadia), for British colonists from America.

1789
Explorer Sir Alexander Mackenzie heads north-west and reaches Great Slave Lake and the Mackenzie River.

1791
The Constitutional Act creates Upper and Lower Canada.

This chapter covers the history of the civilizations, empires, and kingdoms of Asia and Africa from the early 15th to the late 18th century. Powerful empires fought for dominance in Asia, including Muslim sultanates in the west and the great Ming Dynasty that ruled for nearly three hundred years in the Far East. The long line of Ming emperors finally gave way to neighboring Manchus, who succeeded in making the Chinese empire even bigger. The influence of Chinese culture was felt strongly in Japan and Korea, but Japanese emperors lost authority and real power passed into the hands of noble warlords.

African kingdoms were smaller than those of Asia. During this period their rulers came under pressure from Muslim invaders in the north and European explorers and traders along the west coast. In both Africa and Asia, different religions and European ambitions had great influence on the civilizations they touched.

A decorative turban pin made for the Moghul emperor Shah Jahan (reigned 1628–58).

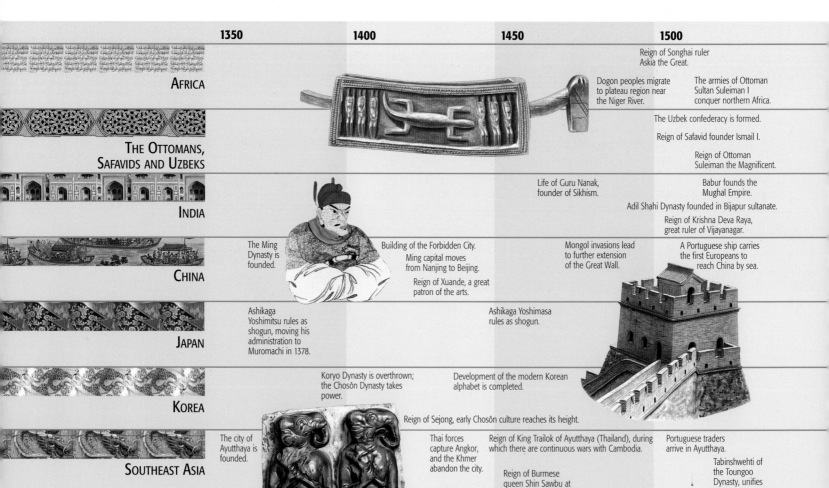

	1350	1400	1450	1500
AFRICA			Dogon peoples migrate to plateau region near the Niger River.	Reign of Songhai ruler Askia the Great. The armies of Ottoman Sultan Suleiman I conquer northern Africa.
THE OTTOMANS, SAFAVIDS AND UZBEKS				The Uzbek confederacy is formed. Reign of Safavid founder Ismail I. Reign of Ottoman Suleiman the Magnificent.
INDIA			Life of Guru Nanak, founder of Sikhism.	Babur founds the Mughal Empire. Adil Shahi Dynasty founded in Bijapur sultanate. Reign of Krishna Deva Raya, great ruler of Vijayanagar.
CHINA	The Ming Dynasty is founded.	Building of the Forbidden City. Ming capital moves from Nanjing to Beijing. Reign of Xuande, a great patron of the arts.	Mongol invasions lead to further extension of the Great Wall.	A Portuguese ship carries the first Europeans to reach China by sea.
JAPAN	Ashikaga Yoshimitsu rules as shogun, moving his administration to Muromachi in 1378.		Ashikaga Yoshimasa rules as shogun.	
KOREA		Koryo Dynasty is overthrown; the Chosôn Dynasty takes power.	Development of the modern Korean alphabet is completed. Reign of Sejong, early Chosôn culture reaches its height.	
SOUTHEAST ASIA	The city of Ayutthaya is founded.	Thai forces capture Angkor, and the Khmer abandon the city.	Reign of King Trailok of Ayutthaya (Thailand), during which there are continuous wars with Cambodia. Reign of Burmese queen Shin Sawbu at Pegu; trade flourishes.	Portuguese traders arrive in Ayutthaya. Tabinshwehti of the Toungoo Dynasty, unifies Burma.

Asian and African Empires

Black wooden figurine of the founder hero of the Luba Empire in south-central Africa.

	1550	1600	1650	1700	1750
		Mai Idris Alooma rules Kanem-Bornu.	Gold-trading states emerge in present-day Ghana.	The Kongo Kingdom is defeated by the Portuguese.	Changamire Dombo founds the Rozwi Kingdom.	
			Chieftaincies unify to form the Kuba Kingdom.	Reign of Wegbaja, who turns Abomey into the powerful state of Dahomey.	Gondar (Ethiopia) is a thriving center of Christian art. Oyo takes control of the kingdom of Dahomey.	
	Reign of the great Uzbek ruler Abd Allah Khan II.	Allied Christian navy defeat the Ottoman imperial fleet at the Battle of Lepanto.		Ottomans besiege Vienna for a second time without success.	
		Reign of Savafid leader Abbas the Great.		Isfahan falls to Afghan invaders.	
		Isfahan becomes Safavid capital.			
	Reign of Akbar, the greatest ruler of the Mughal Empire.	Mughal capital moves to Agra.	Reign of Shivaji, founder of the Maratha Empire.	Nadir Shah's Persian army defeat the Mughals.	Afghans defeat the Maratha.
			War between the Rajputs and Mughals.		The British appoint their first governor general of India.
		The Manchu Jin Dynasty is founded.		The Qing stop a Mongol invasion of Tibet.	The Chinese invade Burma.
			Reign of the first Qing emperor.		
	Spanish Jesuit missionaries arrive in Japan.	Yoshiaki is deposed as the last Ashikaga shogun.	Expulsion of Portuguese traders.		Peasant uprisings break out.
		Toyotomi Hideyoshi is chief imperial minister.			
		Two Japanese invasions fail, but leave much of Korea in ruins; scholars and craftworkers are taken away to Japan.	Manchu nomads overrun northern Korea.	The arts thrive during the reign of Yongjo.	
		Siamese king Naresuan captures the Khmer capital Lovek.	Javanese ruler Mataram asks the Dutch to help fight rebels in return for trading rights.		King Rama I establishes the Chakri Dynasty in Thailand.
		Laos is ruled by Burma (Myanmar)			

Kingdoms and Empires

Many civilizations became established and developed in Africa and Asia during the period from 1400–1800. Some declined and even collapsed during the period, and others were overrun by invaders or absorbed by other empires. There was often conflict between neighboring powers, as ruling dynasties vied for control. Religious missionaries and ambitious traders traveled across the continents, spreading their beliefs and cultural traditions.

Portrait of the Ottoman sultan Selim II (reigned 1566–74) wearing his feathered royal turban.

African Kingdoms

Between the 16th and 18th centuries, important kingdoms came to power in Sub-Saharan Africa. Some were successful and grew, while Islam spread down the east coast from North Africa. South of the Congo River in central Africa, several Bantu-speaking kingdoms developed, including those of the Luba and Lunda peoples. In the southeast, the territory of the Mwenemutapa Kingdom eventually became part of the Rozwi Empire.

An Akan ceremonial sword (from present-day Ghana). The handle was made of wood covered with gold leaf.

Muslim Empires

In the early 16th century four Muslim powers dominated west and south Asia—the Ottomans, Safavids, Uzbeks, and Mughals. In 1517 the Ottoman Turks gained control of Egypt and then expanded their empire along the coastal region of North Africa. The Safavids, who were Shiite rivals to the Ottomans, united tribes in Persia. The Uzbek confederation of central Asia also fought the Safavids and Mughals, who moved down to the Indian subcontinent in search of new territory.

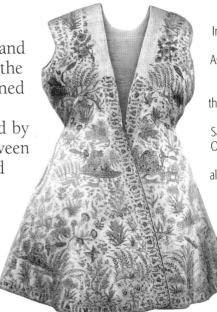

An embroidered muslin hunting jacket of the Mughal emperor Jahangir (reigned 1605–27).

Far-Eastern Dynasties

The largest and dominant empire of the Far East was China, which was ruled by two great imperial dynasties—the Ming (1368–1644) and the Qing (1644–1912). They had a great influence on the rulers and cultures of Korea and Japan, where noble warlords exercised real power.

A mounted bowman of the Manchu, who formed the Qing Dynasty of China.

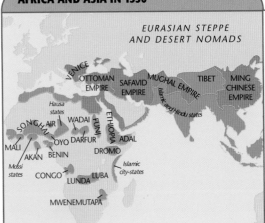

AFRICA AND ASIA IN 1530

EURASIAN STEPPE AND DESERT NOMADS

VENICE / OTTOMAN EMPIRE / SAFAVID EMPIRE / MUGHAL EMPIRE / TIBET / MING CHINESE EMPIRE / Hausa states / Islamic and Hindu states / SONGHAI / AIR / WADAI / FUNJ / ETHIOPIA / MALI / OYO / DARFUR / ADAL / AKAN / BENIN / DROMO / Mossi states / CONGO / LUNDA / LUBA / Islamic city-states / MWENEMUTAPA

Empires
The map shows the important empires and kingdoms of the two continents around 1530. The Far East was dominated by the largest empire of all, Ming China, while western Asia was split between the Mughals, Safavids, and Ottomans. None of the African kingdoms was as large, and much of the continent did not come under any centralized power.

A 16th-century stoneware jar used to hold fresh water during the Japanese tea ceremony.

Right: This Sikh emblem contains a ring, a double-edged sword, and two crossed daggers. Sikhism was founded in northern India in the late 15th century.

The Role of Religion

The great world religions influenced both the politics and culture of the empires. India was the birthplace of Hinduism and Buddhism, and Buddhist monks took their beliefs to the Far East. Christian missionaries also traveled to Africa and Asia. At the same time, Islam continued to spread from southwest Asia and had a great impact on Africa.

Above: Self-portrait by Hakuin (1686–1769), who helped revive Zen Buddhism in Japan.

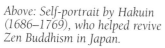

The Madar-i Shah madrasa in Isfahan (in modern Iran) was built in 1706–14 by the last Safavid ruler.

The gold-producing Akan states included Asante. This gold sword ornament takes the form of a fish.

Yoruba Kingdoms

Yoruba-speaking peoples created several city-states, of which the most powerful were Ife and Oyo. The Oyo Empire was at the height of its power between 1650 and 1750, dominating the region between the Volta River (in present-day Ghana) and the Niger River (in Nigeria). Oyo craftsmen produced stunning works of bronze and terra-cotta, but their kingdom's power began to decline from the mid-1700s.

This ivory ceremonial sword was carried by a chief of the small Yoruba state of Owo.

Western and Northern Africa

Several important kingdoms and empires developed and expanded in northwest Africa between 1500 and 1800. This meant that most farmers and traders came under the rule of a king and a central government. Some successful empires thrived, but they had to accept the influence of Islam as it spread steadily south from the Mediterranean coast. At the same time, European traders made their way inland from the Atlantic coast in a determined search for gold, ivory, and slaves.

Magreb States

In the early 16th century the Turkish sea captain Barbarossa helped join the coast of present-day Algeria to the Ottoman Empire. By then Morocco was also ruled by a dynasty of Islamic rulers, and Tunisia became part of the Ottoman Empire in 1574. Muslims controlled the whole of the Maghreb coastal region, from where pirates raided Mediterranean towns and shipping as part of the wars against Spain.

The kasbah (citadel or fortress) at Telouet, in Morocco. These fortresses acted as residences for local leaders and were used to defend nearby cities.

WESTERN AND NORTHERN AFRICA

1493–1528
Reign of Songhai ruler Askia the Great.

1520–1566
Reign of Ottoman Sultan Suleiman I (the "Lawgiver" or the "Magnificent"), whose armies conquer northern Africa.

1580–1617
Mai Idris Alooma rules Kanem-Bornu and extends his empire.

1591
The Songhai are defeated by a Moroccan army in the Battle of Tondibi.

1630–1690
Denkyira and other Akan gold-trading states emerge in present-day Ghana.

c. 1645–1685
Reign of Wegbaja, who turns Abomey into the powerful state of Dahomey.

1701–1712
Reign of Osei Tutu as ruler of Asante, whose territory increases greatly.

1724–1748
Oyo takes control of the kingdom of Dahomey and demands tribute.

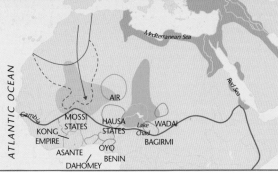

WESTERN AND NORTHERN AFRICA

Mediterranean Sea

ATLANTIC OCEAN

Red Sea

AIR

Gambia

MOSSI STATES

HAUSA STATES

Lake Chad

WADAI

KONG EMPIRE

ASANTE

OYO

BENIN

BAGIRMI

DAHOMEY

- Ottoman Empire,
- Kanem Bornu Empire, greatest extent
- Songhai Empire, greatest extent
- - - - Moroccan expansion
- → Moroccan invasion
- — Southern limit of Islamic influence

Empires and Kingdoms

The Songhai Empire dominated West Africa in the 16th century, until it was attacked by Moroccan invaders. The nearby Kanem-Bornu Empire (north of Lake Chad) was at its greatest around 1600, but then began to decline. The map shows these kingdoms at their greatest extent, as well as the kingdoms of Asante and Oyo. Islamic influence grew during this period.

The Dogon Peoples

The Dogon group of peoples migrated north to the plateau region near the Niger River in present-day Mali towards the end of the 15th century. They lived in villages, pressed up against cliffs and hills, where they were safe from invaders. The Dogon mainly lived as farmers, and their craftsmen worked in wood and metal. They believed that a creator god named Amma sent an ark into the world to organize and populate it.

This Dogon wooden vessel, more than 6.5 feet (2 m) long, represents the original creator's ark.

The Dahomey

The Fon people's kingdom of Dahomey, in the south of present-day Benin, was most powerful during the 18th century. It was founded as the smaller Abomey around 1600, and this later became the capital city and a province of the larger kingdom. Dahomey took many captives as the king expanded his boundaries. Some were forced to work as farmers for the royal court or the army, while others were sold as slaves to the Europeans.

The Dahomey king was protected by a large group of female bodyguards. These warriors, known as Amazons to the Europeans, also served in battle against neighboring kingdoms.

This late 17th-century Qur'an shows African influences on the Arabic script.

TIMELINE

1527–1543
Muslims from neighboring Adal destroy many of Christian Ethiopia's churches, monasteries, and libraries.

c. 1625
King Shyaam a-Mbul a Ngoong unifies chieftaincies into the Kuba Kingdom.

1631
Portuguese conquer the Swahili port of Mombasa.

1632–1667
Reign of Emperor Fasiladas in Ethiopia.

1652
The Dutch found Cape Colony in the south.

1665
The Portuguese defeat Kongo at the Battle of Mbwila.

c. 1684–1706
Life of Kimpa Vita (Dona Beatriz) in the Kongo Kingdom.

c. 1690
Changamire Dombo conquers territory around the Zambezi River and founds the Rozwi Kingdom.

1706
Beginning of the chaotic "Age of Princes" in Ethiopia.

Eastern, Central, and Southern Africa

Between the 16th and 18th centuries, large political units also developed in the southern half of Africa. Several states grew up around the great East African lakes, including Rwanda, where Tutsi herdsmen provided leaders who dominated Hutu farming communities. Further south were the large Bantu-speaking states of Lunda and Luba, as well as the kingdoms of Mwenemutapa and Rozwi. Some of these African states fought with each other, and by the end of the period they were all under pressure from European raiders and traders.

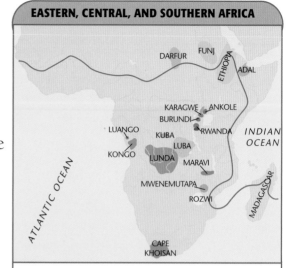

EASTERN, CENTRAL, AND SOUTHERN AFRICA

— Southern limit of Islamic influence

Empires and Kingdoms
From the early 1600s the Bantu-speaking Lunda people had one of the largest and most powerful kingdoms. By the 18th century, some groups had broken away to form their own, smaller empires. Similarly, there were many small kingdoms on the island of Madagascar, including Merina, which was founded toward the end of the 16th century on a central plateau and later expanded.

Kongo
Kongo lay in west-central Africa, around the Congo River (across parts of present-day Angola, Congo, and DR Congo). During the 16th century its Bantu-speaking people fell out with the Portuguese, who increased their slaving raids. The kingdom declined, was defeated by the Portuguese in 1665, and broke up into warring chiefdoms. Early in the 18th century, a young Kongolese woman named Kimpa Vita introduced the cult of St. Anthony and tried to stop the cycle of internal wars. She failed and was burned at the stake.

An 18th-century Kongolese brass pectoral of St. Anthony of Padua. The saint was known as Toni Malau ("Anthony of good fortune").

People of the Kuba kingdom wore special masks at dancing ceremonies. The king honored someone else by choosing him to wear the royal mask, which was crowned with a feather headdress.

Ethiopia
The Christian kingdom of Ethiopia was attacked and badly damaged by Muslims during the 16th century. The Ethiopians were finally helped to repel the Muslims by the Portuguese, and in 1632 Emperor Fasiladas moved his capital to Gondar. By 1700 the city was a thriving center of Christian art and scholarship, but by then the empire's central government was in decline. A state of feudal anarchy, dominated by powerful regional warlords, took over from imperial authority.

The castle at Gondar was built when the new Ethiopian capital was founded.

Right: Ethiopian wooden statue.

This wooden bowl was used by the Venda-speaking people of southern Africa. It was filled with water, to which maize kernels were added for divining purposes.

Kuba

The Kuba Kingdom, in the interior of present-day DR Congo in central Africa, was formed in the 17th century from a number of smaller chieftaincies. It was run by the Bushoong people, who brought with them their own artistic and ceremonial traditions. These included wooden helmet masks representing their founding ancestor, Woot, and their king. Kuba craftsmen also worked with copper, iron, and brass, making useful tools and ceremonial weapons.

Southern States

There were many small states in the southern regions. The Mwenemutapa Kingdom lay between the Zambezi and Limpopo rivers (in present-day Zimbabwe and Mozambique). In the 17th century the state lost power when the Portuguese deposed its king. By the end of the century, the territory was part of the Rozwi Empire, which stretched into present-day Botswana and South Africa.

The Ottoman Golden Age

The Ottomans were named after their founder and first ruler, Osman (or Uthman, c. 1258–1326). He was the chief of a nomadic Turkic tribe of central Asia that fled from the Mongols and settled in northwest Anatolia (modern Turkey). He and his Muslim successors fought the Christian Byzantines, and after capturing their capital of Constantinople, went on to enjoy a period of great power and importance in the 16th century.

Selim I (ruled 1512–20) was known as "the Grim" because of the violent way in which he dealt with his rivals.

The Sultan's Men

A highly disciplined force of infantrymen acted as the sultan's bodyguards. They were known as Janissaries, or "new troops." The force was originally made up mainly of young Christian prisoners of war from the Balkans. They were given a Muslim education and military training, and were taught to speak Turkish.

A group of Janissaries in marching order.

Sultan's Palace

In the 1460s Mehmed the Conqueror had a sultan's palace built in his new capital, overlooking the Bosphorus. Surrounded by high walls and four courtyards, the Topkapi Palace housed the sultan along with his family, harem, advisers, ministers, and religious officials. More than 4,000 slaves lived within the walls of the palace, which served as the center of government. By the 16th century the palace also housed an imperial art studio and library.

In this illustration of the Topkapi Palace, the sultan listens in a private room to the deliberations of his ministers.

Osman's Successors

The Ottoman rulers fought relentlessly against the Christian Byzantines. Osman's son Murad (ruled 1360–89) captured the Byzantines' second city, Edirne (in modern Turkey). But the greatest prize was claimed in 1453, when the seventh sultan, Mehmed II, captured their first city—Constantinople—and made it the Ottoman capital. The Ottomans renamed the city Istanbul.

Hagia Sophia, the 6th-century Byzantine Church of Holy Wisdom in Constantinople, was turned into a mosque when the city was taken.

The ceremonial monogram of Suleiman the Magnificent.

Ottoman Society

The Ottomans called Suleiman I "the Lawgiver," because he reformed the empire's legal system. The ruling class was made up of the imperial family, landowners, military leaders, and religious officials. Everyone else paid taxes to the empire, and craftworkers were members of recognized guilds, which set prices and upheld quality. Mosques served as religious and social centers, but Muslim leaders were generally tolerant of other religions.

Public baths were an important feature of daily life in the towns, and some were designed by great Ottoman architects. There were separate days for men and women.

THE OTTOMAN EMPIRE C. 1640

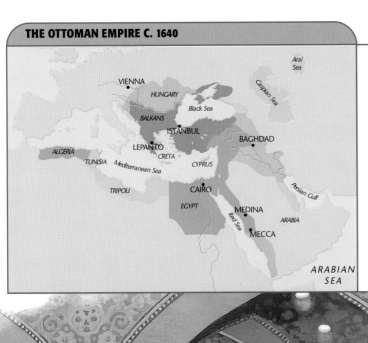

VIENNA
HUNGARY
Aral Sea
Caspian Sea
BALKANS
Black Sea
ISTANBUL
LEPANTO
ALGERIA
CRETA
TUNISIA Mediterranean Sea
CYPRUS
BAGHDAD
TRIPOLI
CAIRO
Persian Gulf
EGYPT
MEDINA
Red Sea
ARABIA
MECCA
ARABIAN SEA

Growth of the Empire

The Ottoman Empire experienced a golden age in the 16th century during the reign of its tenth ruler, Suleiman I. The empire was at its richest and most powerful, and Suleiman was known as "the Magnificent" in the Western world. He was recognized as a great soldier and administrator. Imperial armies invaded Hungary, Persia, and northern Africa, and the Ottoman navy dominated much of the Mediterranean and Red Seas. The map shows how the empire had expanded by the 17th century.

- 1300–1481
- 1515–1520
- 1520–1566
- 1566–1683

THE OTTOMANS

1444–1446, 1451–1481
Reign of Mehmed II, named "the Conqueror" after he captured Constantinople.

1448
Murad II defeats a Hungarian force led by nobleman John Hunyadi in the Battle of Kosovo.

1481–1512
Reign of Bayezid II, during which the empire becomes the leading naval power in the Mediterranean region.

1517
Selim I defeats the Mamelukes and gains control of Egypt, Palestine, and Syria, almost doubling the size of the empire.

1520–1566
Reign of Suleiman the Magnificent, when the empire reaches its peak.

1526
Ottomans capture Belgrade and defeat Hungary at the Battle of Mohacs.

1529
Suleiman lays an unsuccessful siege to the Habsburg capital of Vienna.

1534
Suleiman takes Baghdad from the Persians.

1571
Allied Christian navy of the Holy League defeats the imperial fleet of galleys at the Battle of Lepanto.

The Ottoman Decline

After the reign of Suleiman the Magnificent, the Ottoman Empire entered a long period of stagnation and then decline. There was corruption in government and among the ruling class, and low pay and high taxes affected workers throughout the empire. Several sultans made attempts to bring in reforms and restore success, but the problems were made worse by military defeats. The imperial army and navy were often still successful, but they lost many important battles, and gradually the empire was forced to give up most of its European lands.

An Iznik-ware dish.

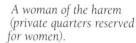

A woman of the harem (private quarters reserved for women).

Causes of Decline

In the late 16th century, Dutch and British success in closing international trade routes through the Middle East affected the Ottomans. Their guilds were unable to compete with cheap European goods, so Ottoman industry declined and workers were poorly paid. At the same time taxes were increased, central government became weaker, and there were problems with food supply. Corruption and theft increased, and there were revolts in the provinces.

A print showing 17th-century Algiers. The Ottomans continued to defend the city by land and sea.

Ottoman Style

The basic Ottoman clothing style was the long, loose tunic called a caftan, which was worn in variations by both men and women. While women wore a veil or scarf to cover their face, Muslim men wore a white turban. People of high rank favored a large turban, and the imperial family had feather decorations. Christians were denoted by wearing a blue turban, and Jews wore yellow. The town of Iznik (ancient Nicaea) became famous for its beautiful pottery bowls, jugs, and dishes, and later for wall tiles.

This 18th-century Turkish School painting shows Selim III receiving an ambassador at the Gate of Felicity in the Topkapi Palace.

The Tulip Period

The period 1717–30, during the reign of Ahmed III, is called the Tulip Period. The flowers became fashionable in Istanbul at a time when Grand Vizier Ibrahim Pasha encouraged the imperial court to take on a more European style. The period is also associated with an art movement similar to European Rococo, and the paintings of masters such as Abdulcelil Levni used softer colors than previously. The court poet Ahmed Nedim wrote lyrical poems and songs that were full of grace.

Portrait of Ahmed III by Levni.

Warfare

A series of military defeats led to a great loss of territory and power. At the end of the 17th century, a disastrous defeat by an alliance led by Holy Roman Emperor Leopold I led to a great loss of European territory that had been in Ottoman possession for two centuries. This marked the beginning of the Ottoman retreat from Europe, which was hastened by further losses to Austria-Hungary, Russia, and others.

Reforms

During the 17th and 18th centuries sultans and their ministers tried to restore the government and social systems that had been so successful earlier. Corrupt officials were executed, provincial revolts were put down, new coinage was introduced, and trade and industry were encouraged. Nevertheless, power remained in the hands of a selfish ruling class, and the reforms were only partly successful.

Turkish pistol case.

The Safavids and the Uzbeks

Mosaic from the dome of the Lutfallah mosque in Isfahan, completed in 1619.

The Safavids were descended from the head of the 13th-century Persian Sufi order of Safawiyah. Their founder proclaimed Shi'ism to be the state religion throughout his empire at the beginning of the 16th century. The Turkic-Mongol Uzbek tribes, who occupied lands to the northeast of the Safavid Empire, were Sunnite Muslims. This religious difference heightened tensions between the hostile neighbors, who vied for territory. By the end of the 17th century, both the Safavid Empire and the Uzbek confederation were in decline.

THE SAFAVIDS AND THE UZBEKS

1500–10
Reign of Uzbek ruler Muhammad Shaybani Khan, who creates the Uzbek confederacy.

1501–24
Reign of Safavid founder Ismail I.

1514
Ottoman army defeats Safavids at the Battle of Caldiron and occupies their capital of Tabriz (in present-day Iran).

1557–98
Reign of the great Uzbek ruler Abd Allah Khan II.

1588–1629
Reign of Abbas the Great.

1598
Isfahan becomes Safavid capital.

1599
The Uzbek Shaybanid dynasty is succeeded by the Ashtarkhanids, leading to decline.

1603
Safavids defeat the Ottomans and regain Tabriz, Herat (in modern Afghanistan), and Baghdad (Iraq).

1722
Isfahan falls to Afghan invaders.

The Safavids

Founding ruler Ismail was first shah of Azerbaijan and then of Persia. Before the end of the 16th century, the greatest Safavid ruler—Abbas I—came to power. He established his imperial capital at Isfahan and turned it into a center of culture, created a standing army to oppose both the Uzbeks and the Ottomans, developed a single coinage, and encouraged trade with Europe and Mughal India. He and his successors also gave new life to Persian art and architecture.

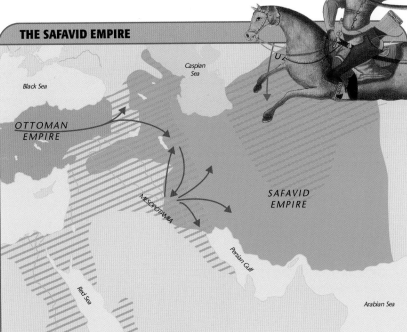

THE SAFAVID EMPIRE

Caspian Sea

Black Sea

OTTOMAN EMPIRE

MESOPOTAMIA

SAFAVID EMPIRE

Persian Gulf

Red Sea

Arabian Sea

This mural detail shows Ismail I stabbing an Ottoman horseman at the Battle of Caldiron, which the Safavids lost. According to legend, Ismail's sword could cut a man in two.

Between the Ottomans and the Uzbeks

The Safavid Empire disputed territory with the Ottomans to the west and the Uzbeks to the northeast. The Safavids won a victory over the Uzbeks in 1510, but four years later were defeated by the Ottomans, which checked their expansion west. There was a continuing struggle with their two rivals, and during the reign of Abbas the Great the Safavids pushed as far as Mesopotamia in the west and Transoxania in the east.

- Area invaded by Ottoman forces 1514-1638
- Ottoman Empire before 1514
- Safavid Empire
- Maximum range of armies of Uzbek khans
- → Major Ottoman campaign
- → Uzbek invasion 1587

Centers of Trade

The Safavid capital Isfahan and Uzbek Bukhara were both great centers of trade. At Isfahan, a new public square was built in the heart of the city during the 1590s. The square itself was used for ceremonial purposes, and it was also surrounded by two-storied rows of shops. Under the Uzbek Shaybanids, Bukhara replaced Samarkand as the trading hub of Central Asia. The city had large bazaars and a separate horse market.

The Uzbeks

The first ruling dynasty of the combined Uzbek tribes, the Shaybanids, held power throughout the 16th century. They ruled from their capital of Bukhara (in modern Uzbekistan), where they built mosques and other impressive buildings. The Shaybanid khans were also great patrons of the arts. After their demise, the Uzbek confederation split into three separate khanates—Bukhara (including Samarkand), Khiva (to the northwest), and Kokand (in the Ferghana valley).

Safavid gunpowder flask.

The Last of the Safavids

Decline began to set in after the death of Abbas the Great. Shah Abbas II (reigned 1642–66) ran his government well and succeeded in regaining central authority. But his successors allowed more power to those religious scholars who believed they should have more say in running the state. There was a series of revolts, and in 1722 Shah Husayn was forced to abdicate by invading Afghans.

Abd Allah Khan II, who expanded Uzbek territory in the late 16th century.

The covered bazaars of Bukhara were filled with busy stalls and workshops. Merchants and craftworkers sold local goods as well as produce such as silk imported from the east.

Origins of the Mughal

Miniature of Babur, who was an accomplished poet and writer of memoirs as well as a great military leader.

The Mughals (sometimes called Moguls) were named after their Mongol ancestors. They came originally from central Asia, traveling south to the Indian subcontinent at the beginning of the 16th century. The early Mughal rulers continued to follow Islam but were tolerant of other religions. They allowed the subcontinent's Hindu majority to go on following their own culture, creating a blend of Persian and Indian influences. The empire expanded rapidly during the 16th century, and great rulers such as Akbar organized its structure and government well.

A lady of the harem dressing her hair. Mughal leaders and noblemen had more than one wife and often had a large number of children.

Humayun's tomb in Delhi took nine years to build. It was made of red sandstone and white marble.

Founding the Empire

Babur (1483–1530), a Turkic warrior ruler from Ferghana (in present-day Uzbekistan), was descended from two great Mongol leaders, Genghis Khan and Timur. In 1501 he lost Samarkand to one of his greatest opponents, Muhammad Shaybani Khan of the Uzbeks (see page 56). Babur decided to head south, capturing Kabul and Kandahar, and finally his army won a great victory over the sultan of Delhi. This marked the foundation of the Mughal Empire.

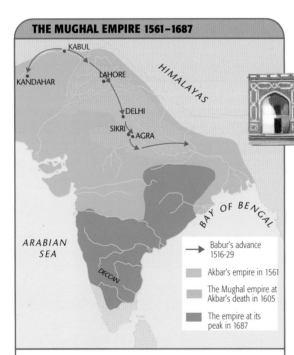

THE MUGHAL EMPIRE 1561–1687

KABUL
KANDAHAR
LAHORE
HIMALAYAS
DELHI
SIKRI
AGRA
ARABIAN SEA
BAY OF BENGAL
DECCAN

→ Babur's advance 1516-29

Akbar's empire in 1561

The Mughal empire at Akbar's death in 1605

The empire at its peak in 1687

Imperial Expansion
Babur's territory was limited to the plain of the Ganges River, and his successors gradually expanded the empire to the west and south. By the time of Akbar's death in 1605, the Mughals controlled the whole of the subcontinent, from the Gulf of Arabia to the Bay of Bengal. Later in the century, the empire stretched much further south into the Deccan and reached its peak.

Civil War and Restoration

In 1539–40 Babur's son Humayun, the second Mughal emperor, was twice defeated in battle by a force of invading Afghan Surs. Humayun was forced to take refuge in Persia, where he received military aid from the Safavid Shah Tahmasp. Having retaken Kandahar and Kabul, Humayun went on to capture Lahore and Delhi, where civil war had broken out. After a gap of 15 years, Humayun resumed his rule in 1555. He died the following year in an accident.

Jahangir

Akbar's son Salim assumed the title of Jahangir ("world conqueror") when he succeeded his father in 1605. Despite rebelling against Akbar during his lifetime, Jahangir adopted many of his father's policies and expanded the empire further. The new ruler's patronage of the arts led to great developments in Mughal painting and music.

This miniature was commissioned by Jahangir in 1620 to show his dream of friendship with his great rival, Abbas I (on the left). Two years later, Abbas took Kandahar from Jahangir.

THE EARLY MUGHAL EMPIRE

1526
Babur founds the Mughal Empire.

1535
Humayun (ruled 1530–40, 1555–56) invades Gujarat.

1556–1605
Reign of Akbar, the greatest ruler of the Mughal Empire.

1569
Akbar founds Fatehpur Sikri, near Agra, as his capital.

1576
Completion of the conquest of Bengal.

1598
Mughal capital moves to Agra.

1605–27
Reign of the fourth emperor, Jahangir.

1614
Jahangir captures the great Rajput fortress of Rajasthan.

1622
The Mughals lose the fortress of Kandahar to Safavid ruler Abbas I after a 45-day siege.

Akbar

The founder's grandson, Akbar, became ruler at 13. He soon set about expanding Mughal territory, and at the same time set up an effective system for organizing and governing the empire, including new methods of tax collection. Akbar became known for his justice and religious toleration. Despite some resistance from senior orthodox Muslims, his approach won the support and loyalty of many Hindus.

Akbar's household rejoices at the birth of his second son, Murad. Scene from an illustration accompanying the Akbarnama, a biography written by Abu l-Fadl in the 1590s.

The Mughal Decline

The Mughals never recovered their power after the death of their last great emperor, Aurangzeb, early in the 18th century. During his reign the Marathas, a Hindu people from western India, fought the Mughals for territory and succeeded in expanding their own influence. The Marathas themselves had great rivals for power in the Afghans and the British. This left the Mughals with little authority, and by the end of the 18th century, they had no real empire left.

Silver rupees from Aurangzeb's imperial mint at Surat.

A 17th-century Mughal sword.

From Peak to Decline

Aurangzeb was the last of the great Mughal emperors. He fought off invasions in the north and expanded the empire to the south. But he created great discontent by executing a Sikh guru, reintroducing a tax on non-Muslims, and destroying Hindu temples. These intolerant acts undid much of his predecessors' work and weakened the Mughals' authority. His reign left the empire with considerable problems and led to its rapid decline.

Wars of Succession

The Mughal succession was often disputed with great violence. Jahangir's son Khurram had his brothers killed in order to gain the throne as Shah Jahan. His reign was a troubled one, and when he fell ill in 1657, his four sons contested the throne by making war on each other. Aurangzeb emerged the victor, claimed the title and imprisoned his father in the Agra fort. Shah Jahan died there 8 years later.

This miniature of Shah Jahan on horseback was painted by a court artist. His reign was a golden age of Mughal art and architecture.

Mughal Empress

Jahandar Shah's short reign (1712–13) began when he defeated his brothers and ended when he was overthrown by his own nephew. During his time as emperor Jahandar gave his favorite wife Lal Kunwar, who was famous for her beauty and musical skills, a title meaning "chosen of the palace." She acted as an empress and soon made sure that her whole family received special status and favors. Lal Kunwar even accompanied the emperor into battle.

This 18th-century painting shows a Mughal prince and consort in their palace garden.

Mughal ruler Muhammad Shah (on the left) with Persian leader Nadir Shah.

The Last Mughal Emperors

The Mughals never recovered from the humiliation of the sack of Delhi, and their empire fell apart under pressure from the Marathas and the British. By the mid-18th century the Mughals governed only a small area around Delhi. By the end of the century Shah Alam II held power only inside his palace. He ended up living under the protection of the British, who captured Delhi in 1803.

The Sack of Delhi

During the weak rule of Muhammad Shah, the Mughals were invaded by Nadir Shah, a military leader who had assumed power in Persia in 1736. The Persian army defeated Muhammad Shah at Karnal and went on to sack Delhi. Nadir Shah ordered a general massacre and then took an enormous amount of booty, including gold, jewels (such as the famous Koh-i-noor diamond), and the golden Peacock Throne that had been made for Shah Jahan.

During their sack of Delhi, Nadir Shah's men loaded horses, elephants, and camels with treasure, including the Peacock Throne.

Dynasties and Kingdoms of India

Before the arrival of the Mughals, several great dynasties ruled the sultanate of Delhi. There were kingdoms and empires in other parts of the subcontinent, some Muslim and others Hindu. There was constant conflict between different peoples and regions. When Afghan invaders finally defeated the Marathas in the 18th century, the Sikhs were able to establish themselves as rulers of the Punjab region. By that time the British East India Company controlled Bengal and had a strong foothold in the subcontinent.

This painting from Rajasthan of the Hindu goddess Radha dates from about 1760.

Mughal conflict

From early in the 16th century, independent Muslim sultanates and Hindu kingdoms came into conflict with the growing Mughal empire. As the Mughals expanded their influence, they fought and conquered others, advancing into the Deccan at the beginning of the 17th century. The Mughals conquered Ahmadnagar in 1636, and 50 years later went on to capture the powerful kingdom of Bijapur.

Gol Gumbaz, the domed tomb of Muhammad Adil Shah (ruled 1626–56) in Bijapur.

Rajput Painting

The Rajputs of the northwestern region developed their own style of art in the 16th and early 17th centuries. Rajput rulers were great art patrons, and their preferred style was traditional and romantic. Favorite subjects were the great Hindu god Krishna and his companion Radha. Many paintings were kept in boxes or albums, which were passed around for viewing.

Maratha Empire

The Marathas founded their Hindu empire in western India (in the present-day state of Maharashtra) in 1674, when Shivaji united warrior chiefs into a federation. They increased their empire by conquest, fighting the Mughals for territory during the reign of Aurangzeb (see page 60). But the Marathas failed to take Delhi, and in 1761 were defeated by an invading Afghan army. This caused the decline of their empire.

Maratha founder Shivali, who was known as a tough warrior and a tolerant ruler.

Bijapur ruler Ali Adil Shah II (reigned 1657–72) is fanned by a servant.

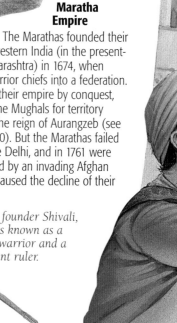

EMPIRES AND SULTANATES

INDEPENDENT HIMALAYAN STATES

LAHORE

THE RAJPUT KINGDOMS

SIND

BIHAR

MALWA

BENGAL

GUJRAT

ARABIAN SEA

GONWANA

BERAR

ORISSA

AHMADNAGAR

BIDAR

BIJAPUR

GOLCONDA

HINDU EMPIRE OF VIJAYANAGAR

INDIAN OCEAN

- - - - Other boundaries

▨ Akbar's kingdom 1561

▨ Mughals 1605

Muslim and Hindu Powers

By the middle of the 16th century the earlier Bahmani sultanate of the Deccan had been succeeded by the five Muslim states of Bijapur, Ahmadnagar, Golconda, Berar, and Bidar. The Rajputs, who claimed descent from ancient tribes and were within the warrior caste of Hindu society, fought hard against Mughal domination. In the south, the Hindu empire of Vijayanagar had become powerful during the first half of the century, but it suffered a devastating defeat by a combined Muslim sultanates' force in 1565.

Late 16th-century ivory relief of two heroic brothers from the Hindu epic Ramayana.

Sikh Community

Gobind Singh was the tenth Sikh Guru (religious teacher). During the Sikh New Year festival of Baisakhi, in 1699, he formed a new community called the Khalsa (meaning "pure"). The Guru called for volunteers prepared to die for their faith, and five men came forward. They were taken one by one into a tent, but emerged unscathed, to become the first members of the Khalsa.

Gobind Singh initiated the first members into the Khalsa order by giving them a drink of sweetened water.

TIMELINE

1451–89
Reign of Bahlul Lodi, first ruler of the Lodi Dynasty in Delhi.

1469–1538
Life of Guru Nanak, founder of Sikhism.

1489–1511
Reign of Yusuf Adil Shah, founder of the Adil Shahi Dynasty in the sultanate of Bijapur.

1509–29
Reign of Krishna Deva Raya, great ruler of Vijayanagar.

1517–26
Reign of last Lodi ruler Ibrahim, who is killed by Mughal founder Babur.

1577
Amritsar is founded by Ram Das, fourth Guru of the Sikhs.

1579–1626
Reign of Ibrahim Adil Shah II, who extends the Bijapur Kingdom south to Mysore.

1674–80
Reign of Shivaji, founder of the Maratha Empire.

1675–1708
Gobind Singh is Sikh Guru.

1679–1709
War between the Rajputs and Mughals.

1761
Afghans destroy northern Maratha power at the Battle of Panipat.

1774
The British appoint their first governor general of India.

The Early Ming Dynasty

T he first emperor of the Chinese dynasty that took over from the Mongols in the 14th century chose the dynastic name Ming, meaning "brilliant." The new ruler set out to wipe out the memory of foreign occupation and restore the empire's past greatness. This was largely achieved by successive Ming emperors, who were to go on to rule China for nearly 300 years. Their capital moved from Nanjing to Beijing, where the imperial court was housed in a rectangular city within the city.

Portrait of Emperor Hongwu (reigned 1368–98), who was a harsh ruler and famously ugly.

This stone sculpture of a Ming general was one of many colossal statues that lined the road to the imperial cemetery near Beijing.

TIMELINE

1368
Zhu Yuanzhang (1328–98) founds the Ming Dynasty as Emperor Hongwu.

1380
Hongwu has his prime minister executed for plotting against him; the emperor later abolishes the post altogether.

1403–24
Reign of Yongle.

1405–33
Naval commander Zheng He leads seven voyages from eastern China to the Indian Ocean.

1406–21
Building of the Forbidden City.

1417
Confucian text The Great Compendium of the Philosophy of Human Nature is published.

1421
The capital moves from Nanjing to Beijing.

1426–35
Reign of Xuande, a great patron of the arts at the imperial court.

1436–49, 1457–64
The interrupted reigns of Emperor Zhengtong/ Tianshun.

Founding the Dynasty

The Mongols had ruled China for 89 years when their Yuan Dynasty came to an end. In 1368 rebel leader Zhu Yuanzhang, who controlled central and southern China, declared himself emperor (taking the title Hongwu, meaning "vast military power") and founded the Ming Dynasty. Hongwu captured Beijing, and by 1387 his troops had driven the Mongols out of the provinces.

This watchtower, now restored, was built during the Ming period as part of the extended Great Wall.

The Third Emperor

Hongwu was succeeded by his young grandson, who ruled as Jianwen (1399-1402). During the reign of Yongle, the fourth son of Hongwu, Beijing was completely rebuilt –including the construction of the Forbidden City–and became the official capital. Yongle had a good military and scholarly education, and he was a strong ruler.

Mongol Threat

The Mongols remained a threat to the Ming Empire. Yongle himself led five campaigns against them, and he died during the last of these. The Ming emperors strengthened existing parts of the Great Wall and added new sections to protect their northern borders against invaders. They built extra walls at passes and in valleys, adding large watchtowers and beacon towers.

This painting of the Sun was made in 1425 by Emperor Hongxi, who took an interest in astronomy.

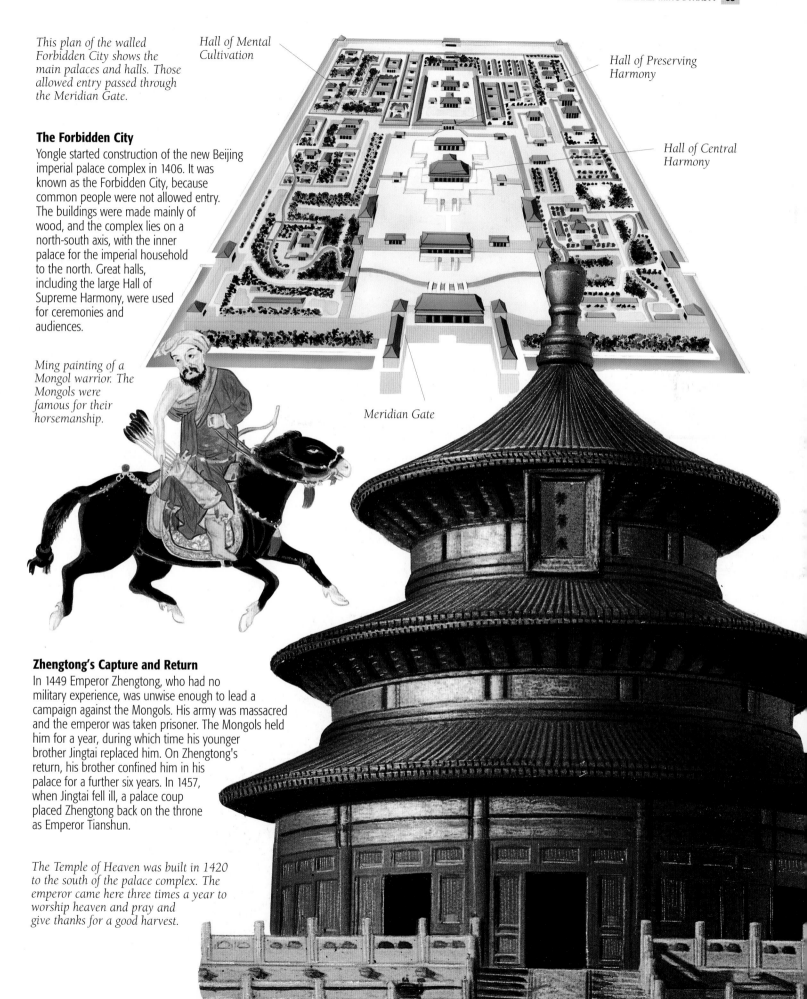

This plan of the walled Forbidden City shows the main palaces and halls. Those allowed entry passed through the Meridian Gate.

Hall of Mental Cultivation

Hall of Preserving Harmony

Hall of Central Harmony

The Forbidden City

Yongle started construction of the new Beijing imperial palace complex in 1406. It was known as the Forbidden City, because common people were not allowed entry. The buildings were made mainly of wood, and the complex lies on a north-south axis, with the inner palace for the imperial household to the north. Great halls, including the large Hall of Supreme Harmony, were used for ceremonies and audiences.

Ming painting of a Mongol warrior. The Mongols were famous for their horsemanship.

Meridian Gate

Zhengtong's Capture and Return

In 1449 Emperor Zhengtong, who had no military experience, was unwise enough to lead a campaign against the Mongols. His army was massacred and the emperor was taken prisoner. The Mongols held him for a year, during which time his younger brother Jingtai replaced him. On Zhengtong's return, his brother confined him in his palace for a further six years. In 1457, when Jingtai fell ill, a palace coup placed Zhengtong back on the throne as Emperor Tianshun.

The Temple of Heaven was built in 1420 to the south of the palace complex. The emperor came here three times a year to worship heaven and pray and give thanks for a good harvest.

The Ming Empire

Despite increasing trade and an expanding economy, the Ming emperors and their imperial government gradually became weaker. Threats from the north remained, and though there was more contact with the rest of the world through trade, the emperors generally remained conservative and inward-looking. High taxes caused unrest, and famine and drought led to open revolt. This eventually caused the downfall of the dynasty, as rebels within the empire opened the way for Manchus from the north to take over.

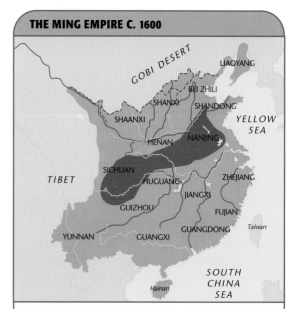

THE MING EMPIRE C. 1600

Trade Routes

During the 16th century maritime trade became more important and ports grew. Ningbo gave access to and from Japan, Quanzhou to Taiwan, and Guangzhou to Southeast Asia. Cotton textiles, silk, porcelain, and tea were the main exports, and American silver was imported via Manila. In 1557 the Portuguese were allowed to establish a permanent trading base at Macao. But relations between the Chinese and European merchants were not always good.

- Ming territory c. 1590
- Popular uprising 1636-41
- - - - Great Wall
- —— Chinese trade routes under the Ming Empire

Philosophy and Religion

During the early Ming period, leading figures in the empire followed the interpretation of Confucianism that had been made by the 12th-century philosopher Zhu Xi. Emperor Hongzhi (reigned 1488–1505), for example, received a strict Confucian education. By this time Buddhism and Taoism were less influential, though Emperor Jiajing (reigned 1522–67) was a Taoist who tried to suppress Buddhism. His son and successor Longqing expelled the Taoists from the imperial court.

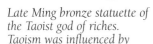

Late Ming bronze statuette of the Taoist god of riches. Taoism was influenced by Chinese folk religion.

This 17th century illustration on parchment shows the emperor Jaijing on his ship. During the long journeys, his officers checked the condition of the canal network.

Rebellion

Severe famine in 1628 led to despair. Army deserters and laid-off soldiers formed bandit gangs, and others rebelled against imperial rule. Tax increases in 1639, followed by floods, made the situation worse. Workers rioted and tenants rose up against their landlords. One rebel leader, Li Zicheng, finally captured the capital and Emperor Chongzheng committed suicide. This was the perfect opportunity for the Manchus, who drove the rebels out and seized power.

Peasants rebelled against landowners. In this scene, former servants loot an estate. The landowner can do nothing as his wife is forced to serve the rebels.

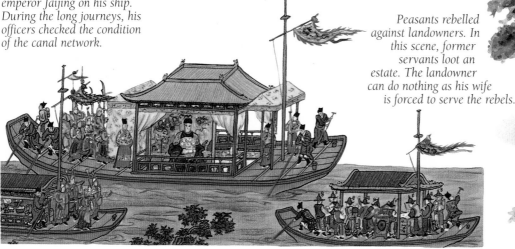

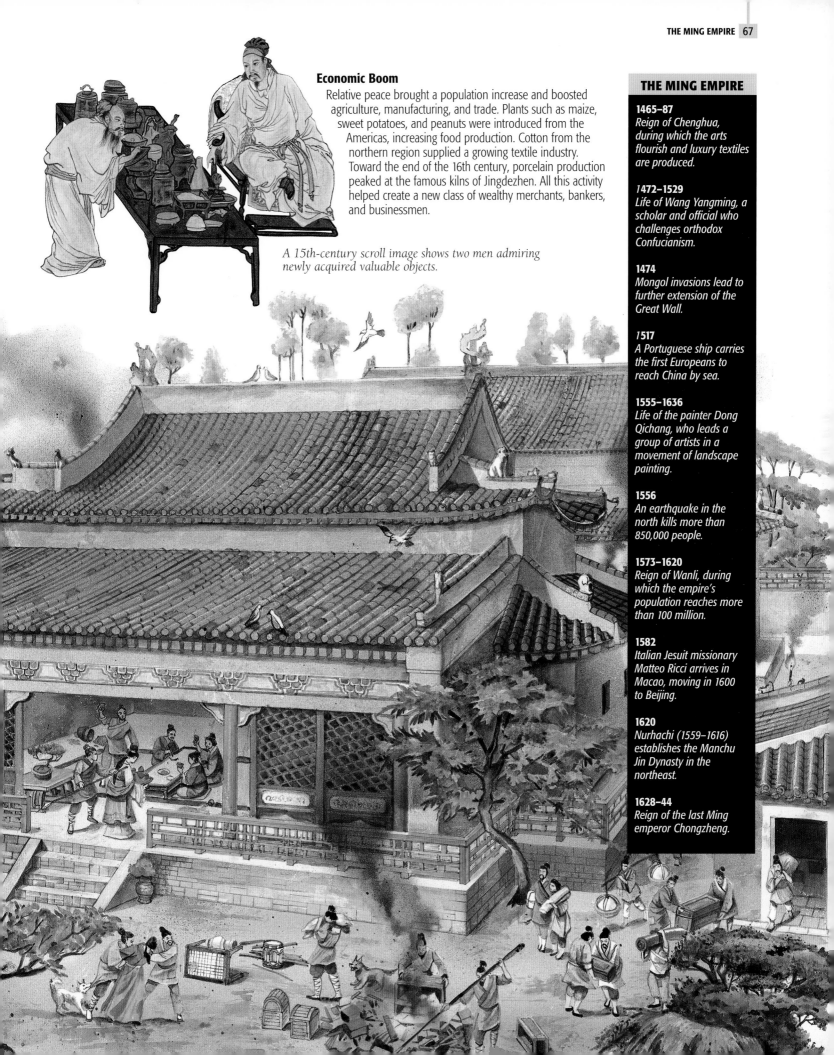

Economic Boom

Relative peace brought a population increase and boosted agriculture, manufacturing, and trade. Plants such as maize, sweet potatoes, and peanuts were introduced from the Americas, increasing food production. Cotton from the northern region supplied a growing textile industry. Toward the end of the 16th century, porcelain production peaked at the famous kilns of Jingdezhen. All this activity helped create a new class of wealthy merchants, bankers, and businessmen.

A 15th-century scroll image shows two men admiring newly acquired valuable objects.

THE MING EMPIRE

1465–87
Reign of Chenghua, during which the arts flourish and luxury textiles are produced.

1472–1529
Life of Wang Yangming, a scholar and official who challenges orthodox Confucianism.

1474
Mongol invasions lead to further extension of the Great Wall.

1517
A Portuguese ship carries the first Europeans to reach China by sea.

1555–1636
Life of the painter Dong Qichang, who leads a group of artists in a movement of landscape painting.

1556
An earthquake in the north kills more than 850,000 people.

1573–1620
Reign of Wanli, during which the empire's population reaches more than 100 million.

1582
Italian Jesuit missionary Matteo Ricci arrives in Macao, moving in 1600 to Beijing.

1620
Nurhachi (1559–1616) establishes the Manchu Jin Dynasty in the northeast.

1628–44
Reign of the last Ming emperor Chongzheng.

The Early Qing Dynasty

The Manchus were quick to seize their opportunity to capture Beijing, take over from the Ming Dynasty, and expand their northern territory into a vast empire. During the 17th and 18th centuries, they were able to extend Qing control even further. The Manchus made up a small percentage of their new empire's population, and there was some resistance to their customs. The Qing emperors adopted many of the Ming forms of government and administration, but they kept their own military system based on separate "banner" units.

Painting from 1760 of one of the emperor's warrior bodyguards.

A 17th-century statuette of a European.

Below: This scroll painting by Giuseppe Castiglione shows Kazakh envoys presenting horses as tribute to Qianlong. It was painted in a style that combined Chinese and European techniques.

A Qing emperor's court boots.

The Manchus

The Manchus were descendants of the Jurchens from Manchuria (to the northeast of the Ming Empire). Their ancestors had ruled northern China in the 12th century, and in 1620 their chieftain Nurhachi started a new Manchu Dynasty. His son Huang Taiji (reigned 1626–43) ruled from their capital Shenyang and adopted the Chinese dynastic name Qing, meaning "pure." By 1644 Huang's six-year-old son Shunzhi ruled the new Qing Empire of China.

Longest Reign

The second Qing emperor, Kangxi, succeeded his father at the age of eight and assumed full power six years later. His reign (1661–1722) was the longest in this or any other Chinese dynasty. As both a good administrator and military commander, Kangxi toured and inspected his vast empire. He also led the Qing army against the Mongols, who continued to threaten the Chinese borders. He had a great love of literature and was a patron of the arts.

The young Kangxi at his studies. As emperor he set up studios for artists and architects in the Forbidden City.

This porcelain statuette of Guanyin, a Buddhist figure known in the West as the goddess of mercy, shows Western influences.

Qianlong's Empire

Kangxi's grandson Qianlong expanded the Qing Empire to its greatest extent. Success and wealth brought a further population boom, and farming production and manufacturing went up. Tea, cotton, and porcelain exports all increased. But rapid expansion also brought problems, and these were made worse in the emperor's later years by dependence on his corrupt minister Heshan.

Jesuits at Court

Kangxi welcomed Jesuit missionaries at his court, admiring the Europeans' artistic and technical skills and appointing them as astronomers, cartographers, and physicians. Qianlong continued the tradition and even commissioned Jesuit architects to design his summer palace outside Beijing. The Jesuits were careful to blend their European ideas with Chinese styles.

THE QING EMPIRE

SIBERIA

MANCHURIA

MONGOLIA

ZUNGHARIA

KOREA

GOBI DESERT

Yellow River

EAST TURKESTAN

TIBET

Yangtzi River

HIMALAYAS

BURMA

ANNAM

Expansion

The Qing Empire expanded greatly in the 18th century, under Kangxi, Yongzheng, and Qianlong. A series of campaigns led to Tibet being brought under Chinese control, and in 1755–65 Qianlong's armies went west and swept through Central Asia. By then the empire covered present-day Mongolia and parts of Russia, and Chinese dominance was recognized in Korea, Vietnam, and Burma.

Additional area under Manchu Dynasty in 1760

Manchu expansion by 1644

Manchu homeland

Manchu vassal state

Area under Ming dynasty

--- Great wall

Japan in the Muromachi Period

In the early 14th century central military authority and government moved from Kamakura to Kyoto. A new family of shoguns came to power, and they continued to exercise authority over the imperial family. The period of rule by the Ashikaga shoguns (1338–1573) is called after its center of power, Muromachi. After a disastrous civil war in the 15th century, the shogunate lost authority and provincial warlords fought each other for land and power. This split Japan into hundreds of separate feudal states.

Takauji was a powerful warrior as well as a skilled statesman.

The Muromachi Shogunate

Takauji's grandson Yoshimitsu (1358–1408) moved his headquarters to the Muromachi district of Kyoto, giving the shogunate its name. Yoshimitsu was a powerful shogun, who brought the two rival imperial courts together again. Nevertheless, during his rule provincial military governors gained more influence, raising taxes from local landowners.

The Ashikaga Family

The Ashikaga family had become one of the most powerful in Japan during the 13th-century Kamakura period. Having driven the emperor from Kyoto, Ashikaga Takauji (1305–58) had himself appointed shogun by a rival emperor in 1338. This marked the beginning of the Ashikaga shogunate. Takauji was a cultured man who wrote poetry and helped the development of Zen Buddhism.

Yoshimitsu had this Golden Pavilion built outside Kyoto in 1394.

Increasing Trade

Yoshimitsu stopped southern feudal lords from raiding the Chinese coast and set up formal trade with Ming-dynasty China and Korea. He even adopted the title "King of Japan" in his dealings with the Ming government. Increased trade at home and abroad helped create a new class of Japanese merchants, as farming, commerce, and mining all grew and improved.

Onin War

Civil war broke out in 1467 between rival regional warlords. They took the opportunity to take sides in a dispute over the succession to the shogunate. Yoshimasa had made his younger brother his heir, but then the shogun's wife gave birth to a son. Full-scale war broke out around Kyoto and lasted for ten years. The shogun abdicated in favor of his son, but the shogunate was greatly weakened.

An ashigaru foot-soldier. These men formed the shogun's personal army.

Decorated samurai swords. The warrior class of samurai supported the provincial feudal lords.

TIMELINE

1336
Ashikaga Takauji's rebel forces drive Emperor Go-Daigo (reigned 1318–39) from Kyoto to Yoshino; there are two rival imperial courts until 1392.

1363–1443
Life of Zeami Motokiyo, a great playwright of No theater under the patronage of Yoshimitsu. 1368–94 Ashikaga Yoshimitsu rules as shogun, moving his administration to Muromachi in 1378.

1449–73
Ashikaga Yoshimasa rules as shogun.

1483
Yoshimasa builds the Silver Pavilion as his retirement retreat in the Eastern Hills of Kyoto.

1488
A Poem of One Hundred Links is composed by three poets, Sogi (1421–1502), Shohaku (1443–1527), and Socho (1448–1532).

1543
Portuguese sailors in a Chinese boat become the first Europeans to visit Japan.

1549
Spanish Jesuit missionary Francis Xavier (1506–52) arrives in Japan.

1573
Yoshiaki is deposed as the last Ashikaga shogun.

Cultural Developments

There was a flowering of Japanese culture in the 14th century. Masked No theater followed on from ancient forms of dance drama and festival rituals. A form of "linked verse" developed, in which three or more poets supplied alternating verses. Zen Buddhists encouraged these arts, as well as those of ink painting, flower arrangement, and the tea ceremony.

A No mask. All the actors were male, but they sometimes wore female masks.

The ritual of the tea ceremony was a study in refinement and elegance.

No dramas were popular with the nobility. A performance was usually made up of five serious, stylized plays separated by comic interludes.

The Oda Regime

Born into a noble family, Oda Nobunaga (1534–82) was a powerful, ambitious warrior. Originally a supporter of the shogun Ashikaga Yoshiaki, Nobunaga turned against him and finally deposed him in 1573. After occupying Kyoto, Nobunaga built Azuchi Castle, selected able generals, and fought his way to domination over central Japan.

The Unification of Japan

From 1574 great efforts were made to reunify the warring regions of Japan. The years 1574 to 1600 are often called the Azuchi-Momoyama period. The name refers to castles built by the country's first great unifiers: Azuchi (beside Lake Biwa) was built by Oda Nobunaga, and Momoyama (in Kyoto) by his successor Toyotomi Hideyoshi. The third unifier, Tokugawa Ieyasu, moved his power base to Edo (modern Tokyo). In 1603 Ieyasu became shogun, founding the Tokugawa shogunate that was to rule unified Japan until 1867.

Oda Nobunaga, who equipped many of his followers with muskets.

Society

In the 17th century Japanese society was governed by a strict system of military authority. Much of the power lay with the regional feudal lords, who in their own region made laws and collected taxes. The rest of society was divided into four classes: samurai warriors at the top, followed by farmers, artisans, and merchants. Despite their supposedly low status, many merchants came to enjoy great wealth.

Painted wooden statuette of Zen Buddhist priest Ishin Suden (1569–1633), who helped draft new laws.

Ieyasu and Edo

Tokugawa Ieyasu (1542–1616) was a noble from eastern Japan, who became an ally of Hideyoshi and ruled as one of the regents for the shogun's heir. He controlled a large army, defeated his rivals in battle, and founded the Tokugawa shogunate. Ieyasu ran his government from Edo, which became the unified country's political center, though Kyoto remained the official capital throughout the Tokugawa period.

A Christian is killed during the outbreak of violence in 1638.

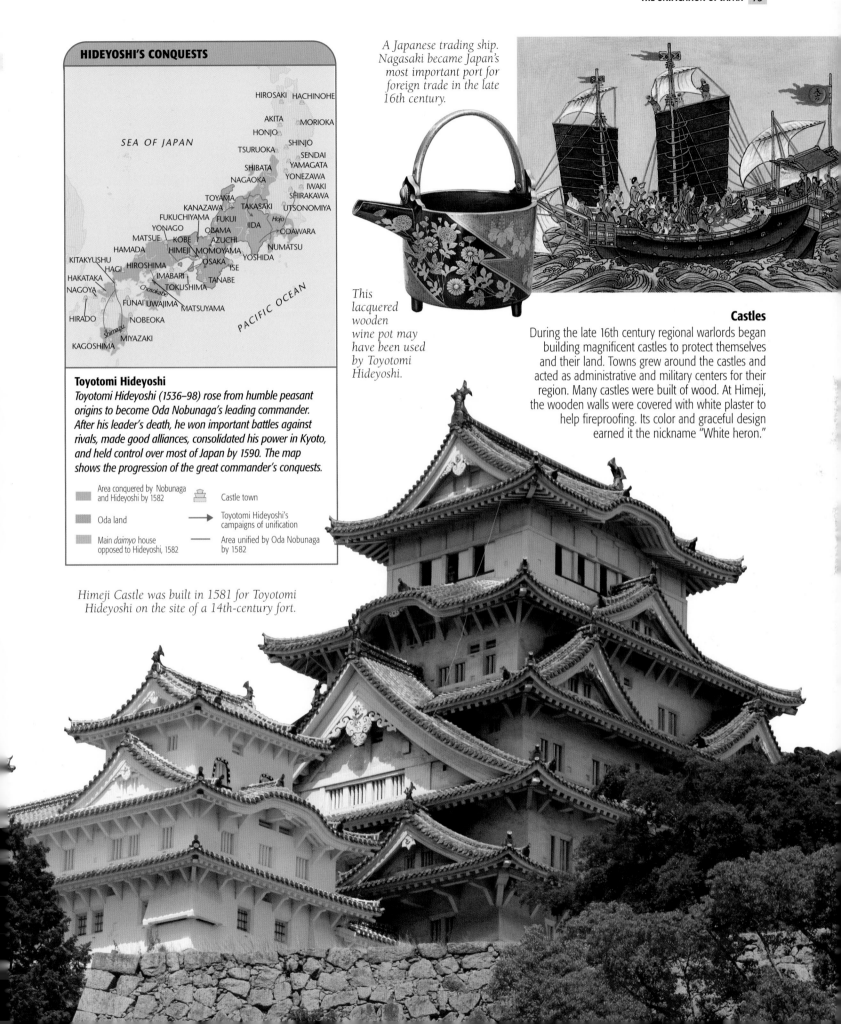

HIDEYOSHI'S CONQUESTS

SEA OF JAPAN

HIROSAKI HACHINOHE
AKITA MORIOKA
HONJO
TSURUOKA SHINJO
SENDAI
SHIBATA YAMAGATA
NAGAOKA YONEZAWA
IWAKI
TOYAMA SHIRAKAWA
KANAZAWA TAKASAKI UTSONOMIYA
FUKUCHIYAMA FUKUI *Hojo*
YONAGO OBAMA IIDA ODAWARA
MATSUE KOBE AZUCHI NUMATSU
HAMADA HIMEJI MOMOYAMA
KITAKYUSHU HIROSHIMA OSAKA YOSHIDA
HAGI IMABARI ISE
HAKATAKA *Chosokabe* TOKUSHIMA TANABE
NAGOYA FUNAI UWAJIMA MATSUYAMA
HIRADO NOBEOKA
Shimazu MIYAZAKI
KAGOSHIMA

PACIFIC OCEAN

Toyotomi Hideyoshi

Toyotomi Hideyoshi (1536–98) rose from humble peasant origins to become Oda Nobunaga's leading commander. After his leader's death, he won important battles against rivals, made good alliances, consolidated his power in Kyoto, and held control over most of Japan by 1590. The map shows the progression of the great commander's conquests.

Area conquered by Nobunaga and Hideyoshi by 1582	Castle town
Oda land	Toyotomi Hideyoshi's campaigns of unification
Main *daimyo* house opposed to Hideyoshi, 1582	Area unified by Oda Nobunaga by 1582

Himeji Castle was built in 1581 for Toyotomi Hideyoshi on the site of a 14th-century fort.

A Japanese trading ship. Nagasaki became Japan's most important port for foreign trade in the late 16th century.

This lacquered wooden wine pot may have been used by Toyotomi Hideyoshi.

Castles

During the late 16th century regional warlords began building magnificent castles to protect themselves and their land. Towns grew around the castles and acted as administrative and military centers for their region. Many castles were built of wood. At Himeji, the wooden walls were covered with white plaster to help fireproofing. Its color and graceful design earned it the nickname "White heron."

This Chosôn porcelain jar, with an iron brown glaze, is decorated with a dragon design.

Chosôn Society

The elite, scholarly class of Chosôn society was known as yangban, meaning "two groups" (referring to civilian and military officials). Members of this land-owning class were expected to cultivate the Confucian moral standards of others during the course of their duties. Many were accomplished artists. Beneath them in the hierarchy were craftsmen, peasants, and merchants. At the bottom of the social order were lowly butchers and gravediggers, as well as slaves.

Painting from a late Chosôn Album of Scenes from Daily Life, which focused on people's everyday lives.

KOREA

MING CHINESE EMPIRE

Korea Bay

KOREA

SEA OF JAPAN

YELLOW SEA

JAPAN

Japanese Invasion
In 1592 Japan's ruler Toyotomi Hideyoshi (see page 73) sent a large army to invade Korea. With support from Ming China and great resistance by their navy, the Koreans forced the Japanese to withdraw. In 1597 the Japanese invaded again, but after Hideyoshi's death in the following year, they again withdrew. The map shows the regions where the Japanese campaigns took place and the area that they occupied.

Area of Korea occupied by Japan 1593-98 → Campaigns in Korea 1592
Main area of Korean resistance to Hideyoshi → Korean and Ming Chinese counteroffensives
→ Toyotomi Hideyoshi's campaigns of unification

Korea's Chosôn Dynasty

When a new dynasty came to power in Korea in 1392, its founder took up the ancient name of Chosôn for his kingdom. The dynasty of Yi rulers had close cultural ties with Ming China, to which it paid tribute. This was transferred to the Manchus (and their Chinese Qing Dynasty) after they ravaged the Chosôn capital Hanyang. The Chosôn rulers officially ended support for Buddhism and made theirs a united, Confucian state. Korean scholars made their own contribution to the theories of Confucianism.

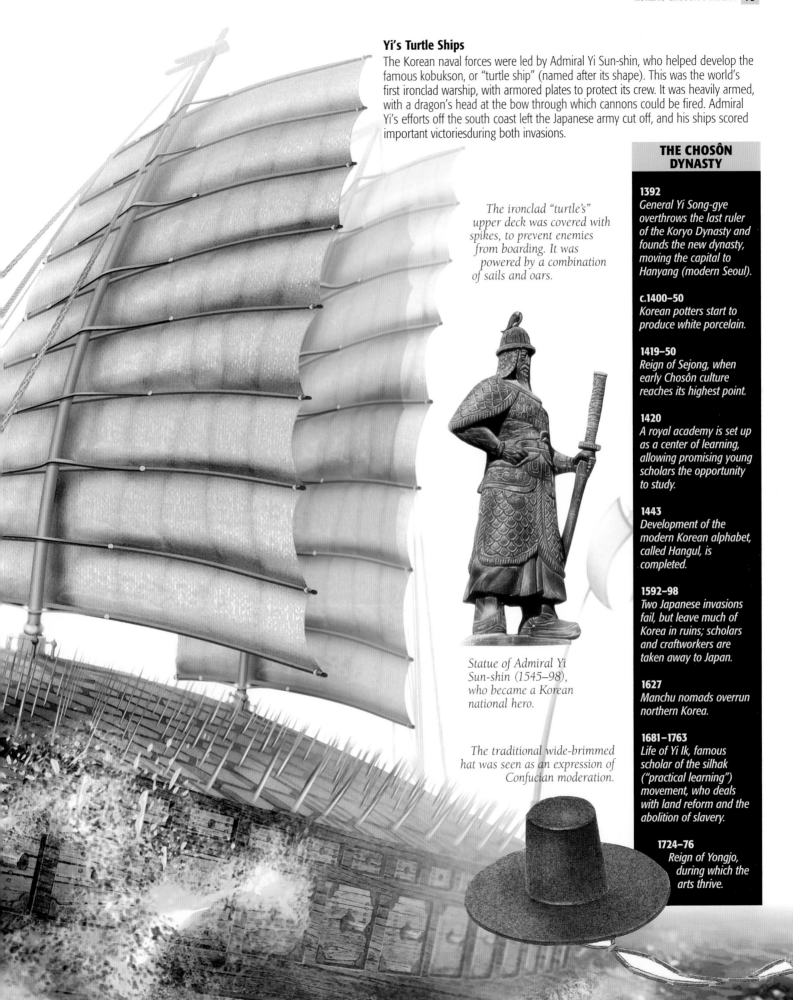

Yi's Turtle Ships

The Korean naval forces were led by Admiral Yi Sun-shin, who helped develop the famous kobukson, or "turtle ship" (named after its shape). This was the world's first ironclad warship, with armored plates to protect its crew. It was heavily armed, with a dragon's head at the bow through which cannons could be fired. Admiral Yi's efforts off the south coast left the Japanese army cut off, and his ships scored important victoriesduring both invasions.

The ironclad "turtle's" upper deck was covered with spikes, to prevent enemies from boarding. It was powered by a combination of sails and oars.

Statue of Admiral Yi Sun-shin (1545–98), who became a Korean national hero.

The traditional wide-brimmed hat was seen as an expression of Confucian moderation.

THE CHOSÔN DYNASTY

1392
General Yi Song-gye overthrows the last ruler of the Koryo Dynasty and founds the new dynasty, moving the capital to Hanyang (modern Seoul).

c.1400–50
Korean potters start to produce white porcelain.

1419–50
Reign of Sejong, when early Chosôn culture reaches its highest point.

1420
A royal academy is set up as a center of learning, allowing promising young scholars the opportunity to study.

1443
Development of the modern Korean alphabet, called Hangul, is completed.

1592–98
Two Japanese invasions fail, but leave much of Korea in ruins; scholars and craftworkers are taken away to Japan.

1627
Manchu nomads overrun northern Korea.

1681–1763
Life of Yi Ik, famous scholar of the silhak ("practical learning") movement, who deals with land reform and the abolition of slavery.

1724–76
Reign of Yongjo, during which the arts thrive.

CAMBODIA, BURMA, AND THAILAND

1350
The city of Ayutthaya is founded by Ramathibodi I on an island at the mouth of the Pa Sak River (in modern Thailand).

1431
Thai forces under Siamese King Boromoraja II capture Angkor, and the Khmer abandon the city.

1448–88
Reign of King Trailok of Ayutthaya (Thailand), during which there are continuous wars with Cambodia.

1453–72
Reign of Burmese queen Shin Sawbu at Pegu, when trade flourishes.

1511
Portuguese traders arrive in Ayutthaya.

1516–66
Reign of Khmer king Ang Chan, during which his people campaign deep into Thai territory.

1531–50
Reign of Tabinshwehti, second king of the Toungoo Dynasty, who unifies Burma.

1594
Siamese King Naresuan captures the Khmer capital Lovek.

1760
Alaungpaya is wounded and dies on a Burmese campaign against the Siamese capital Ayutthaya (which is captured 7 years later).

1782
Thai general Chaophraya Chakri becomes King Rama I and establishes the Chakri Dynasty.

Cambodia, Burma, and Thailand

From the beginning of the 15th to the end of the 18th century, the mainland region of Southeast Asia was made up of many small kingdoms. They vied with each other for power, and there was constant tension and conflict between Burma (or Myanmar), Siam (modern Thailand), and Cambodia. The many different peoples of the region had their own rich cultures, inherited from earlier empires. The region was never united, but it had one major religion across the kingdoms—Buddhism.

This 15th-century glazed ceramic tile from Burma shows ass-headed demons from the army of the god of death. They tried in vain to prevent the Buddha from attaining enlightenment.

An 18th-century puppet of a Burmese king, from Rangoon.

Burma

The southern region of modern Burma (Myanmar) was dominated by the Mon people, until their kingdom fell to the Burmese Toungoo Dynasty in 1539. They made their capital at Pegu, which became a great center of Buddhism. The Mon rebelled in the mid-18th century, brought down the Toungoom, and captured the capital of Ava, another Burmese kingdom. A king named Alaungpaya (reigned 1752–60) reunified Burma, establishing a new dynasty and founding the city of Rangoon.

Cambodia

The sacking and abandonment of its capital Angkor in 1431 marked the decline of the powerful Khmer Empire of Cambodia. The weakened Khmer court moved south to Lovek (near modern Phnom Penh), where a golden royal palace was built in 1553. During the 15th and 16th centuries the Khmer were almost constantly at war with the Siamese state of Ayutthaya, which further weakened the Cambodian state.

Thailand

The Thai kingdom of Ayutthaya ruled the region around its capital of the same name from the mid-14th to mid-18th century. For much of that time the kingdom was at war with its neighbors, the Burmese and the Khmer. After the city of Ayutthaya was finally destroyed by the Burmese in 1767, a military commander took over, until a new dynasty of kings was founded 15 years later. The capital of the kingdom was Bangkok.

In 1593 King Naresuan of Thailand (reigned 1590–1605) rode his war elephant against the crown prince of Burma during a Burmese invasion. The Thai king was victorious and became a national hero.

CAMBODIA, BURMA, AND THAILAND

MING EMPIRE

Andaman Sea

Gulf of Thailand

Strait of Malacca

SOUTH CHINA SEA

A Diversity of Peoples

The different peoples of the Burma–Thailand–Cambodia region were constantly in conflict with each other. Yet they were united by the religious tradition of Buddhism, following the ancient school of Theravada ("Doctrine of the Elders"). To the east of the region, the earlier Khmer Empire had followed Hindu-Buddhist traditions. Islam dominated Arakan to the northwest and Malaya to the south.

Ayutthaya Kingdom (Siam), mid-15th century

Burmese Kingdom of Toungou at maximum extent, 1555

Burma, 1783

Khmers (Cambodia)

Indonesia, Malaysia, Laos, and Vietnam

Vietnam

The state of Dai Viet had been established in the 10th century. It was strongly influenced—and for some years controlled—by China. The Le Dynasty came to power in 1428, and later in the century conquered the Hindu kingdom of Champa to the south.

By the time the Europeans arrived in the early 16th century, the mainland and islands of Southeast Asia were divided into many different kingdoms and sultanates. There was often conflict among them. This made things easier for the various East India Companies, which sent ships across the Indian Ocean in search of precious goods, especially spices. The route to the Spice Islands led through the strategically important Strait of Malacca, between the Malay Peninsula and Sumatra (in modern Indonesia).

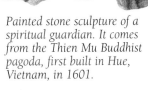

Painted stone sculpture of a spiritual guardian. It comes from the Thien Mu Buddhist pagoda, first built in Hue, Vietnam, in 1601.

Map of the port of Malacca, which controlled the strait linking the Indian Ocean with the South China Sea.

Hat Makmo ("melon stupa"), a Buddhist temple built in 1504 by the consort of Laotian king Visunarat (reigned 1500–20).

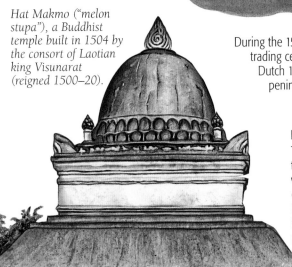

The Malay State

During the 15th century the Muslim port of Malacca became an important trading center. It was a vital capture for the Portuguese in 1511 and the Dutch 130 years later. The Malays established other kingdoms on the peninsula, including Johore. In the 18th century the Buginese from Sulawesi invaded, captured Johore, and established further sultanates. The British arrived towards the end of the century.

Laos

The unified Laotian kingdom of Lan Xang was established in the mid-14th century with Khmer help. Theravada Buddhism was introduced during the reign of the founder Fa Ngum (reigned 1353–74). Except for a period of rule by the Burmese, the kingdom lasted continuously until 1713, when it split into three separate kingdoms—Vien Chan (around the present capital of Laos, Vientiane), Champassak, and Luang Prabang. These kingdoms came under Thai control during the 18th century.

INDONESIA, MALAYSIA, LAOS, AND VIETNAM

c.1403
A Sumatran prince sets up the sultanate of Malacca on the Malaysian coast.

1488–1511
Reign of Mahmud Shah as sultan of Malacca; after the Portuguese invasion, he founds the kingdom of Johore.

1574–1637
Laos is ruled by Burma (Myanmar)

1600–64
East India Companies are formed: British (1600), Dutch (1602), Danish (1616), and French (1664).

1641
The Dutch seize Malacca from the Portuguese.

1677
The ruler of the Javanese kingdom of Mataram asks the Dutch to help fight rebels and gives trading rights in return.

1705–48
Life of the celebrated Vietnamese poet Doan Thi Diem.

1786
The British East India Company sets up a trading base on the Malayan island of Penang.

1778
Vientiane comes under Siamese (Thai) control.

1802
Gia Long becomes emperor of Dai Viet, which he renames Vietnam.

A traditional wooden and leather puppet used in Javanese shadow plays of Hindu epics.

European Presence

After the Portuguese arrived in Malaysia early in the 16th century, European explorers, traders, and settlers made a great impact on the Indonesian islands. Followed by the Dutch and British, the Portuguese opened up the sea route from Europe to the Spice Islands (the Maluku province of Indonesia, or the Moluccas). The map shows the territories controlled by European nations by the 18th century.

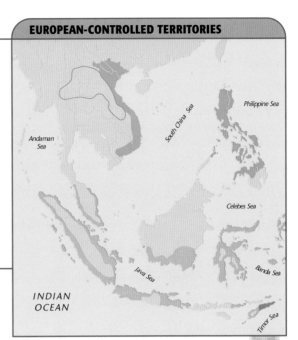

EUROPEAN-CONTROLLED TERRITORIES

Andaman Sea

South China Sea

Philippine Sea

Celebes Sea

Java Sea

Banda Sea

INDIAN OCEAN

Timor Sea

■ Empire of Annam, 1783

■ Spanish territory, 1783

— Lao Kingdom of Lan Chang at maximum extent, 1548

■ Dutch territory, 1783

■ Portuguese territory, 1783

Indonesia

The Hindu Majapahit kingdom of Java dominated the region of present-day Indonesia until the late 15th century. By that time Islam had spread through the islands, and new Muslim trading kingdoms vied with each other for supremacy. In the following century the Portuguese established trading posts, and the first Dutch fleet arrived in 1596, landing at Bantam on the coast of Java. The Dutch East India Company ensured that their nation became the dominant power in Indonesia.

Pilgrims visit the Javanese tomb of Maulana Malik Ibrahim, who died in 1419. He was one of the Wali Sanga ("nine saints of Islam"), who brought Islam to Java.

Art and Culture in East Asia

Chinese cultural styles and artistic techniques made their impression throughout East Asia. The Chinese love of calligraphy and skill in producing decorated pottery, and especially delicate porcelain, influenced the artists and art-lovers of Korea and Japan. Throughout the region rulers and their governments promoted excellence among their artists, setting up official academies and workshops and acting as patrons for painters and poets. Many results of their work can still be seen today.

Illustration for Dream of Red Mansions, *a 120-chapter Chinese novel written by Cao Zhan (1715–64), famous for its sensitive portrayal of female characters.*

Literature

In China, Ming emperors restored competitive literary examinations and scholarly works were held in great respect. The educated elite disliked the colloquial literature that became more popular by the 16th century. Japanese adoption of printing in the 17th century also encouraged popular literature, since the classics existed only as manuscripts. In Korea, the Hangul alphabet developed in the 15th century was used for more popular works, but scholars continued to write in classical Chinese.

This poem was written in the new Korean alphabet by Emperor Sejong (reigned 1419–50).

Painting

Ming-dynasty imperial patronage ensured that painters were highly regarded. Their style gradually became less academic as paintings showed more self-expression, especially in landscapes. Chinese painters influenced Korean artists, who also chose to show more realistic scenes of daily life. In Japan, the famous Kano school of painters reflected the official Confucian view of a well-ordered society, while other painters were more individualistic.

Science and Medicine

The 16th-century Chinese scholar Li Shizhen compiled a comprehensive compendium of more than 8,000 herbal remedies, following ancient prescriptions. Chinese physicians understood blood circulation, using acupuncture to ensure a good flow of chi, or "life force." Many scientific books were taken from China to Korea and Japan, including works on mathematics. By the 17th century Japan was also influenced by European medicine introduced by Jesuit missionaries and Dutch physicians.

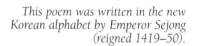

A 17th-century Japanese screen painting of the wind god.

This Chinese ivory figure from the Ming period was used to teach female anatomy to medical students.

This 18th-century Korean screen painting of a bookshelf shows a Confucian respect for learning.

The Nine Dragon Screen

Emperor Qianlong (reigned 1736–95) refurbished and extended the Forbidden City in Beijing (see page 65). One of his additions was a screen wall covered with glazed tiles, which was completed in 1771 to protect the northeast section of the City. Nine writhing dragons appear on the screen in ceramic relief, representing in the highest single number the principle of heaven and the emperor as the son of heaven.

Ceramics

The Chinese ceramics industry flourished during the Ming period, producing porcelain and other wares of exceptional quality. Porcelain production reached its peak at the Jingdezhen imperial kilns in the first half of the 18th century. In Korea, the Chosôn government also supported an official kiln to produce blue-and-white porcelain, but standards never reached the heights of Ming ware. In the 17th century, skilled Japanese potters specialized in vessels for the tea ceremony.

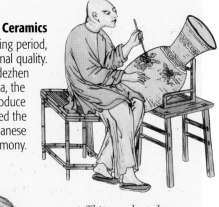

This woodcut shows a Ming artist decorating a large vase before it was glazed and fired.

This detail of the Nine Dragon Screen shows the beauty of the ceramic details.

In addition to the nine large dragons on the screen, there are a further five in the background (the number being midway between 1 and 9). The screen is 91 feet (27.5 m) long and is covered with 270 tiles.

The Industrial Revolution brought about a long period of transition, during which a society dominated by agriculture changed into one characterized by increasing trade, industry, and finance. The invention of new machines drove this so-called revolution and led to the building of factories to house them.

Working conditions in the factories were usually poor, and machine-minders worked long hours for little pay. Industrial towns sprang up, where housing was often overcrowded and unsanitary. Nevertheless, industrial growth brought the benefits of new, cheaper goods, as well as steam-powered methods of transportation. Eventually, social reformers succeeded in improving working conditions, housing, and education for working-class families.

This chapter tells the story of the Industrial Revolution, from its beginnings in Britain, through its spread to other European countries, the United States, Russia, and Japan. The revolution took different forms around the world, depending on natural resources and politics, but its impact was enormous everywhere.

The Industrial Revolution changed the working habits of women. Many took factory jobs.

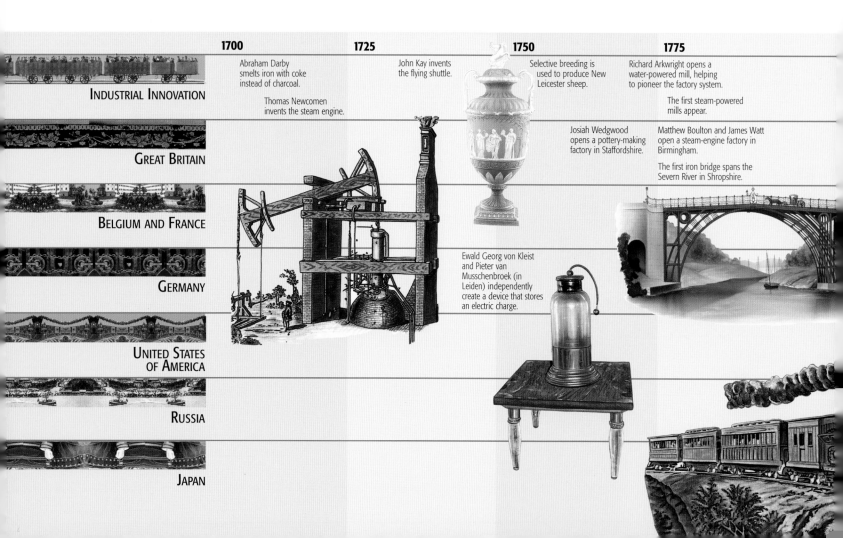

	1700	**1725**		**1750**	**1775**
INDUSTRIAL INNOVATION		Abraham Darby smelts iron with coke instead of charcoal.	John Kay invents the flying shuttle.	Selective breeding is used to produce New Leicester sheep.	Richard Arkwright opens a water-powered mill, helping to pioneer the factory system.
		Thomas Newcomen invents the steam engine.			The first steam-powered mills appear.
GREAT BRITAIN				Josiah Wedgwood opens a pottery-making factory in Staffordshire.	Matthew Boulton and James Watt open a steam-engine factory in Birmingham.
					The first iron bridge spans the Severn River in Shropshire.
BELGIUM AND FRANCE					
GERMANY				Ewald Georg von Kleist and Pieter van Musschenbroek (in Leiden) independently create a device that stores an electric charge.	
UNITED STATES OF AMERICA					
RUSSIA					
JAPAN					

The Industrial Revolution

This American steam engine was made in 1869 to speed up and improve farming methods. It was used to drive mechanical threshers and sawmills.

1800	1825	1850	1875	1900

Steam locomotives are used for public railway.

English landowners are allowed to enclose land without referring to Parliament.

The Leeds–Liverpool Canal is completed.

The Great Exhibition opens in Hyde Park, London.

The coal mines of the Borinage region are updated with conveyor belts, leading to an increase in coal output.

The first Belgian railway links Brussels with Mechelen.

First public railway in France opens between Paris and Saint Germain.

Alfred Krupp introduces the open-hearth steel-making process in his factory in Essen.

Werner von Siemens builds the first electric railroad.

The New York Stock & Exchange Board is established.

The first US passenger train steams along a local line in South Carolina.

Charles Goodyear discovers vulcanization, a process of making rubber stronger.

Edwin Drake strikes oil near Titusville, Pennsylvania.

The first continuous railroad track across the US are completed.

Andrew Carnegie forms the Carnegie Steel Company.

Tsar Alexander II frees Russia's serfs.

The Trans-Siberian Railroad is begun.

The Nobel Oil Extracting Partnership is founded in Baku.

Commodore Perry's squadron arrives in Edo Bay.

The Mitsubishi company is founded, dealing first in shipping and then coal mining.

The Japanese government nationalizes 17 private railway companies.

Nagasaki dockyard opens, with its own ironworks and imported steam hammer.

The first Japanese railroad opens from Tokyo to Yokohama.

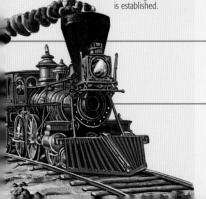

The Importance of the Industrial Revolution

T he industrial revolution did not happen suddenly and it did not change people's lives overnight. It evolved gradually, as one small, new development led to another, bigger one. Nevertheless, in Europe and elsewhere the events of this period changed an agricultural, rural society into an industrial, urban society. The gradual transformation touched everyone, from aristocrats and successful industrialists to peasants and ordinary workers. It affected the lives of men, women, and children, causing significant social as well as economic changes.

Work Changes

Before the industrial revolution, most people in Europe lived on farms and in country villages. In 1800 four out of five Europeans depended on agriculture for their livelihoods. Some farming families regularly moved around the countryside in search of seasonal work. This traditional routine was greatly affected by new agricultural methods which involved less labor. As people moved to the growing towns, their working lives changed dramatically.

A farming family sets out to look for work at haymaking time. Casual workers were expected to have their own tools.

1 A merchant acted as the entrepreneur throughout the process. First he purchased the raw material, in this case wool.

2 The merchant delivered the wool to the working family's cottage. They first sorted, cleaned, and carded the wool.

Cottage Industry

Before industrialization and even after the invention of power-driven machines, many textiles and other goods were made by country people in their own homes. The whole family worked together in this so-called cottage industry, using traditional skills to make cloth or finished goods. Some merchants provided their working families with spinning wheels and mechanical looms. The sequence of illustrations (right) shows how this domestic system worked when making textiles.

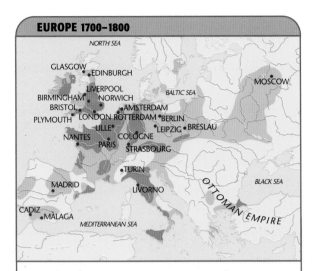

EUROPE 1700–1800

NORTH SEA

GLASGOW
EDINBURGH

LIVERPOOL
BIRMINGHAM NORWICH
BRISTOL AMSTERDAM
PLYMOUTH LONDON ROTTERDAM BERLIN
LILLE COLOGNE LEIPZIG BRESLAU
NANTES
PARIS STRASBOURG

TURIN

MADRID

LIVORNO

CADIZ
MÁLAGA

MEDITERRANEAN SEA

BALTIC SEA

MOSCOW

BLACK SEA

OTTOMAN EMPIRE

Population Growth

During the industrial revolution all classes of society generally lived longer and had larger families than previously. Europe's population grew rapidly, from about 140 million in 1750 to 200 million in 1800 and 430 million by the end of the 19th century. Britain's percentage of those figures grew from 5 percent in 1750 to nearly 9 percent in 1900. The map shows the major European centers of population around 1750.

● Major centers of population

▨ Population over 100 per square mile (1.6 sq km)

▨ Population from 50 to 100 per square mile (1.6 sq km)

▨ Population less than 50 per square mile (1.6 sq km)

Cities had no mains sewerage before 1850. This brass plaque belonged to a London "nightman," who collected waste from domestic cesspits at night.

The busy city streets were full of life—and noise.

Living Conditions

The industrial revolution led to successful members of the middle and upper classes enjoying more comfortable lives, with better diets and improved health. For working-class people the results were mixed. They were forced to work long hours for low pay, and many of the new jobs were extremely monotonous. Nevertheless, their situation gradually improved during the 19th century, and they too were able to enjoy some of the new products on the market.

3 A spinning wheel was used to twist the raw wool into yarn.

4 Finally, the yarn was woven into fabric. This family did their weaving on a Jacquard loom (invented in 1804), which used punched cards to produce patterns in the cloth.

Westminster Bridge, spanning the Thames River in London, shortly before its completion in 1750.

Ideal Conditions

Conditions in Britain favored the change from an agricultural to an industrial society. The country was politically stable, unified, and free from internal customs duties. It had large deposits of coal and iron, both of which were essential for industrialization. During the 18th century canals were built to connect new industrial centers, adding to new roads and bridges, and transportation was soon to be revolutionized by the introduction of steam railroads.

Visitors to the Great Exhibition were amazed by the exhibits and the Crystal Palace that housed them. The building, designed by Joseph Paxton (1803–1865), was almost 2,000 feet (600 m) long, with an iron frame supporting nearly 300,000 panes of glass.

This souvenir box shows the exterior of the Crystal Palace.

These silk shoes were made in London in the 1760s.

Great Britain

The term "Industrial Revolution" was first used in late 19th-century Britain to refer to events in that country that had begun in the previous century. The iron-smelting process was improved, power-driven machinery came into use, canals were built, and factories opened. More British goods were made, and new forms of transportation helped move raw materials and finished products more quickly. By the middle of the 19th century, Victorian Britain was able to stage a Great Exhibition to show the results to its own people and the rest of the world.

London was a bustling trading center. This 19th-century illustration shows St. Katherine's Dock, one of the busiest docks along the Thames.

A Trading Power

Britain was a successful colonial and trading power. Its colonies produced raw materials and themselves became markets for manufactured goods. They helped to stimulate the textile industry, and demand for British goods grew, forcing competing businesses to look for more efficient ways of production to keep prices affordable. Successful entrepreneurs achieved this by developing new machines and factories.

The Great Exhibition

The Great Exhibition of 1851 was designed to show that Britain was the "workshop of the world." The planning committee was headed by Queen Victoria's husband Prince Albert, who opened the exhibition and visited it many times. The Crystal Palace, which contained around 13,000 exhibits, had its own boiler room with steam engines to run the machinery on show.

ENGLAND

1709
Abraham Darby converts a furnace to smelt iron with coke instead of earlier charcoal.

1761
The Bridgewater Canal links the coalmines of Worsley to the city of Manchester.

1774
Matthew Boulton and James Watt open a steam-engine factory in Birmingham.

1785
James Watt's steam engine is first used to power a cotton mill.

1799–1800
The new Combination Acts outlaw trade unions (but are repealed in 1824).

1801
The Act of Union with Ireland creates the United Kingdom of Great Britain and Ireland.

1816
The Leeds–Liverpool Canal is completed.

1851
The Great Exhibition opens on May 1st in Hyde Park, London, and runs until October 11th; more than 6 million people pay to visit the exhibition.

1854
The Crystal Palace, having been taken down and moved from Hyde Park, reopens in Sydenham.

The Factory System

The development of power-driven machines meant that goods could be made more uniformly, more efficiently, and—most important of all to the owner-entrepreneurs—more quickly. Large machines were even more efficient, and they were housed in manufactories, or factories as they came to be known. The textile industry was one of the first sectors to build factories, for its newly developed spinning and weaving machines. Other industries soon followed suit.

Portrait of early industrialist Matthew Boulton (1728–1809).

Organizing Work

Though wages were low, labor was the main production cost in the new factories. Entrepreneurs and factory-owners made sure that workers were properly supervised and disciplined, since they normally now paid for their time rather than the amount of work completed or finished products. New machinery meant that an individual's work became more specialized, since each factory worker concentrated on one single part of the process.

Richard Arkwright (1732–92), who invented a spinning machine that was used in early cotton mills.

Changing the Landscape

Urban centers grew rapidly around the new factories, as working families moved to spreading towns and cities from the country. Since they worked long hours for low pay, traveling to work was out of the question. Dominated by factories, the towns were noisy and dirty. Further out, the growing number of coal mines and ironworks also changed the rural landscape.

Silver tureen made in 1776 at the Birmingham factory of Boulton and John Fothergill.

This 19th-century painting shows a district of Burnley, in Lancashire, dominated by the Lowerhouse print works.

Increased Production

Power-driven machinery meant a greatly increased scale of production, which kept costs down. This interested many different kinds of businessmen, including manufacturers such as Matthew Boulton, who went into partnership with the famous engineer James Watt. Craftsmen such as Josiah Wedgwood (1730–95) also opened factories, so that they could meet the demand that their products created.

THE FACTORY

1769
Josiah Wedgwood opens a pottery-making factory at Etruria, near Stoke-on-Trent in Staffordshire,

1771
Richard Arkwright opens a water-powered mill in Cromford, Derbyshire, helping to pioneer the factory system (see page 96).

1775
Matthew Boulton and James Watt become partners in the steam-engine business.

1779
First steam-powered mills.

1786
Matthew Boulton develops steam-powered coin-minting machinery; Arkwright puts a Watt engine in a cotton mill in Blackfriars, London.

1811–16
During Luddite riots workers destroy factory machines they fear will replace them.

1814
The Times is printed on a steam-driven press.

A Yorkshire miner. His workplace, the colliery, also became more mechanized.

This ornamental vase was made at Wedgwood's large pottery factory.

Spreading Industrialization

Before the existence of factories, textiles and other goods were made in rural homes and small workshops. Many workers were farmers, who added to their income by making products from raw materials provided by a merchant. This cottage industry worked successfully for many, and the earlier methods overlapped with the factory system, which spread across Britain gradually and sporadically.

The Textile Industry

Between the mid-18th and mid-19th century, English factories gradually took over the manufacture of textiles from home workers. Once looms were driven by steam it became much more efficient to group them together in large workrooms. Cotton textiles contributed greatly to the rise of Britain as an industrial nation, as cotton goods became increasingly popular and cheap enough to be afforded by most of the population.

This furnishing fabric of cotton and linen was made in London in 1769. The colors were added using copperplates and woodblocks.

From Wool to Cotton

Britain had developed a thriving wool industry in the late Middle Ages. By the 16th century cotton textiles were being imported, until eventually the British began bringing in raw cotton and spinning and weaving it themselves as a cottage industry. Cotton could be made into a wide variety of fabrics, especially for clothes, as it was comfortable to wear. Technological advances made it possible to mechanize the production of cotton fabric.

Cotton fibers grow out of seed pods of the cotton plant. The fibers can be spun into yarn.

Cotton Processing

The invention of machines revolutionized the cotton industry in Britain. In 1733 John Kay invented the flying shuttle (first used with wool), which increased weaving speed. This meant that more yarn was needed, which spurred the invention of the spinning jenny. Next came the invention of a water-driven spinning machine. These developments, along with the invention of the cotton gin in America, all helped make cotton an important fabric.

INDUSTRIAL ENGLAND

AYR

LANCASTER
PRESTON
WIGAN BLACKBURN
MANCHESTER
CROWE NOTTINGHAM
DERBY
NORWICH
YARMOUTH

IPSWICH
GLOUCESTER COLCHESTER

SALISBURY

EXETER DORCHESTER

NORTH SEA
IRISH SEA
BRISTOL CHANNEL
ENGLISH CHANNEL

● Cotton ● Silk ● Wool

Spreading Factories

Textile-producing factories spread throughout England during the Industrial Revolution. Wool production was centered on West Yorkshire, the West Country, and East Anglia. The map shows the main manufacturing centers for wool, cotton, and silk. Lancashire also became known for its fustian cloth, a sturdy mixture of cotton and linen.

TEXTILES

1779
English weaver Samuel Crompton (1753–1827) develops the spinning mule, a cross between the spinning jenny and the water frame (see page 96).

1791
A Manchester mill orders 400 of Edmund Cartwright's power looms, but is burned down by workers fearing for their jobs.

1793
American inventor Eli Whitney (1765–1825) develops a cotton gin that separates seeds from fibers, speeding up production of the raw material.

1801
French inventor Joseph Marie Jacquard develops a loom that can weave cloth with intricate patterns.

1803
William Horrocks improves Cartwright's power loom and makes his machine of iron.

1809
The English Parliament awards Cartwright £10,000 for the benefits to the nation of his power loom.

1856
William Perkin develops the first synthetic dye.

The Power Loom

A clergyman named Edmund Cartwright (1743–1823) changed the history of weaving after visiting Arkwright's Cromford factory in 1784. The following year Cartwright invented his first version of a power loom. The machinery was driven by steam, which speeded the process up enormously. After improvements, the first power loom was soon installed in Cartwright's factory in Doncaster.

This 19th-century engraving shows power looms in use in the weaving room of a textile mill in 1834. A male supervisor oversees the work of female weavers.

Silk

British silk weavers were constantly competing for quality and price with foreign imported goods. But by the 18th century England was the European leader in silk manufacture. Weavers made damasks, velvet, and satins, as well as silk brocades. The main center was at Spitalfields, in east London, where there were 17,000 looms. As power looms became available, silk cloth became even more popular.

This silk dress from the 1860s was dyed with a synthetic mauve. The first synthetic dye was made from coal tar.

This silk twister's wheel, cross, and reeler dates from about 1770. It was turned by hand to twist single filaments of silk into a stronger thread.

The Agricultural Revolution

Beginning in the 17th century, great changes were made to European agriculture, especially in the Low Countries and Britain. Improved methods led to better yields, as leading farmers began treating agriculture as a science. High yields led to low prices, allowing people to buy more manufactured goods and so helping industry. At the same time, fewer farmhands were needed. By 1850 less than a quarter of the British workforce was in agriculture, and many had moved to towns to work in factories.

A Dutch windmill, which was used to pump water from land and reclaim it for farming.

New Machinery

English farmer Jethro Tull (1674–1741) developed two pieces of machinery that contributed to change and progress. The first was a horse-drawn hoe that lifted weeds and turned over soil. The second was a mechanical seed drill, also drawn by horses, which made rows of holes in the soil and dropped seeds in them. The drill sowed three rows at a time and was very productive.

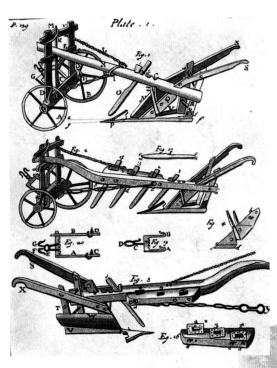

A page from Jethro Tull's book Horse-Hoeing Husbandry, *published in 1731.*

Land Enclosure

The change from open-field strip farming to the rotation system led to more fields being enclosed by fences and hedges. This allowed individual farmers to have complete control over their own fields, working them as units. Farms grew larger, leading to a hierarchy of wealthy landowners, tenant farmers, and landless farm laborers.

Farm laborers, such as this man with his scythe, often moved from farm to farm in search of work.

AGRICULTURE

1701
Jethro Tull develops the seed drill.

1730
Viscount Charles "Turnip" Townshend retires from politics to his Norfolk estate, where he introduces the four-course system.

1755
Robert Bakewell uses selective breeding to produce New Leicester sheep.

1776
Norfolk farming earl Thomas Coke (1752–1852) begins making improvements to farming methods and stockbreeding.

1782
Jethro Tull's seed drill is improved by adding gears.

1783
The first factory for making plows is established in England.

1786
France obtains its first Spanish Merino sheep (officially forbidden from export by Spain); Scottish engineer Andrew Meikle develops a threshing machine.

1836–40
Two General Enclosure Acts allow English landowners to enclose land without referring to Parliament.

Crop Rotation

In the English county of Norfolk, Viscount Townshend introduced a new system of crop rotation that had no fallow year and produced fodder crops. In one field he grew wheat in the first year, clover or ryegrass in the second, oats or barley in the third, and turnips in the fourth year. The clover or ryegrass were grazed by livestock, and the turnips were used as fodder in winter. Manure from the livestock fertilized the fields, which were rotated each year.

Tull's seed drill was a great success, especially since the new system used less seed than old-fashioned sowing by hand.

Feeding the People

The introduction of new rotation methods, machinery, and more animal power increased crop yields significantly. English harvests were good during the first half of the 18th century, and less productive grains such as rye were replaced by higher-yielding wheat or barley. The result was more food for the growing population, including those in the spreading cities.

In the 18th century other European countries tried to increase their crop yields. This illustration shows Frederick the Great encouraging Prussian farmers to grow potatoes.

Stockbreeding

Livestock benefited from the new fodder crops. In the 1760s Leicestershire farmer Robert Bakewell (1725–95) began improving his own animals by selecting breeding stock from those with the best characteristics, such as fine wool or high milk yields. Bakewell successfully bred Leicester sheep, Longhorn cattle, and large white pigs. Others soon followed his example.

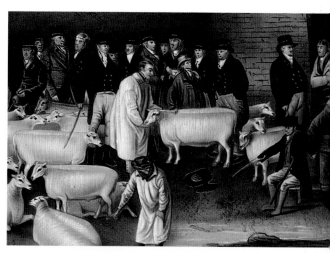

Above: This painting shows Robert Bakewell hiring out his rams to farmers who wanted to improve their own stock.

Steam

English engineer Thomas Savery (1650–1715) invented the first practical steam engine–to pump water from mines–in 1698. Fourteen years later, English blacksmith Thomas Newcomen (1663–1729) developed a more efficient steam pump that had a cylinder fitted with a piston. Since Savery had a wide-ranging patent on his device, Newcomen went into partnership with him.

Sources of Power

At the beginning of the industrial revolution the two power sources in addition to muscle power were wind and water. Windmills and waterwheels were useful, but human workers and animals were still needed for many tasks. The invention of the steam engine changed everything, and soon steam—created by burning coal to heat water—was driving machines in factories and mines throughout Britain. At the same time innovative scientists were investigating alternative forms of energy, such as electricity.

Newcomen's steam engine. Steam from the boiler drove a piston in the cylinder, which moved a wooden beam. The other end of the beam operated a pump plunger in the mine shaft.

Horses were used to haul coal, along with mules, oxen, and even dogs.

Human and Animal Power

Many industrial and agricultural activities relied solely on muscle power. In early coal mines, windmills were sometimes used to pump water away. The coal itself was broken loose with picks and loaded into baskets that were carried on the backs of men and women. Alternatively, the coal was put into wooden sledges or wagons that were pushed or hauled to vertical shafts. The coal was raised to the surface using manpower and, later, horsepower.

Up until the 19th century, many children worked long hours. This child is helping to operate a press.

English chemist Sir Humphry Davy (1778–1829) invented the miner's safety lamp in 1815. Its flame was enclosed in a double layer of wire gauze.

Mining Technology

After successful pumping operations, steam engines were soon being used to power windlasses and haul coal to the surface of mines. But it was not until the 19th century that steam engines were used to pull coal along railway tracks. By then rotary ventilation fans had been introduced and special safety lamps were being used by miners to light up the tunnels. These helped cut down explosions caused by naked flames.

A manual windlass was used to lower children and other workers down the mine shaft.

William Watson's book on electricity was published in 1748.

Ponies, women, and children were often used to haul coal along the narrow, low tunnels.

Electricity

In 1745 the Dutch physicist Pieter van Musschenbroek (1692–1761) and the German cleric Ewald Georg von Kleist independently invented a device that could store an electric charge. It was later called a Leyden jar. Two years later, English scientist William Watson (1715–87) increased the capacity of the Leyden jar by coating it with lead foil. These early discoveries led to an understanding of electricity, which would later be used to power many industrial machines.

The glass Leyden jar was sealed with a cork and partly coated with metal foil on its inner and outer surfaces.

Great Inventions

Many of the great inventions of the industrial revolution came about in the textile industry (see pages 90–91), where each practical innovation was aimed at increasing productivity. Water power was largely replaced by steam, and several inventors were involved over a long period in improving the power and efficiency of the steam engine. By the 19th century steam was being used to power railway locomotives, with enormous possibilities for transport.

By turning the wheel on James Hargreaves' spinning jenny, an operator could spin 8 threads on to separate spindles. This number was later doubled and then increased still further.

Combining the Best Features

The 18th-century inventors were practical people, looking to use technology to advance production. Samuel Crompton was a weaver, and his spinning mule was so called because it was a cross between the earlier jenny and frame. The mule produced a strong, fine yarn that could be used in all kinds of textiles and was particularly suited to muslin. Crompton could not afford to pay for a patent and sold his design to Lancashire manufacturers.

Crompton's spinning mule. The first versions were hand-operated, later machines were water-powered, and they were finally driven by steam.

Advancing the Textile Industry

John Kay's flying shuttle greatly increased the amount of cloth weavers could produce, and the next important invention helped supply weavers with more thread. This was the spinning jenny, a hand-operated frame that could spin 8 threads at once. Five years later, Richard Arkwright patented his water frame, a water-powered spinning machine.

Richard Arkwright designed his spinning machine to be powered by water. It was capable of spinning stronger yarn than the jenny.

Right: Arkwright's Cromford cotton mill was built beside a watercourse flowing from the Derwent River. A waterwheel provided power for the factory's water frames.

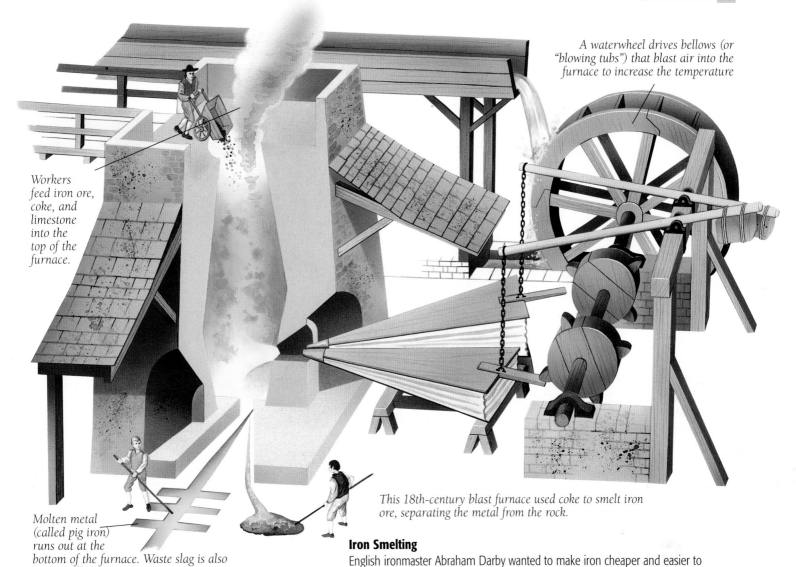

A waterwheel drives bellows (or "blowing tubs") that blast air into the furnace to increase the temperature

Workers feed iron ore, coke, and limestone into the top of the furnace.

Molten metal (called pig iron) runs out at the bottom of the furnace. Waste slag is also tapped off.

This 18th-century blast furnace used coke to smelt iron ore, separating the metal from the rock.

Iron Smelting

English ironmaster Abraham Darby wanted to make iron cheaper and easier to produce. Wood, which was needed for making charcoal, was becoming scarce in early 18th-century England. So Darby converted his furnace at Coalbrookdale, Shropshire, to burn coke instead of charcoal. The coke was made by heating coal (which was plentiful) in an airtight oven. The new furnace was ideal for smelting iron.

Steam Locomotives

In 1814 English engineer George Stephenson designed and built a steam locomotive to run on rails and haul coal from mines. Stephenson then constructed the Stockton and Darlington Railway. In 1829 he built an improved locomotive with his son Robert, which won competitive trials and pulled a special train to open the Liverpool and Manchester Railway a year later. The new engine was called *Rocket*.

The Stephensons' Rocket pulled its own coal and water in a tender. It could travel at 28 mph (46 km/h), which was very fast for the time.

Watt's steam engine.

Improving Steam Engines

Thomas Newcomen developed his steam engine in 1712 (see page 94). Fifty-seven years later, Scottish engineer James Watt produced an engine that used less coal and produced more power. Watt did this by using a condenser to change steam back into water by cooling. In 1782, Watt improved his own engine by developing a double-action machine, using steam to push a piston both ways

The First Iron Bridge

In 1779 Abraham Darby III, grandson of the ironmaker who devised the coke-fired furnace, built the world's first cast-iron bridge. It still stands today, spanning the River Severn in Shropshire. The bridge's five curved arch ribs were each cast in two halves, and the main parts of the bridge were put together in just three months. Cast iron is made by remelting the pig iron that comes from a furnace and pouring it into casting moulds.

The arch of the famous iron bridge, made of nearly 400 tons of cast iron, spans more than 98 feet (30 m).

Iron and Steel

There were rapid developments in the iron industry from the early 18th century, when coke replaced charcoal in furnaces. Cheaper iron meant that it could be used for many of the machines, pipes, and other parts that were needed in the factories that were springing up in industrial cities. The factories were then able to use iron to manufacture household items that were more practical and cheaper than earlier models in brass or other materials. By the mid-19th century, a new method of producing cheaper steel had also been developed.

Producing Steel

Steel is a refined product of iron and is made by removing impurities from the original metal. In 1740 English clockmaker Benjamin Huntsman used coke as a fuel to remelt iron bars in clay crucibles and make molten steel, which he then cast. Huntsman opened a steelworks in Sheffield, and by 1873 that city was making half the world's steel. The big advantage of steel over iron is its greater strength.

Forging Iron

Scottish engineer James Nasmyth (1808–90) was an expert in machine tools. In 1837 the Great Western Steam Company asked him to help forge some huge iron parts for their new steamship Great Britain. In order to be able to do this, Nasmyth designed and built a powerful steam hammer, which he patented in 1842.

A lump of iron ore, which can be smelted to release the metal.

The Bessemer Process

English engineer Henry Bessemer (1813–98) devised an easier and cheaper way of making steel. In 1856 he developed a converter (turning iron into steel), which was a new kind of furnace lined with a rock called ganister. Air was blown through molten iron in the furnace, and the high temperatures removed impurities and carbon, producing molten steel. Bessemer's new process cut the price of steel in half.

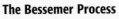

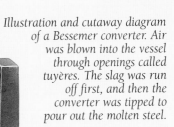

Nasmyth's steam hammer in operation. Steam was used to raise the heavy hammer head, which dropped by its own weight. Extra steam could push the hammer down even harder.

Illustration and cutaway diagram of a Bessemer converter. Air was blown into the vessel through openings called tuyères. The slag was run off first, and then the converter was tipped to pour out the molten steel.

Above. This 19th-century painting shows forge workers hammering hot wrought iron into shape. Wrought iron is softer than cast iron, but less brittle.

Iron was a very useful material for household items. This box iron had a removable slug, which could be heated up in the fireplace.

MINING IN ENGLAND

GLASGOW

NORTH SEA

WORKINGTON

NEWCASTLE-UPON-TYNE
DARLINGTON
STOCKTON

BARROW-IN-FURNES

LEEDS

IRISH SEA

HOLYHEAD
BIRKENHEAD

SHEFFIELD

DERBY

IRONBRIDGE
WOLVERHAMPTON
BIRMINGHAM

SWANSEA
GLOUCESTER
MERTHYR TYDFIL

BRISTOL CHANNEL
BATH

EXETER
REDRUTH PLYMOUTH
ENGLISH CHANNEL
PENZANCE

Coal   Tin
Iron   Copper
Lead

Tapping the Earth's Resources
The map shows the coalfields of England, as well as the mining and smelting sites for important metals. Coal and iron both played a vital role in the Industrial Revolution. Coal was needed as an energy source for steam engines and—as coke—for smelting iron ore (see page 97). By the late 17th century, Britain was producing more than three quarters of the world's coal, from mines spread around the country.

Transportation and Communication

During the first half of the 19th century improved transportation started to changed people's lives. Scottish engineer John McAdam (1756–1836) developed new road surfaces that made travel within and between towns much faster. At the same time steam engines were transforming land and sea transport, with the coming of the railways and the introduction of steamships. Everyday communication was also helped by an improved postal system and by the introduction of an instrument that used electricity to send messages by wire —the telegraph.

The world's first adhesive postage stamp, known as the Penny Black, paid for a letter to be delivered anywhere in Britain.

Steamships

By the 1840s Brunel's propeller-driven iron steamship Great Britain had cabins for 60 first-class passengers and could carry 300 more in lower classes. But the great engineer went on to build a much larger ship, the Great Eastern, which could carry enough coal to steam from Britain to Australia. It was also the only ship big enough to carry the 2,600 miles (4,200 km) of telegraph cable needed to stretch across the Atlantic seabed from Ireland to Newfoundland.

The Great Eastern's steam engines drove a four-bladed propeller and two giant paddle wheels. There were also six masts of sails.

This Wheatstone telegraph receiver dates from 1842.

Right: French-American transatlantic telegraph.

The Telegraph

By 1840 a telegraph system was being used on the railways, speeding up communication. In this system, pulses of electric current caused needles to move and point to individual letters at the receiving end. A system developed by American inventor Samuel Morse speeded things up. The first messages sent along transatlantic cables used Morse code, and they took hours to transmit. But this was still extremely fast international communication for the time.

The excitement of railroad travel is captured in this 1862 painting of Paddington station. Designed by Brunel, the station opened in 1854 as the London terminus of the Great Western Railway.

Two trains on the Liverpool and Manchester Railway show closed, more comfortable first-class carriages (above, with luggage on top), and a second-class service open to the elements.

All Aboard!

The new railroads changed the way people of all classes thought about travel. There were usually three classes of travel, with a great difference in comfort between them. The London to Brighton railroad line opened in 1841, and over the next three decades other seaside resorts grew up along the British coast. The success of the railroads kept prices down, and even working-class passengers could afford a day trip to the seaside.

THE RAILROAD SYSTEM

— Major railroad

NEWCASTLE ON TYNE

NORTH SEA

IRISH SEA

MANCHESTER

LIVERPOOL SHEFFIELD

DERBY

CAMBRIDGE

LONDON

ENGLISH CHANNEL

Expanding Network

The Liverpool and Manchester Railway, opened in 1830, was the first to offer passenger services with a regular timetable. The venture was so successful that it caused an enormous railway-building boom. By 1850, there were nearly 6,300 miles (10,000 km) of railroad track in Britain. The tracks all had a standard gage of 4 feet 8½ inches (1.44 m).

The Commercial Revolution

In Britain the industrial revolution was supported by a successful banking system, including the Bank of England and private financiers. Commerce had previously been strongly regulated under the system of mercantilism that encouraged exports and the establishment of overseas colonies. In the 18th century this was replaced by a capitalist system in which bankers, merchants, and industrialists became more important than landowners. Commercial markets grew wider and became more secure.

This Great Iron Chest was used from the beginning of the 18th century for the safekeeping of bills in the Bank of England.

Bank of England

The Bank of England was set up by a group of London merchants to raise funds for the British government to finance war in the Low Countries. During the 18th century it developed into a commercial bank, taking deposits and issuing banknotes, which at first were partially printed with cashiers making out the exact sum involved. In 1793 the Bank issued its printed £5 note, which still had to be signed by hand by a Bank cashier.

Economic Philosophy

Adam Smith is often regarded as the founder of modern economics. He argued for capitalism, the economic system based on private ownership of the means of production and a free competitive market. Smith maintained that governments should adopt a laissez-faire attitude to the economy, allowing individuals to follow their business interests without interference. He believed that, in order to make money, manufacturers produce things that consumers want to buy, creating wealth and an expanding economy.

Scottish economist and philosopher Adam Smith (1723–90).

Workers were strictly supervised at the Bank of England's press in Threadneedle Street, which started printing its own banknotes in 1808. The notes were printed from engraved copper plates.

BANKING AND TRADE

1694
Foundation of the Bank of England.

1765
Sampson Lloyd and John Taylor set up a private banking business in Birmingham, England– Lloyds Bank.

1773
A group of brokers establish a Stock Exchange in London's Threadneedle Street.

1776
Publication of An Inquiry into the Nature and Causes of the Wealth of Nations by Adam Smith.

1792
The New York Stock Exchange is established.

1826
In Britain the Country Bankers Act allows the establishment of joint-stock banks more than 65 miles (100 km) from London.

1844
The Bank Charter Act recognizes the Bank of England as Britain's central banknote-issuing authority.

Private Banking

By the late 17th century some goldsmiths, merchants, and legal clerks offered their own financial and banking services in London. They accepted deposits of money, made loans, and exchanged foreign coins. Any of their customers could also instruct the financier to pay money from their account to another person. In the British provinces, so-called "country banks" could not compete with the Bank of England until restrictions on them were lifted in 1826.

This handwritten document of 1725 is addressed to a London goldsmith. It requests a payment of £70 to be made to a named individual, in the same way as a modern check would do.

Growing Businesses

The industrial revolution stimulated manufacturing, which helped all kinds of businesses to grow. Company owners sold shares in their businesses to shareholders, and the resulting capital allowed small specialist companies to expand into wider areas. For further expansion, manufacturers raised long-term capital by mortgaging factory buildings and machinery to banks and other institutions.

This 18th-century engraving shows the Royal Exchange in London, built in 1669, where merchants met to conduct business.

Belgium and France

Newly independent Belgium, under King Leopold I (whose niece became Britain's Queen Victoria six years after his accession), was quick to follow Britain in its move toward industrialization. This was particularly evident in the French-speaking southern regions of the country. France itself also expanded its economy, especially after 1852, and both countries developed transportation systems to move people, raw materials, and the new goods produced. This helped trade between the two countries and their neighbors.

This Belgian coin shows King Leopold II, during whose reign (1865–1909) there was great colonial expansion.

Belgian Industry

Early in the 19th century industry developed fast in the southern Belgian region of French-speaking Wallonia, while Dutch-speaking Flanders remained largely agricultural. The coal mines of the Borinage region increased production, and iron and steel developed around Charleroi. The Belgian government encouraged a system of free private enterprise, and Belgian banks invested heavily in Walloon industry.

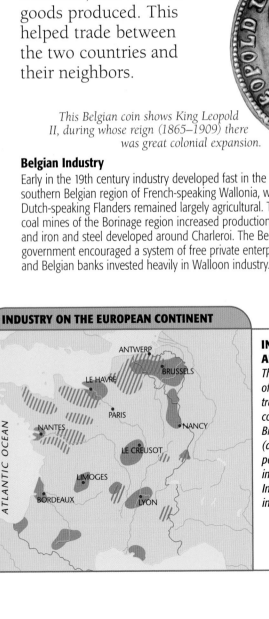

INDUSTRY ON THE EUROPEAN CONTINENT

INDUSTRY IN FRANCE AND BELGIUM

The map shows how the face of France and Belgium was transformed by industry during the course of the 19th century. As in Britain, the presence of coalfields (and their usefulness for steam power) tended to further the industrialization of a region. In France, industry developed most in the north and east.

Heavy industry

Major textile manufacturing

The 16th-century Maison du Roi ("King's House") in central Brussels was restored in the 1870s.

New Transport Links

Belgium developed an excellent network of roads, railroads, and canals, connecting the industrial south with Brussels and, most importantly, the port of Antwerp. The Charleroi–Brussels Canal was part of a waterway system that linked rivers. From the outset the Belgian railroads were state-owned, and in 1843 a line connected Antwerp to Cologne, helping Belgian exports.

View of the 1900 Exposition Universelle in Paris. It lasted 7 months and attracted more than 50 million visitors.

Expositions Universelles

Universal Expositions (or World's Fairs) helped Parisians and others celebrate French industrial expansion. The first was held in Paris in 1855, just four years after London's Great Exhibition (see page 87). The 6-month Exposition showcased French wine production and attracted 4.5 million visitors.

There were further successful fairs in 1867, 1878, and 1889, when the main symbol was the newly completed Eiffel Tower. Several bridges and railway stations were built specially for the 1900 Exposition.

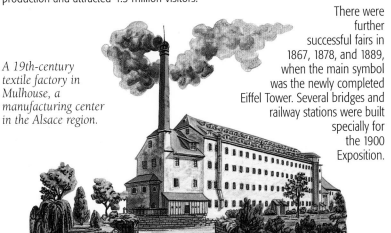

A 19th-century textile factory in Mulhouse, a manufacturing center in the Alsace region.

The Second Empire

French industrial production doubled during the period of its Second Empire (1852–70). French industry turned to steam power, as many more railway tracks were laid so that the network covered the whole country. The textile industry grew, and cotton manufacture was second only to Britain. Great French investment banks were founded, and successful shops grew into grand department stores in Paris. The capital itself was renovated and redesigned by the administrator Georges-Eugène Haussmann.

Germany

By the mid-19th century, Germany's growing railroads were causing an increased demand for coal and iron. North German industrial centers expanded, and Prussia's victory over France and unification in 1871 led to the foundation of large, successful companies. Though there was a worldwide depression just two years later, more than four-fifths of the new German firms survived. Adding to steel-making and engineering, German scientists, inventors, and industrialists helped their country dominate the new chemical and electrical industries.

Founder Years
The period 1871–73 in Germany is known as the Gründerjahre ("founder years"), because so many enterprises were founded after unification. More than 850 joint-stock companies were established, requiring more investment in two years than had been made in the previous two decades. Much of this came from investment banks that were created to finance industry rather than provide credit for individuals.

The Krupp Factory
Alfred Krupp (1812–87) took over his father's cast-steel factory in Essen at the age of 14. The family firm was the first on the European continent to introduce the Bessemer process (see page 98), making railway tracks and axles. In 1851 the factory produced a cast-steel cannon that was shown at the Great Exhibition in London (see page 86). This led to Krupp becoming Europe's leading arms manufacturer, and the success of its guns in the Franco-Prussian War led to the nickname "arsenal of the empire."

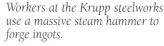

Workers at the Krupp steelworks use a massive steam hammer to forge ingots.

One of Krupp's huge cannons on exhibition in 1867.

Baron Justus von Liebig (1803–73), who helped found the study of organic chemistry.

Chemicals

Justus von Liebig established a laboratory for chemical research at the University of Giessen in 1827. This led to more labs and technical colleges being founded in Germany and helped create its world-famous chemical industry. In 1863 Friedrich Bayer (1825–80) founded a factory in Elberfeld to produce dyestuffs and pharmaceutical products. The company was hugely successful and still exists today.

The Siemens Telegraph Company laid the first long-distance telegraph, from Berlin to Frankfurt, in 1848. This painting shows the cable being laid between Berlin and Cologne.

The Siemens pointer telegraph of 1847.

The Electrical Industry

As a young man Werner von Siemens (1816–92) invented an improved telegraph transmitter. In 1847 he founded a company in Berlin to set up telegraph lines, and 19 years later Siemens discovered the principle of the electric dynamo. His company grew into a manufacturing giant and became international when one of the founder's brothers went to England and another to Russia. Today, Siemens AG is an enormous global conglomerate.

Growing Industry and Railroads

The map shows the development of railroads and industry from 1870. The German railway network, which had started modestly in Bavaria in 1835, nearly doubled in size between 1865 and 1875. Iron and steel were used to build railroads and locomotives, as well as for industrial machinery, merchant ships, and armaments. The electrical and chemical industries grew enormously in the late 19th century.

GERMANY

NORTH SEA

BALTIC SEA

HAMBURG

BERLIN

RUSSIAN EMPIRE

BRESLAU

FRANKFURT

DRESDEN

AUSTRIA — HUNGARY

— Railroad ||| Iron working   ▨ Coalmining   — Boundary 1871

The United States of America

The transformation of the United States (and Germany) into industrial nations is sometimes known as the second industrial revolution. In the US, developments largely took place after the end of the Civil War in 1865. Coal, iron, and steel production increased, railroads were built across the continent, factories opened, and industry advanced much faster than agriculture. By the end of the 19th century, the US had grown into the world's leading producer of many industrial products.

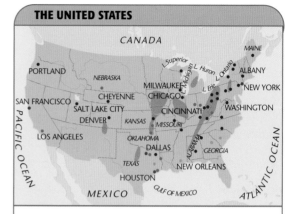

Whitney's cotton gin (short for "engine") revolutionized the cotton industry in the US and Europe.

THE UNITED STATES

A Land Rich in Natural Resources
An abundance of raw materials was an important factor in the industrial growth of the United States. As in Britain, coal was a vital resource: in 1800 the US produced 98,000 tons of coal; by 1850 the figure was 7.6 million tons, and by 1900 it was 245 million tons. Metals were mined, including all-important iron, as well as oil and gas. The growing railroad network made it easier to transport materials.

- Coal
- Iron
- Oil and gas
- Cotton

Cotton

After the American inventor Eli Whitney developed a cotton gin to separate seeds from fibers quickly and efficiently, the United States became the world's leading cotton grower. The slave population grew in the south to pick and gin cotton, contributing to the causes of the Civil War. In 1860 agricultural goods still made up more than two-thirds of US exports. After 1865, large numbers of cotton mills sprang up in the south to make cotton cloth.

This distinctive kind of American locomotive was first built in Philadelphia in 1837.

An early Singer sewing machine. I.M. Singer & Co. was established in New York in 1851, and soon became the most famous manufacturer of sewing machines.

Iron and Steel

English colonists had brought iron-making skills and techniques with them to the New World. By 1864 the Bessemer process (see page 98) was being used in the United States to turn iron into steel. This development supplied the material that helped the growth of railroads and manufacturing industries. In 1873, Andrew Carnegie established the first large-scale US steel plant in Braddock, Pennsylvania. By the early 20th century, the US was producing more steel than Germany or Britain.

Scottish-born Andrew Carnegie (1835–1919) (left) emigrated with his family at the age of 12. He made his fortune in steel manufacture and became a noted philanthropist.

The First Oil Wells

When the news spread that Edwin Drake had struck oil, prospectors rushed to Pennsylvania. Oil wells soon sprang up near Titusville along a river that came to be known as Oil Creek, and boom towns were founded. At first the new oil industry was chaotic, but businessmen such as John D. Rockefeller brought order to the production, refining, and distribution of "black gold."

Portrait of John Davison Rockefeller (1839–1937), who formed the hugely successful Standard Oil Company in 1870.

Wooden derricks in the Oil Creek region of Pennsylvania. In 1861 the Phillips well (on the right) produced 4,000 barrels of oil a day.

(see page 98)

INDUSTRY IN THE UNITED STATES

1817
The New York Stock & Exchange Board (later Stock Exchange) is established.

1830
The first US passenger train steams along a local line in South Carolina.

1839
Connecticut inventor Charles Goodyear discovers vulcanization, a process used to make rubber stronger.

1859
Edwin Drake (1819–80) strikes oil near Titusville, Pennsylvania.

1861–65
The American Civil War between the northern Union and the southern Confederacy.

1869
Railway lines meet at Promontory, Utah, to complete the first continuous track across the US.

1876
Alexander Graham Bell displays his telephone at Philadelphia's Centennial Exhibition.

1879
Thomas Edison (1847–1931) invents the light bulb.

1882
Electric lighting illuminates New York City; John D. Rockefeller controls the US oil-refinery business.

1892
Andrew Carnegie combines three of his firms and forms the Carnegie Steel Company.

Russia

At the start of the second half of the 19th century, the Russian tsar and leading figures in his empire set about trying to catch up with progress made by the leading European countries. They introduced a program of industrialization, fuelled as elsewhere by coal and also by oil, and including an expanding railroad network. But in Russia discontent grew among workers in the growing cities, and the empire's industrial revolution soon led to strikes and the 1917 Bolshevik revolution.

Coal miners worked long hours in harsh conditions. These men are watched over by armed soldiers as they work.

Trans-Siberian Railway

In 1889 Count Witte (then in the Ministry of Communications) set up a railway department in the Ministry of Finance. Two years later the first track was laid to open the cold, vast region of Siberia to Muscovites and others. By 1904 the track was complete all the way from Moscow to Vladivostok, on the Pacific coast, a distance of more than 5,600 miles (9,000 km). It helped open up Siberia for settlement and industry.

Social and Economic Change

Following the freeing of the serfs, Russian industrialization accelerated during the last decades of the 19th century. A new class of businessmen rapidly developed, but there were still great difficulties for ordinary people as old-fashioned agricultural methods continued while modern factories were coming into operation. Rapid changes continued, as French and Belgian capital was invested in the steel industry, the British invested in Russian oil (see opposite), and Germany in electricity.

A postcard of Vladivostok, which was founded as a Russian naval port in 1860.

Postage stamp of 1922 showing a gushing Baku oil well.

Portrait of finance minister Count Witte (1849–1915), who helped modernize the empire, expanding the railroads and developing industry.

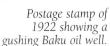

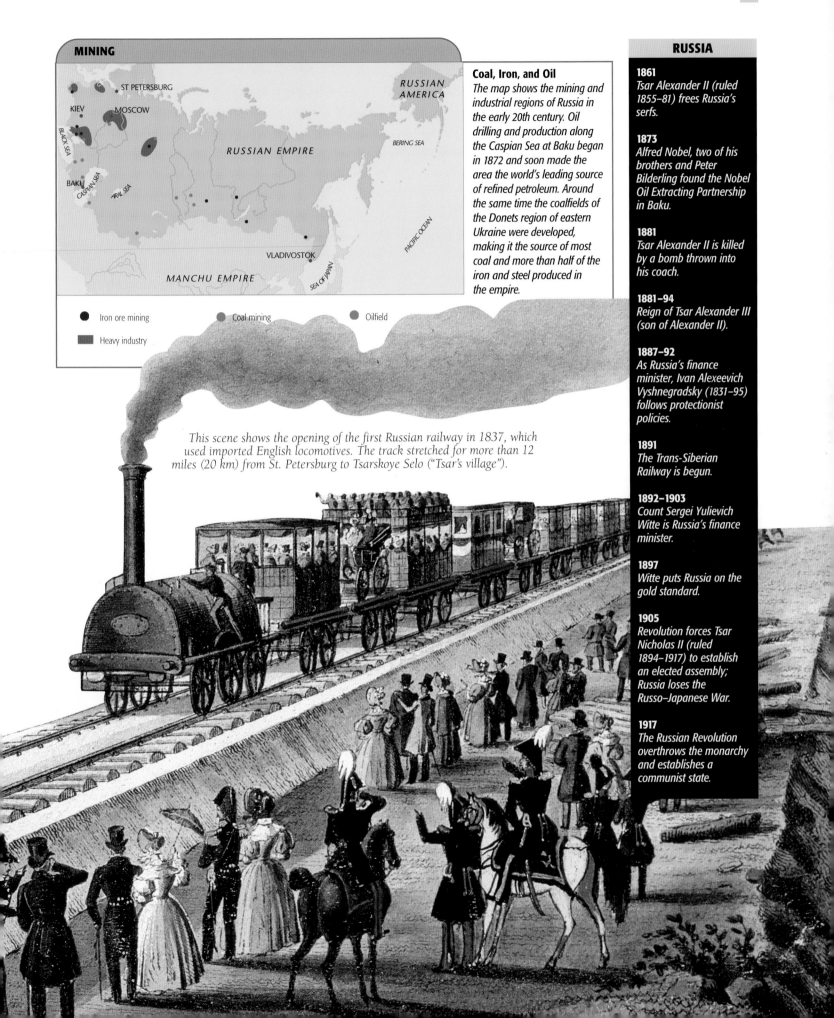

MINING

Coal, Iron, and Oil
The map shows the mining and industrial regions of Russia in the early 20th century. Oil drilling and production along the Caspian Sea at Baku began in 1872 and soon made the area the world's leading source of refined petroleum. Around the same time the coalfields of the Donets region of eastern Ukraine were developed, making it the source of most coal and more than half of the iron and steel produced in the empire.

ST PETERSBURG

KIEV

MOSCOW

RUSSIAN AMERICA

RUSSIAN EMPIRE

BERING SEA

BLACK SEA

BAKU

CASPIAN SEA

ARAL SEA

PACIFIC OCEAN

VLADIVOSTOK

MANCHU EMPIRE

SEA OF JAPAN

● Iron ore mining

● Coal mining

● Oilfield

▬ Heavy industry

This scene shows the opening of the first Russian railway in 1837, which used imported English locomotives. The track stretched for more than 12 miles (20 km) from St. Petersburg to Tsarskoye Selo ("Tsar's village").

RUSSIA

1861
Tsar Alexander II (ruled 1855–81) frees Russia's serfs.

1873
Alfred Nobel, two of his brothers and Peter Bilderling found the Nobel Oil Extracting Partnership in Baku.

1881
Tsar Alexander II is killed by a bomb thrown into his coach.

1881–94
Reign of Tsar Alexander III (son of Alexander II).

1887–92
As Russia's finance minister, Ivan Alexeevich Vyshnegradsky (1831–95) follows protectionist policies.

1891
The Trans-Siberian Railway is begun.

1892–1903
Count Sergei Yulievich Witte is Russia's finance minister.

1897
Witte puts Russia on the gold standard.

1905
Revolution forces Tsar Nicholas II (ruled 1894–1917) to establish an elected assembly; Russia loses the Russo–Japanese War.

1917
The Russian Revolution overthrows the monarchy and establishes a communist state.

Japan

Japan was an isolated country until international trade links were forcefully opened during the mid-19th century. This was quickly followed by a revolution that put an end to the old feudal system. These changes led to the industrialization of Japan, as politicians and businessmen learned European methods and imported machinery. The growing national industries were sold to private companies, some of which quickly grew into large enterprises. The new Japanese leadership also developed its military force, building naval shipyards and modernizing weapons.

Commodore Matthew Calbraith Perry (1794–1858) meeting a representative of the Japanese emperor.

Open for Trade

Four US Navy warships arrived in Edo (now Tokyo) Bay in 1853, under the command of Commodore Perry. The commodore carried a letter from the US president to the Japanese emperor, asking Japan to open its ports to international trade. This was not immediately successful, but Perry returned a year later with eight ships and negotiations then began. A treaty was soon signed, opening two (and later, more) Japanese ports.

Mihorabashi railway station. The advanced Japanese rail system and a nationwide telegraph network contributed to the country's industrial modernization.

INDUSTRIAL JAPAN

Railroad

Industrial areas

HOKKAIDO

SEA OF JAPAN

HONSHU

SHIKOKU

KYUSHU

PACIFIC OCEAN

Rise of Industry

Traditional industries—such as ceramics, textiles, and silk manufacture—were expanded and modernized. During the period 1868–98, exports multiplied tenfold, though imports grew even faster. From 1890, the emphasis switched to heavy industry, including manufacturing, machine-building, shipbuilding, iron and steel, and the chemical industry. This was helped by the expanding railroad network. The map shows the main centers.

Textiles

Traditional Japanese textile manufacture was gradually mechanized. Spinning mules were imported from Britain and France, and in 1883 a steam-powered cotton-spinning factory opened in Osaka. Some of the growing factories included dormitories and hospitals for workers, and schools for their children. By the end of the Meiji era, factory-produced cotton and silk had become major Japanese exports.

The Meiji Era

The end of feudal rule in Japan was brought about by a non-violent revolution known as the Meiji Restoration (1866–1868). Though this nominally returned full authority to the emperor, the political leaders held real power and set about modernizing industry, strengthening the military, and enriching the nation. They achieved this by copying the successful methods adopted in Europe and North America, and by importing expensive machinery for their new factories.

A Japanese helmet of the Meiji era. Samurai swords were replaced by European-style rifles. In 1894–1895 a war with China gained Japanese control of Formosa (now Taiwan), southern Manchuria, and Korea.

Japanese factory-workers produced silk to compete in export markets with China. By the 1870s many human-powered drive-wheels had been replaced by steam power.

Painting of 1834 of the German Ruhr valley town of Burg Wetter, where factories were built around the medieval castle.

Moving to Town

During the early period of the Industrial Revolution some workers migrated according to the seasons. They stayed in the country during the harvest season, and moved to town when they needed other work. Many stayed in town permanently, however, attracted by the offer of constant work in the new factories. Some towns specialized in one form of industry: there were "mill towns" and "coke towns," and even "company towns" as individual firms expanded.

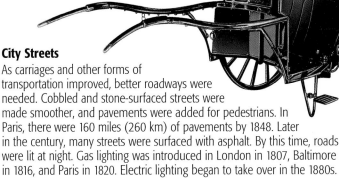

The two-wheeled hansom cab was a popular method of urban transportation from the 1830s.

City Streets

As carriages and other forms of transportation improved, better roadways were needed. Cobbled and stone-surfaced streets were made smoother, and pavements were added for pedestrians. In Paris, there were 160 miles (260 km) of pavements by 1848. Later in the century, many streets were surfaced with asphalt. By this time, roads were lit at night. Gas lighting was introduced in London in 1807, Baltimore in 1816, and Paris in 1820. Electric lighting began to take over in the 1880s.

Left: In this cartoon, some Londoners marvel at the new gas lighting, while others are more sceptical.

Drains and Sewers

Before the problems of waste removal were tackled in the mid-19th century, streets were dirty and smelly. Disease was rife in congested cities, where cholera, typhus, and smallpox were all big killers. In the 1850s, proper sewerage and drainage systems were dug beneath the streets of Paris and London. This was an enormous undertaking and an impressive engineering achievement, using the latest technology. By 1878 the Parisian sewer system was 375 miles (600 km) long.

Urbanization

Industrialization led to urban growth, which occurred most rapidly in the birthplace of the industrial revolution —Britain. By the beginning of the 19th century 24 percent of the British population was already living in towns of 10,000 or more people. In the rest of Europe the figure was less than 10 percent. The new town-dwellers faced problems of poor housing, water supplies, and sanitation, leading to an urgent need for modernization and social planning.

Sandstone tunnels were dug beneath the streets of Paris. They contained storm drains, a main sewer with sidewalks, iron mains pipes for drinking water, and a separate supply of non-drinkable water. Some sections were even built for tourists, who were at first by suspended carts and later by carriage.

Chicago streets were paved with tarred pine blocks in 1859. The flat surface of blocks was covered with pitch and gravel.

Growing Cities

The world's cities grew bigger as railroads made it possible for wealthier people to move further out to the suburbs. Ordinary workers stayed near their place of work, around the city center, and poverty led to many of these areas turning into slums. In more prosperous districts buildings grew taller. The use of steel for constructing the framework of tall buildings was introduced in Chicago in the 1880s and soon spread throughout North America.

By 1870 the streets of Paris had been widened, helping the movement of horse-drawn omnibuses and trams. These larger, faster vehicles made pedestrian pavements even more important. Buildings grew taller as the age of the Parisian department store began.

Working Families

Industrialization and the growth of cities had a great impact on the family life of working-class people. The place of work moved away from the home to the factory, where in many cases men, women, and children had to work long hours in order to make ends meet. Home life suffered as women were faced with the burden of factory work being followed by domestic chores and childcare. Other women went into domestic service in middle-class households, where life was very different. Few middle-class women were required to work in paid employment.

The family was seen as central to the middle-class ideal of a stable life. All family members were expected to try and better themselves.

Tokens such as this were issued to factory workers to buy food.

The Working Classes

The hierarchical structure of society into upper, middle, and lower or working classes was reinforced by the Industrial Revolution. Skilled craftsmen, shopkeepers, and higher domestic servants were at the upper end of the working class, and unskilled laborers at the lower. Generally the lower working classes had no education. Industrialization also created a new class of manual worker—the machine-minder, who received a short period of training and became familiar with one part of a factory process.

Child Labor

Many children were sent to work at a very young age, and had to put in long hours. In the British textile industry of 1861, nearly a fifth of the workforce was under 15. In mines, the figure was 12 percent. Small children were used for cleaning machinery, such as removing fluff from under power looms. Since the machines were kept running, it was dangerous work. In other factories, children worked as assistants to adult machine-minders.

This unfortunate boy got his foot caught in machinery.

Factory Hours

Factory conditions were often hard, and hours were always long. Many people, including children, worked 16 hours a day. In 1833 the British government recommended changes in the textile industry: 9–11 year olds' hours were cut to 8 a day, and under-18s to 12 a day. Things were not much better for a whole class of domestic servants. Many worked 80 hours a week for very little pay, but they had the advantage of being well fed and were given clothing and shelter.

In this illustration of 1868, men, women and children make their way home after a long day's work at a Massachusetts textile factory.

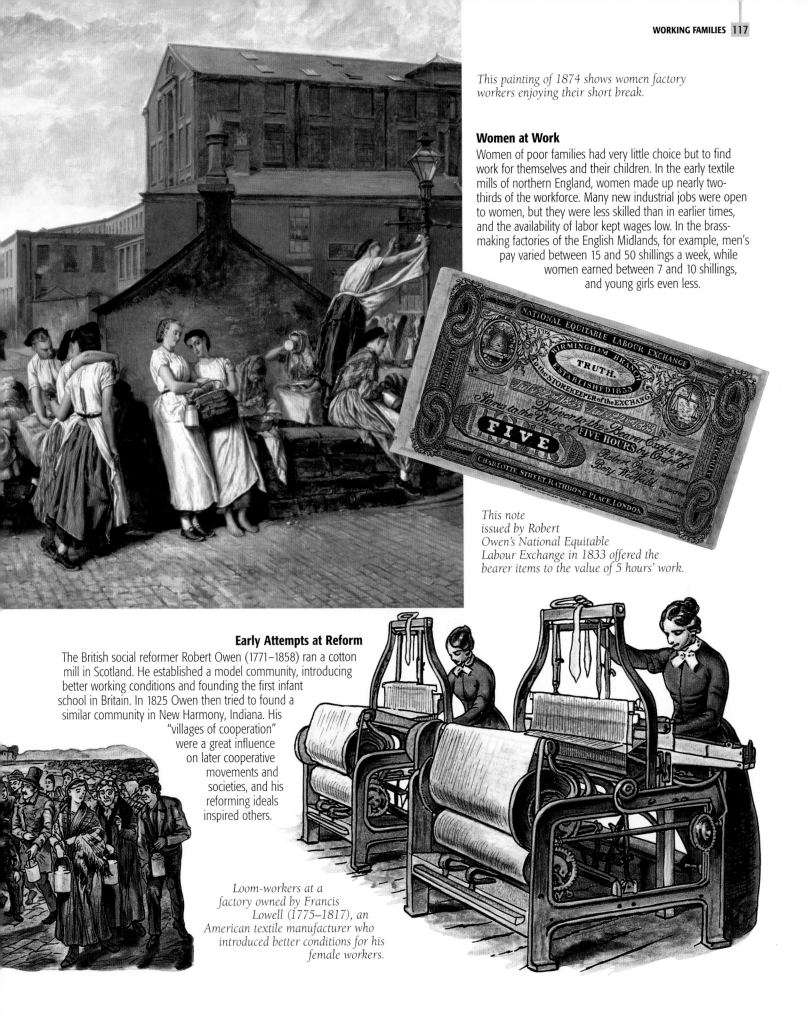

This painting of 1874 shows women factory workers enjoying their short break.

Women at Work

Women of poor families had very little choice but to find work for themselves and their children. In the early textile mills of northern England, women made up nearly two-thirds of the workforce. Many new industrial jobs were open to women, but they were less skilled than in earlier times, and the availability of labor kept wages low. In the brass-making factories of the English Midlands, for example, men's pay varied between 15 and 50 shillings a week, while women earned between 7 and 10 shillings, and young girls even less.

This note issued by Robert Owen's National Equitable Labour Exchange in 1833 offered the bearer items to the value of 5 hours' work.

Early Attempts at Reform

The British social reformer Robert Owen (1771–1858) ran a cotton mill in Scotland. He established a model community, introducing better working conditions and founding the first infant school in Britain. In 1825 Owen then tried to found a similar community in New Harmony, Indiana. His "villages of cooperation" were a great influence on later cooperative movements and societies, and his reforming ideals inspired others.

Loom-workers at a factory owned by Francis Lowell (1775–1817), an American textile manufacturer who introduced better conditions for his female workers.

Trade Unions and Social Reform

It was some time after the great changes brought about by the Industrial Revolution that workers began to organize themselves into useful groups. The first aim was to improve pay and conditions, and this was largely achieved by the growing labor movement. Social reformers and political revolutionaries put forward theories as to how the so-called class conflict could be resolved. In practice, trade unionists improved their members' working lives, and liberal-minded politicians changed laws to help working-class families and their children's education.

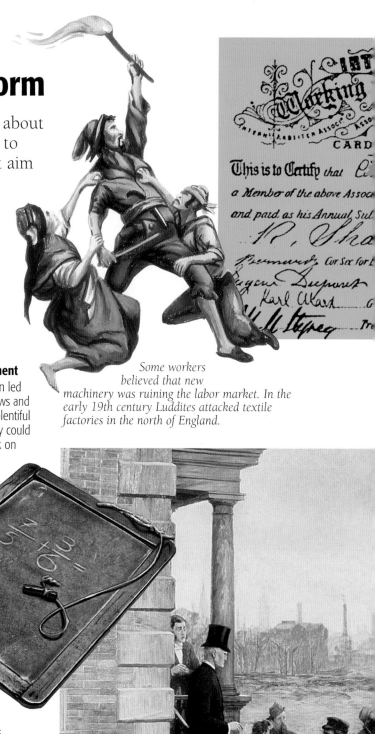

Some workers believed that new machinery was ruining the labor market. In the early 19th century Luddites attacked textile factories in the north of England.

The Labor Movement

The dramatic changes in ordinary people's working lives caused by industrialization led to a movement by groups of workers to improve their economic position. New laws and rights were needed, because factory owners and other employers abused the plentiful labor market by offering low pay and poor conditions. Workers realized that they could use collective action and, if necessary, strikes as weapons, while employers fell back on old-fashioned laws to protect their interests.

Education

Children's working conditions and education were linked in 19th-century Britain. Factory Acts reduced working hours, and the Elementary Education Act of 1870 set up school boards across the country. Boards were free to decide whether education was compulsory from ages 5 to 10 in their district, but this was enforced nationally in 1880. At first board schools cost parents a few pence each week, encouraging many to keep their children at work. Fees were generally abolished in 1891.

A schoolchild's writing slate, which could be wiped clean and used over and over again.

Social Reform

For some reformers the labor movement was part of a class struggle that they saw leading to a workers' revolution. The German philosopher Karl Marx and social scientist Friedrich Engels believed that the industrial proletariat (or wage-earning workers) would inevitably win their struggle with the capitalist bourgeoisie (owner-employers) and create a new society free of class conflict and oppression. These ideas influenced thinkers and politicians all over the world.

Karl Marx (1818–83) was a leading figure in the First International. His revolutionary theories encouraged socialists and communists.

Friedrich Engels (1820–95) introduced Marx to the British labor movement.

Membership card of the International Working Men's Association (or First International), an organization of labor groups founded in London in 1864.

Trade Unions

Workers formed trade unions in order to use their bargaining power as a group, which was much greater than that of individuals. In Britain early unions of the 1850s faced strong opposition from employers, who refused to recognize them. Unions themselves were separate until the Trades Union Congress of 1868 formed a national organization. The TUC was made up of unions of skilled workers until 1889, when it started to accept general unions.

Membership certificate of the first successful national trade union, the Amalgamated Society of Engineers, formed in 1851.

BE UNITED AND INDUSTRIOUS

LABOR MOVEMENT

1848
Publication of the 119 by Marx and Engels.

1867
First volume of Marx's 119 is published.

1868
First meeting of the Trades Union Congress (TUC) takes place in Manchester.

1869
The first US national workers' organization, the Noble Order of the Knights of Labor, is founded in Philadelphia.

1871
The Trade Union Act recognizes unions by law.

1875
The German Social Democratic Party (SPD) is founded.

1886
A nationwide strike of factory workers in the US demands an 8-hour working day; the American Federation of Labor (AFL) is founded in Columbus, Ohio.

1889
The Great Dock Strike in London secures wage increases and overtime pay.

1892
French workers strike 261 times against 500 companies.

1900
The Labour Representation Committee is founded in London (renamed the Labour Party in 1906).

This painting of 1886 by German-born artist Robert Koehler (1850–1917) is called simply The Strike. Koehler based it on events he had seen in Germany, England and the USA.

The 18th century in Europe was an age of enlightenment and revolution. The movement known as the Enlightenment, which took place during the so-called Age of Reason, developed from the beliefs and theories of great French thinkers and writers. They furthered scientific advances and advocated a liberal approach to social reform.

Some of Europe's monarchs adopted many of the proposed reforms in theory, but internal struggles and international conflicts made them difficult to carry through. Unfortunately these great ideas had little effect on the lives of ordinary people, and dissatisfaction caused by the growing class conflict laid the foundations for revolution.

This chapter covers the major nations, empires, monarchs, and wars, and details developments in science, art, architecture, and music. By the end of the 18th century, the French Revolution had changed a nation and was making its impact felt throughout the continent and the world.

Frederick the Great was an "enlightened despot" and one of the greatest rulers in European history.

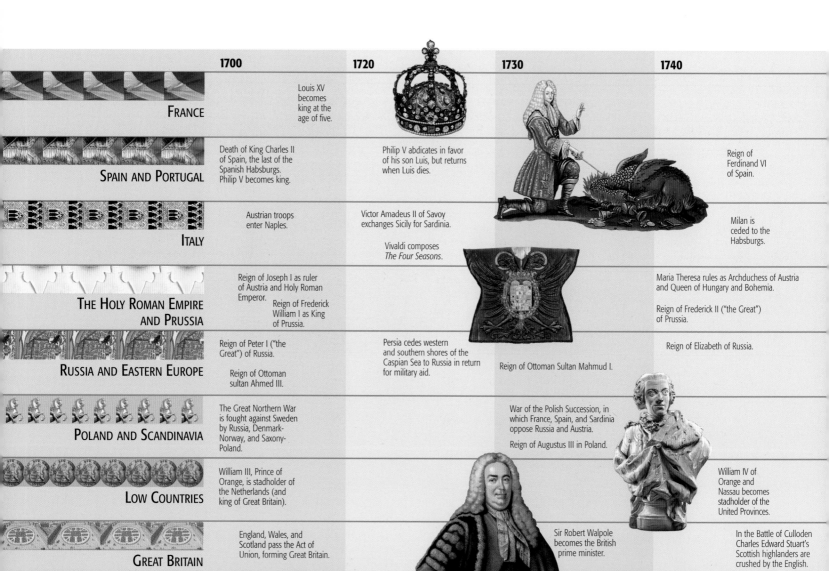

	1700	1720	1730	1740
FRANCE	Louis XV becomes king at the age of five.			
SPAIN AND PORTUGAL	Death of King Charles II of Spain, the last of the Spanish Habsburgs. Philip V becomes king.	Philip V abdicates in favor of his son Luis, but returns when Luis dies.		Reign of Ferdinand VI of Spain.
ITALY	Austrian troops enter Naples.	Victor Amadeus II of Savoy exchanges Sicily for Sardinia. Vivaldi composes *The Four Seasons.*		Milan is ceded to the Habsburgs.
THE HOLY ROMAN EMPIRE AND PRUSSIA	Reign of Joseph I as ruler of Austria and Holy Roman Emperor. Reign of Frederick William I as King of Prussia.			Maria Theresa rules as Archduchess of Austria and Queen of Hungary and Bohemia. Reign of Frederick II ("the Great") of Prussia.
RUSSIA AND EASTERN EUROPE	Reign of Peter I ("the Great") of Russia. Reign of Ottoman sultan Ahmed III.	Persia cedes western and southern shores of the Caspian Sea to Russia in return for military aid.	Reign of Ottoman Sultan Mahmud I.	Reign of Elizabeth of Russia.
POLAND AND SCANDINAVIA	The Great Northern War is fought against Sweden by Russia, Denmark-Norway, and Saxony-Poland.		War of the Polish Succession, in which France, Spain, and Sardinia oppose Russia and Austria. Reign of Augustus III in Poland.	
LOW COUNTRIES	William III, Prince of Orange, is stadholder of the Netherlands (and king of Great Britain).			William IV of Orange and Nassau becomes stadholder of the United Provinces.
GREAT BRITAIN	England, Wales, and Scotland pass the Act of Union, forming Great Britain.		Sir Robert Walpole becomes the British prime minister.	In the Battle of Culloden Charles Edward Stuart's Scottish highlanders are crushed by the English.

Enlightenment and Revolution

Louis XVI was executed by guillotine in Paris in 1793. His severed head was held up to the huge crowd.

1750	1760	1770	1780	1790
Denis Diderot's *Encyclopédie* is published.		The reign of Louis XVI begins.	The National Assembly approves the Declaration of the Rights of Man.	Storming of the Bastille, the French Revolution begins.
				Louis XVI is executed. The Reign of Terror begins.
Reign of Joseph I in Portugal, during which period the Marquess de Pombal is chief minister.	Reign of Charles III of Spain.		Reign of Maria I and consort Peter III (to 1786) in Portugal.	
		Reign in Tuscany of Grand Duke Peter Leopold, who transforms administration and law.		The last ruler of Venice is deposed, and the city falls to Austria.
The Seven Years' War, in which Maria Theresa is forced by Prussia to give up claims to Silesia.			Reign of Frederick William II of Prussia.	Reign of Leopold II as Holy Roman Emperor and king of Hungary and Moravia.
The composer Mozart is born.	Reign of Joseph II as Holy Roman Emperor.			Reign of Francis II as the last Holy Roman Emperor.
Tensions and rising taxes lead to a revolt in Sarajevo (in Bosnia-Herzegovina) against the Ottoman sultan.	Reign of Catherine II, "the Great" of Russia.	Reign of Ottoman Sultan Abdulhamid.	Russian annexation of the Crimea from the Turks.	Reign of Paul I of Russia.
	First Russo–Turkish War.		Second Russo–Turkish War.	
	Reign of Christian VII over Denmark and Norway.	First partition of Poland between Russia, Prussia, and Austria.		Second and third partitions of Poland.
				Denmark frees its serfs.
			Patriot Revolution.	Period of the Batavian Republic
			Prussian troops occupy Amsterdam.	The Dutch East India Company is dissolved.
The Seven Years' War leads to Britain winning control of France's North American empire.	Reign of George III.			

The Eighteenth Century

The institution of absolute monarchy was threatened in many countries during the 18th century. The new philosophy of the Enlightenment spread from France, where before the end of the century social revolution toppled the king and created a republic. Nationalism continued as a powerful force everywhere, however, fuelling wars between European nations. In Britain, the Industrial Revolution was getting underway, and scientific advances were made across the continent.

Right: Portrait of Isabella Godin, who traveled to the Amazon region as the wife of a scientific explorer.

This longcase clock was made in France about 1755. By mid-century, inventors had developed most of the devices found in modern mechanical clocks.

Scientific Studies

At the beginning of the century Isaac Newton (1642–1727), widely considered one of the greatest scientists of all time, and others were making great discoveries in astronomy, mathematics, and other subjects (see pages 150–151). Their work built on and furthered the scientific revolution that had begun in the 16th century. The great thinkers of the Enlightenment period believed that an understanding of scientific processes was essential for all educated people.

A New Philosophy

Leading 18th-century thinkers presented a view of the world based on reason, scientific enquiry, and individualism, rather than on traditional values. This movement came to be known as the Enlightenment, and the period as the Age of Reason (see pages 124–125). Important rational thinkers believed that their approach enlightened others, bringing them greater knowledge and understanding about the world around them.

Feeding the poor in the early 18th century. In 1709 a long period of freezing weather caused food shortages in Paris.

Growing Unrest

Living conditions did not improve for most of Europe's poor people. Many farming families moved to the growing towns, where work and decent accommodation were not always available. At the same time successful business people of the new middle class were beginning to enjoy a wealthy lifestyle. Poverty and class conflict caused growing unrest among the working classes, leading to social revolution toward the end of the century.

Left: Decorated title of the Declaration of the Rights of Man of 1789 (see pages 154–155).

Great thinkers of the age gathered in the fashionable salons of Paris, where they discussed issues of the day.

MAJOR WARS

1701–14
War of the Spanish Succession (see page 128).

1733–38
War of the Polish Succession (see page 142).

1740–48
War of the Austrian Succession (see page 132).

1756–63
Seven Years' War (Britain and Prussia against Austria, France, and Russia).

1778–79
War of the Bavarian Succession (between Austria and Prussia, in which no battles were fought).

1792–1802
French Revolutionary Wars (see pages 156–157).

London financiers organize the Bank of England, which was set up at the end of the 17th century to raise money to finance war against France.

Right to the Throne

Ideas of monarchy changed dramatically in many parts of Europe. The changes were most pronounced in France. In 1700 Louis XIV was conducting his reign of splendor. By 1795 Louis XVI had been executed, the French monarchy had ended, and Napoleon Bonaparte was putting down a rebellion against the republican government. Before then, many so-called "enlightened despots" (see page 124) had introduced social and political reforms.

Frederick the Great extended Charlottenburg Palace in Berlin in the 1740s.

On the Battlefield

Four European wars of the 18th century were caused by disputes over who should succeed to the throne. They are the Wars of the Spanish, Polish, Austrian, and Bavarian Successions (for dates, see above). These and other wars had profound social effects, as monarchs and governments did everything they could to raise funds to support armies and finance campaigns.

Right: Painting by John Wootton of the Battle of Blenheim, fought in Bavaria in 1704. This was an important battle in the War of the Spanish Succession.

The Enlightenment

The Enlightenment, or Age of Reason, was an 18th-century philosophical and intellectual movement in Europe. Leading philosophers and writers, especially in France, put forward a view of the world that was based on reason and scientific enquiry. They believed that this approach helped people to help themselves, by improving their individual lives as well as society as a whole. This rational approach brought about important advances in the sciences and mathematics, and influenced European leaders in their approach to their subjects.

Knowledge, Freedom, and Happiness: Rational Goals

The enlightened thinkers of the Age of Reason believed the main goals of rational human beings to be knowledge, freedom, and happiness. They celebrated the power of reason, which allows all men and women to understand the universe and improve their own condition. The French philosopher and jurist Montesquieu put forward the belief that an understanding of rational laws could lessen the problems of society and improve people's lives.

Right: Denis Diderot (1713–84), and a page from the Encyclopédie *on the art of writing. Both Rousseau and Voltaire wrote articles for the* Encyclopédie.

Sculpture by Claude Michel of Baron de Montesquieu (1689–1755), whose major work was The Spirit of the Laws.

Religion and Deism

The philosophers of the Enlightenment accepted the existence of a creator God on the basis of reason. They believed that this supreme being created the universe and its physical laws, but then did not intervene in it. This rationalistic approach to religion and creation—known as deism—went against conventional religious faith, including Christianity. Some deists developed openly critical views of the Christian church and its practices.

The Powers of Reason

The group of French philosophers and writers known as the *philosophes*, which included Diderot, Rousseau, and Voltaire, believed in the ultimate power of reason. They held that the application of human reason showed the way to truth. Diderot was the chief editor of the 28-volume *Encyclopédie* (1751–72), to which more than 200 scholarly experts contributed. This monumental work presented a rational approach to the sciences, arts, and professions.

Enlightened Despots

Enlightenment ideas captured the attention of several European rulers and influenced their approach to power. These so-called "enlightened despots" included Catherine the Great of Russia (see pages 138–139), Frederick the Great of Prussia (see pages 134–135), and Joseph II of Austria (see page 133). They remained authoritarian rulers (or despots), but used their power to introduce enlightened reforms.

This crown coin of 1787 shows Joseph II, Holy Roman Emperor from 1765 to 1790. He introduced reforms in education and law.

The Swiss philosopher Jean-Jacques Rousseau (1712–78) influenced deist ideas. His novel Émile *offended the ecclesiastical authorities.*

The Salons

In the salons of Paris, well-connected women hosted fashionable gatherings that fostered philosophical and political debate. The *philosophes* were welcome guests, and these events helped them bring their ideas to the attention of influential men and women in French society. The Marquise de Pompadour, mistress of Louis XV, was helpful in resisting efforts to censor the *Encyclopédie*.

Left: At the Parisian salon of Marie-Thérèse Geoffrin, an actor reads a Voltaire play beneath a bust of the author. Encyclopaedists Jean d'Alembert and Denis Diderot are among those present.

France on the Eve of Revolution

The three kings of 18th-century France—Louis XIV, XV, and XVI—were faced with a society being fed revolutionary ideas about government and power by the country's enlightened thinkers. Reforms were needed, but they were generally opposed by the country's clergy and aristocracy. Life for the peasants and workers who paid most taxes became even harder as France's financial crisis deepened. There were food shortages, and the starving people protested by turning against their rulers. Revolution was in the air.

The bejewelled crown of Louis XV, which he wore at his coronation in 1722.

The *Ancien Régime*

The ideas of 18th-century French philosophers challenged the notion of absolute monarchy. Many people no longer believed that a king or queen ruled by divine right, and they looked forward to a new order. Late in the century they began to refer to the political and social system that they wished to replace as the *ancien régime*, or "old order." This was clearly a term of disapproval.

This painting by Louis de Boulogne of the young king exercising power is entitled Louis XV Granting Patents of Nobility to the Municipal Body of Paris.

King Louis XV

The great-grandson of Louis XIV (ruled 1643–1715), the young Louis XV succeeded him on his death but was not crowned until seven years later. For some years France was governed by a regent. In 1743 Louis took over rule without a chief minister, but he was weak and indecisive. He was seen as living in luxury while the people endured great hardship. Colonial losses in the Seven Years' War increased the king's unpopularity.

The Three Estates

French society was made up of three estates (or orders): The First Estate was made up of the clergy and the Second Estate of the nobility. The Third Estate comprised everyone else, including prosperous middle-class merchants, lawyers, officials, and—the largest group—peasants and workers. Most of the country's taxes came from the Third Estate, which caused great resentment, especially when they saw them wasted on foreign wars and court extravagance.

Above: People had to queue for rationed bread. Failed harvests caused rising prices and food shortages for the Third Estate.

Right: This cartoon illustrates the burdens of the Third Estate. A peasant literally carries the weight of a clergyman and a noble.

THE ANCIEN RÉGIME

1715–74
Reign of Louis XV, who becomes king at the age of five; the Duke of Orleans acts as regent until 1723.

1726
Louis's former tutor Cardinal de Fleury becomes head of government.

1733–38
War of the Polish Succession, in which France is allied to Spain.

1740–48
War of the Austrian Succession, in which France is allied to Prussia.

1756–63
The Seven Years' War, which ends with the loss to Britain of French colonies in Canada and India.

1770
Dauphin Louis, grandson of Louis XV, marries Marie Antoinette of Austria.

1774–92
Reign of Louis XVI.

1789
The king is forced to call an assembly of the States General (the first since 1614).

Women of the Court

Louis XV was married to Maria Leszczynska, daughter of the exiled king of Poland. In 1745, he gave one of his young favorites the title Marquise de Pompadour and made her his official mistress. The king was influenced by her political advice, which included involvement in the Seven Years' War. There were other favorites, including the Comtesse du Barry, who took over as royal mistress in 1769. This situation caused constant jealousy and scheming at court.

Portrait of Louis XVI in his royal robes.

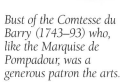

Bust of the Comtesse du Barry (1743–93) who, like the Marquise de Pompadour, was a generous patron the arts.

Failed Reforms

Louis XVI appointed Robert Turgot to run the country's finances, but his attempts to reduce the public debt were opposed by both clergy and nobility. Louis replaced him with banker Jacques Necker, but his proposed reforms also met opposition from Marie Antoinette and the aristocracy. Wars increased the national debt, and the king was forced to call an assembly of the States General, representing the three estates. The following month, the Third Estate declared itself a National

The War of Spanish Succession

Charles II's lack of an heir led to the Spanish crown being taken by the Bourbon Duke of Anjou (grandson of Louis XIV) as Philip V. This led to the War of the Spanish Succession (1701–14), when a grand alliance of England, the Dutch Republic, and the Holy Roman Emperor declared war on Spain and France. Philip was finally recognized as king in 1713, but he lost many territories to Austria and Britain under the Treaty of Utrecht. He turned to creating a centralized administration in Spain.

Spain and Portugal

The Bourbon rule of Spain led to many disastrous battles, but it also helped bring Aragon, Catalonia, and Valencia under royal control. During the 18th century the Bourbon rulers introduced many reforms, such as lower taxes. There were strong family ties with the French, and great conflict with Britain, over Gibraltar, Minorca, and power in the Americas. Portugal had been ruled by the Braganza Dynasty since 1640, but the most important administrator of enlightened reforms was a government minister, the Marquess de Pombal.

Philip V is portrayed here conquering heresy in the form of a dragon.

Spain's Enlightened Despot

Philip V's son and successor, Charles III, was one of Europe's "enlightened despots" (see page 8). He introduced many of the changes that came to be known as the Bourbon Reforms. He and his advisers developed the Spanish economy, encouraging manufacture and freeing up trade. Resenting the power of the Jesuits, Charles expelled them from Spain and its colonies in 1767.

Right: Detail by Goya of the Count of Floribanda (1728–1808), a minister of Charles III who pushed through his reforms.

SPANISH BOURBON TERRITORIES 1789

- LA CORUÑA
- PARMA
SPAIN
- VALENCIA
NAPLES -
MEDITERRANEAN SEA
PALERMO -
- ORUNO
KINGDOM OF NAPLES

Recovered Possessions

The War of the Polish Succession (1733–38) led to Spain gaining the Kingdom of Naples and Sicily, which was ruled by the future Spanish king Charles III. Under the peace treaty, Parma and Piacenza were given to Austria. But both territories, along with Guastalla, were restored to Spain by the terms of the Treaty of Aix-la-Chapelle at the end of the War of the Austrian Succession in 1748. The map shows the European territories of Bourbon Spain in 1789.

▨ Spanish Bourbon Territories, 1789

Huge waves followed a terrible earthquake on 1 November 1755, overwhelming ships in Lisbon harbor. Flooding and fires destroyed much of the city and killed about 60,000 people.

Portugal

By formal agreement there was steady trade between Portugal and England during the 18th century, which helped both countries. Portugal succeeded in retaining its independence from Spain under the rule of John V (1706–50) and his successor Joseph. Real power was in the hands of the Marquess de Pombal, who as a believer in enlightened despotism reformed Portuguese administration and modernized education. Pombal also organized the rebuilding of Lisbon after the earthquake of 1755.

ITALY

1707
Austrian troops enter Naples.

1720
Victor Amadeus II of Savoy exchanges Sicily for Sardinia.

1727–31
Antonio Farnese rules the duchy of Parma and Piacenza.

1748
Milan is ceded to the Habsburgs.

1759–67
Bernardo Tanucci leads a council of regency to rule Naples-Sicily until Ferdinand IV (son of Charles VII) comes of age.

1765
Administrative reorganization in Milan with creation of a Supreme Economic Council.

1765–90
Reign in Tuscany of Grand Duke Peter Leopold, who transforms administration and law.

1768
The republic of Genoa hands its last overseas possession, Corsica, to France.

1797
The last doge (or ruler) of Venice is deposed, and the city falls to Austria.

1799
Lucca falls to the French.

Rome's Trevi Fountain was commissioned by Pope Clement XII in 1732. Designed by Nicolo Salvi, it was completed in 1762.

The Papal States

The Papal States had lost political and economic strength during the 17th century, and this trend continued. Successive popes tried to centralize power, but they failed to improve the poor economic situation. Corruption and bribery were rife, and the papacy's influence declined within the region and throughout Europe. Rome itself had brilliant squares, palaces, and official buildings, but much of the city was still poorly paved and had little sanitation.

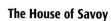

Right: This Venetian coin of 1789 bears the name of the last doge, Ludovico Manin.

Italy

Many of the Italian states were greatly affected by events following the Wars of the Spanish Succession and Polish Succession (see pages 128–129). Peace settlements and treaties resulted in most falling into Spanish and Austrian hands. Some of the less powerful states did manage to retain their independence. Despite its declining political influence, including that of the Papal States, the Italian region remained an important focal point for the arts and sciences.

The House of Savoy

The House of Savoy (originally from the western Alps region) had acquired Piedmont in the 14th century. By the Treaty of Utrecht in 1713, Victor Amadeus II's status was raised from duke to king, as ruler of Sicily. In 1720 the Savoyard king was forced by the Austrian Habsburgs to exchange Sicily for Sardinia (then a Spanish possession). He and his successors ruled from their capital of Turin, in Piedmont, and their kingdom is often called Piedmont-Sardinia.

Left: The Basilica of Superga, on a hill to the east of Turin, was commissioned by Victor Amadeus II. It was designed by the Sicilian architect Filippo Juvarra in 1717 and completed in 1731.

Detail from a Goya painting of Charles III in hunting pose.

Spanish and Austrian Control of Italian Lands

Much of the Italian peninsula came under the control of the Spanish and Austrian Habsburgs. The map shows these lands, as well as the Papal States and other independent states. Some regions changed hands several times. The duchy of Parma and Piacenza, for example, was held by the Farnese family until 1731, when it passed to Don Carlos (the future Charles III of Spain). Two years later it came under Austrian control, but was returned to the Spanish Bourbons in 1748.

ITALY IN THE 18TH CENTURY

SAVOY
MILAN
PARMA
GENOA
VENICE
FLORENCE
TUSCANY
ADRIATIC SEA
ROME
NAPLES
SARDINIA
MEDITERRANEAN SEA
PALERMO
SICILY

Hapsburg Territory, 1715	Savoy, 1715	To Spain, 1748
To Hapsburgs, 1737	To Savoy, 1720	To Spain 1735

Tuscany

In 1737, on the death of Gian Gastone de' Medici, the title of Grand Duke of Tuscany passed to Francis Stephen, Duke of Lorraine (husband of Maria Theresa, later Holy Roman Emperor Francis I). This began the rule of the Habsburg-Lorraine family. Under Francis and his son Grand Duke Leopold I (later Holy Roman Emperor Leopold II), there was a period of reform. The church's privileges were reduced and internal trade barriers were lifted.

Independent States

Some of the northern states remained independent. The republics of Venice and Genoa were no longer the great powers that they had once been, but they did not embrace reform. The nobility continued to govern Venice, while Genoese trade had sunk to its lowest level by 1750. The commune of Lucca, in the northwest of Tuscany, had conflicts with powerful neighbors, but succeeded in keeping its independence until 1799.

This detail from a painting shows Holy Roman Emperor Francis I with two of his daughters in 1756.

Below: This painting by Canaletto shows the return of the Venetian state galley, the bucintoro. On Ascension Day every year until 1789, the galley was rowed out into the Adriatic Sea in a ceremony to wed Venice to the sea.

The Holy Roman Empire

By the start of the 18th century the former power of the Holy Roman Empire was all but gone. Though the emperors were in theory elected, the imperial crown was in practice inherited within the Habsburg Dynasty of Austria. Problems arose over the inheritance of power by a woman, Maria Theresa, leading to yet another European war of succession. Throughout the period there was conflict between Austria and Prussia, although there was agreement toward the end of the century over the division of Poland and concerns about revolutionary France.

Charles VI's seal on the Pragmatic Sanction.

Charles VI's Pragmatic Sanction
Old laws prohibited a woman from inheriting kingdoms or empires. In 1713 Charles VI, having no son, drew up an imperial edict making his daughter Maria Theresa heir to all his Austrian territories. The emperor announced this publicly in 1724, and the major states agreed to recognize the edict. But on Charles' death in 1740, several broke their promise, leading to the War of the Austrian Succession.

Marie Therese's Inheritance
The map shows the changes in Austrian Habsburg possessions during the 18th century. Having lost Silesia to Frederick II of Prussia in 1748, Maria Theresa strengthened her power in her own territory and built up a large army. She allied herself with France and Russia, but lost all claims to Silesia in the Seven Years' War.
In 1772 she succeeded in gaining the territory of Galicia and Lodomeria during a partition of Poland.

HAPSBURG LANDS

POLAND

HOLY ROMAN EMPIRE

SILESIA

GALICIA AND LODOMERIA

FRANCE

KINGDOM OF HUNGARY

OTTOMAN EMPIRE

▨ Austrian Hapsburg territory, 1700	▨ 1737
▨ Silesia	▨ 1772–1805
▨ Peace of Utrecht 1713–1714	— Border of Holy Roman Empire 1783
▨ 1718–1720	

Francis I
Francis Stephen, the Duke of Lorraine, married Maria Theresa in 1736. When doing so, he agreed to give up Lorraine, but gained the duchy of Tuscany (see page 131). Nine years later, the duke became Holy Roman Emperor, but he was overshadowed by his powerful wife. He was not influential in government, leaving administration to the successful chancellor and foreign minister Kaunitz.

Count Wenzel Anton von Kaunitz, who was Austrian state chancellor from 1753 to 1792.

Maria Theresa and Frances had a large family of sixteen children. Their youngest daughter was Maria Antonia (or Marie Antoinette, future queen of France).

The Josephinum, in Vienna, was founded by Joseph II in 1785 as a medical academy. Today the building houses a Museum of Medical History.

Joseph II

From 1765 to 1780 Joseph II co-ruled with his mother, Maria Theresa. After her death, Joseph (one of Europe's "enlightened despots") tried to rationalize the imperial government. He reorganized the army, abolished serfdom, encouraged religious toleration and equality, and granted freedom of the press. Under his rule artistic life in Vienna flourished. His social reforms brought him into conflict with the clergy and nobility, but made him very popular with ordinary citizens.

Leopold II

Joseph II's younger brother Leopold was one of the most capable of the "enlightened despots." He succeeded his father Francis as Duke of Tuscany in 1765 and, after his brother's death in 1790, was elected emperor. Leopold upheld the reforms granting religious freedom to non-Catholics and emancipating the peasants, but in other areas he failed to carry through reforms. He was concerned by revolutionary events in France and concluded an alliance with Prussia before his death in 1792.

Above: The double-headed eagle was a symbol of power adopted by the Holy Roman Empire. All power was lost by the end of the 18th century.

Below: This painting shows Joseph II with his generals at a military camp.

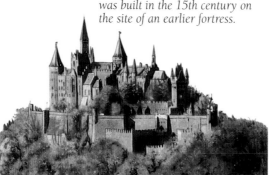

The ancestral Hohenzollern Castle, in Swabia (southwest Germany), was built in the 15th century on the site of an earlier fortress.

The Hohenzollerns

The Hohenzollern family, originally from Swabia, rose to power in the state of Brandenburg. During the early 16th century they acquired the duchy of Prussia. In 1701 the Hohenzollern ruler Frederick III, elector of Brandenburg, assumed the title "king in Prussia" with the agreement of Holy Roman Emperor Leopold I. The Prussian kings kept their title of electors of Brandenburg until the end of the Holy Roman Empire.

Frederick William I

During his reign, Frederick William I (son of the founding Prussian king) created a more unified, efficient, and prosperous state. He streamlined the bureaucracy of government and ended corruption. Frederick William concentrated on military affairs and especially building up his army, introducing a form of conscription in 1733. He succeeded in leaving his son, Frederick II, a centralized state with solid finances and an excellent army.

The Rise of Prussia

Prussia became a powerful force in the 18th century. With a government based on authority and discipline, it had a famously strong, efficient army. Frederick the Great used his power both to expand the kingdom and to further the arts and sciences. He was one of Europe's most important "enlightened despots," believing in progress but ruling autocratically. By the end of his rule Prussia was a large, unified kingdom, stretching from the old border with Hanover in the west to the new, reduced Poland in the east.

The Prussian Army

Frederick William I (nicknamed the "sergeant king") expanded the Prussian army from 38,000 men to about 83,000. As well as introducing conscription, he recruited from all over Europe. His army was famed for its loyal officers and disciplined infantry. They were trained by Prince Leopold of Anhalt-Dessau, a fearsome field marshal who introduced the iron ramrod and modern bayonet. Frederick II carried on the military tradition with his cavalry, which became the strongest mounted force in Europe.

Right: A Prussian grenadier in Frederick II's army. The new-style helmet replaced a peaked cap and was more practical for a grenade-thrower.

Detail from a Prussian grenadier's cap.

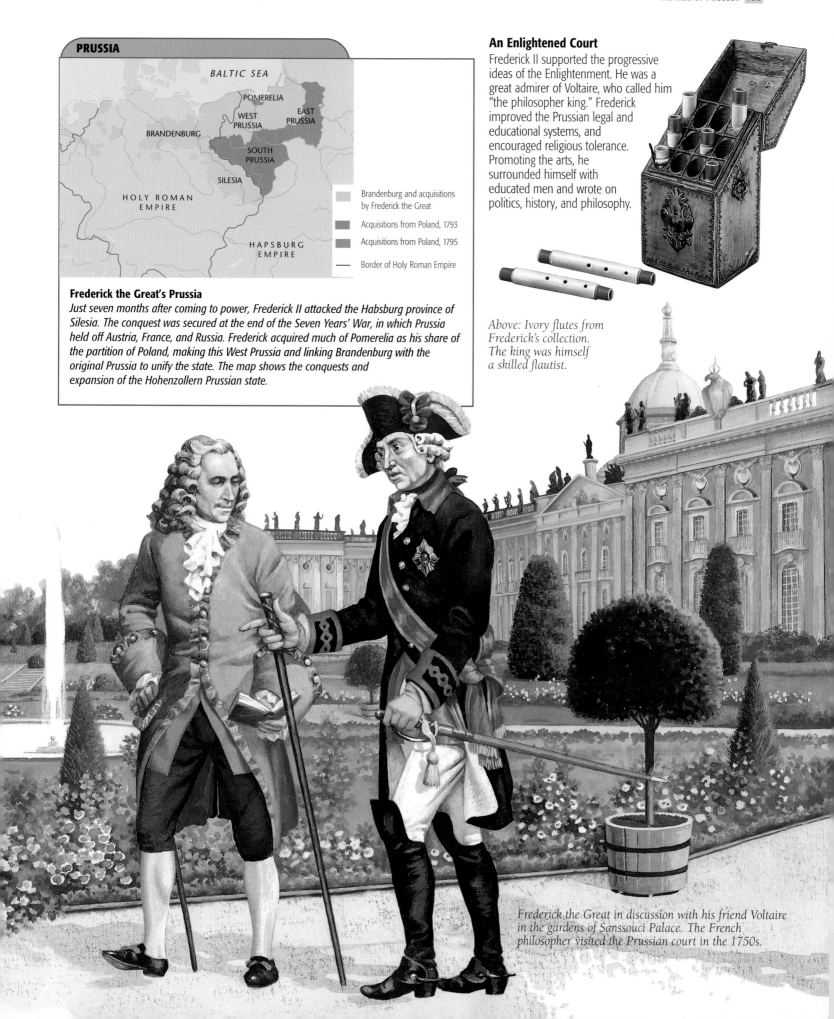

PRUSSIA

BALTIC SEA

POMERELIA

WEST
PRUSSIA

EAST
PRUSSIA

BRANDENBURG

SOUTH
PRUSSIA

SILESIA

HOLY ROMAN
EMPIRE

HAPSBURG
EMPIRE

Brandenburg and acquisitions
by Frederick the Great

Acquisitions from Poland, 1793

Acquisitions from Poland, 1795

Border of Holy Roman Empire

Frederick the Great's Prussia
Just seven months after coming to power, Frederick II attacked the Habsburg province of Silesia. The conquest was secured at the end of the Seven Years' War, in which Prussia held off Austria, France, and Russia. Frederick acquired much of Pomerelia as his share of the partition of Poland, making this West Prussia and linking Brandenburg with the original Prussia to unify the state. The map shows the conquests and expansion of the Hohenzollern Prussian state.

An Enlightened Court
Frederick II supported the progressive ideas of the Enlightenment. He was a great admirer of Voltaire, who called him "the philosopher king." Frederick improved the Prussian legal and educational systems, and encouraged religious tolerance. Promoting the arts, he surrounded himself with educated men and wrote on politics, history, and philosophy.

Above: Ivory flutes from Frederick's collection. The king was himself a skilled flautist.

Frederick the Great in discussion with his friend Voltaire in the gardens of Sanssouci Palace. The French philosopher visited the Prussian court in the 1750s.

Russia Comes to Power

As an important statesman and reformer, Peter the Great was responsible for bringing wider power to Russia in the early 1700s. His successors allowed more power to guards, nobles, and favorite advisers. The developing court culture was important to the autocratic rulers and aristocrats. There were many intrigues and coups at the highest level of society, but life did not generally improve for the growing empire's serfs.

In 1697 Peter the Great (in the striped tunic) disguised himself and worked as a ship's carpenter at the Dutch port of Zaandam. He later visited the British dockyard at Deptford.

Modernization

Peter the Great used his knowledge of Western technology and government to modernize Russia and make it a major European power. He created the first effective Russian regular army and expanded his territory to the Baltic Sea, gaining Ingria, Estonia, and Livonia. Having founded St. Petersburg, he made it his capital in 1712. Peter reformed Russian government and administration, as well as trade and industry, but dealt harshly with anyone who opposed him.

Above right: Practical and educational books flourished under Peter I. This page is from a children's book.

The Navy

Peter I was always fascinated by ships and shipbuilding. He became a skilled shipwright, which enabled him to oversee the construction of the Russian navy. Hundreds of galleys joined with 52 battleships and many other craft to make up Peter's powerful fleet. This was used to annex part of the Baltic coast. The tsar had special schools set up to train young men for naval service.

Catherine I

Peter's second wife, a Lithuanian woman of humble birth, joined the Russian Orthodox Church in 1703 and took the name Catherine. She married the tsar in 1712 and succeeded him through the power and support of guard regiments. Catherine gave control to a Supreme Privy Council made up of her late husband's advisers, who continued many of his policies.

This portrait is considered a flattering likeness of Empress Catherine I.

Above: A satirical woodcut of mice taking their tormentor, a large cat, to its burial. The cat represented Peter the Great, and the mice were those he persecuted.

Anna

After Peter II died on the day set for his wedding to a princess, the Supreme Privy Council offered the throne to Peter the Great's niece, Anna. The new empress promptly abolished the Council, but left affairs of state to a cabinet and German advisers. Anna treated opponents brutally and oversaw a reign of terror against peasants who could not pay their taxes.

Anna's gold and silver crown glittered with precious stones.

Detail of a painting of Elizabeth in 1743.

Elizabeth I

Elizabeth came to power in a coup, when guards arrested the infant emperor Ivan IV (then aged 15 months) and his mother and regent Anna Leopoldovna (niece of the late Empress Anna). The new empress left most matters to her trusted advisers, but she did encourage education and the arts. During her reign Russia stuck to a pro-Austrian foreign policy and fought successfully against Prussia in the Seven Years' War.

In 1754 Elizabeth commissioned her court architect Bartolomeo Rastrelli to rebuild the Winter Palace at St. Petersburg (right) in a baroque style. Rastrelli had completed the Summer Palace ten years earlier. Elizabeth's palaces were meant to compete with Versailles.

PETER THE GREAT'S SUCCESSORS

1696–1725
Sole reign of Peter I ("the Great") after his sister acted as regent (1682–89) and his half-brother as co-tsar (1689–96).

1700–21
The Great Northern War is fought against Sweden by Russia, Denmark-Norway, and Saxony-Poland.

1713
Russia loses Azov at the end of the Turkish War (1710–13).

1723
Persia cedes western and southern shores of the Caspian Sea to Russia in return for military aid.

1725–27
Reign of Catherine I, widow of Peter I.

1727–30
Reign of Peter II, grandson of Peter I, crowned at the age of 11.

1730–40
Reign of Anna, niece of Peter I.

1740–41
Regency during the reign of infant Ivan VI.

1741–62
Reign of Elizabeth, daughter of Peter I and Catherine I.

1752
The Catherine Palace is completed at Tsarskoe Selo by Rastrelli.

1755
Foundation of the University of Moscow.

Catherine The Great

Catherine the Great was very much influenced by the ideas of the Enlightenment, and she counts as one of the most important "enlightened despots." Having read widely among the major French philosophers of the age, including Montesquieu and Voltaire, she had many reforming ideas. Like Peter the Great before her, she expanded the Russian empire physically and gave it greater political significance in Europe during her 34-year reign.

An English cartoon of Catherine being offered Warsaw and Constantinople by the devil.

Catherine Takes the Throne

In 1744 Princess Sophie of Anhalt-Zerbst, a small German principality, was received into the Russian Orthodox Church and took the name Yekaterina (Catherine). The following year she married Empress Elizabeth's nephew Peter, heir to the Russian throne. Six months after her weak husband succeeded Elizabeth as Peter III in 1762, guards officers overthrew the emperor with Catherine's approval. At the age of 33 she became Empress Catherine II, later known as "the Great." Eight days later her husband was murdered.

The rebel Pugachov was captured and taken in an iron cage to Moscow, where he was beheaded.

Pugachev's Rebellion

In 1773 a former Cossack officer named Yemelyan Pugachov, claiming to be the dead emperor Peter III, started a peasant uprising. Pugachov's promise to free the serfs led to a rebellion that spread rapidly through the south-eastern provinces. The rebels killed at least 1,500 nobles and more than 1,000 government officials and were heading for Moscow before Catherine sent troops to crush them.

Copper kopeck of 1789, showing the imperial crown over Catherine's monogram.

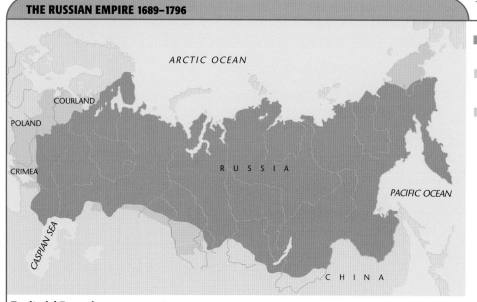

THE RUSSIAN EMPIRE 1689–1796

ARCTIC OCEAN

COURLAND

POLAND

CRIMEA

R U S S I A

CASPIAN SEA

PACIFIC OCEAN

C H I N A

- Russia, in 1689
- Expansion under Peter the Great, 1689–1725
- Expansion by time of Catherine the Great's death, in 1796

Territorial Expansion

Catherine continued the expansion of the empire that had begun with Peter the Great. The partitions of Poland gave Russia valuable territory in the west, and the third partition included annexation of the Baltic duchy of Courland. In the south, the taking of the Crimea from the Ottoman Turks gave the empire new territories along the Black Sea shore. The map shows Russian expansion during the reigns of Peter and Catherine.

Above: The neoclassical Green Dining Room, in the Catherine Palace at Tsarskoe Selo, was designed by the Scottish architect Charles Cameron in 1773.

Artistic Patronage

Catherine was an enthusiastic patron of the arts. She herself wrote satires, historical articles, and opera libretti, and corresponded with the French encyclopaedists (see page 124), including Diderot and Voltaire. She encouraged the translation of foreign works into Russian, and subsidized public performances of plays. The empress promoted the neoclassical style in architecture and decoration.

Above: The Tauride Palace in St. Petersburg was built in 1789 by the Russian architect Ivan Starov for Grigory Potemkin.

Portrait of Alexei Bobrinskoy painted in 1769

Catherine commissioned this colossal bronze statue of Peter the Great from French sculptor Étienne-Maurice Falconet. It was put up in St. Petersburg in 1782.

(see page 124)

REIGN OF CATHERINE THE GREAT

1762
Six-month reign of Peter III, nephew of the late Empress Elizabeth.

1762–96
Reign of Catherine II, "the Great."

1767
Catherine prepares her Instruction, a document that recommends liberal government reform and a new legal code.

1772
First partition of Poland between Russia, Prussia, and Austria.

1775
Reorganization of Russia into provinces and districts.

1782
Catherine appoints a Commission on National Education that leads to the founding of many schools.

1783
Annexation of the Crimea from the Turks; an imperial opera and ballet theater is established in St. Petersburg, with the Kirov ballet company.

1787
Catherine makes a grand journey to the Crimea arranged by her former lover, Grigory Potemkin.

1793–95
Second and third partitions of Poland.

1796–1801
Reign of Paul, son of Catherine the Great.

Catherine's Children

Catherine's first child Paul, born in 1754, succeeded her as emperor. In 1757 Catherine gave birth to a daughter, Anna. Her third child, Alexei Bobrinskoy, was born during her husband's short reign in 1762.

THE TURKISH WARS

1703–30
Reign of Ottoman sultan Ahmed III (period also known as the Tulip Time).

1730–54
Reign of Sultan Mahmud I, who is advised by Comte de Bonneval, a French convert to Islam.

1739
Treaty of Belgrade, peace settlement between the Ottoman Turks and Russia (plus allied Austria).

1750
Tensions and rising taxes lead to a revolt in Sarajevo (in Bosnia-Herzegovina) against the Ottoman sultan.

1757–74
Reign of Sultan Mustafa III.

1768–74
First Russo–Turkish War.

1774–89
Reign of Sultan Abdulhamid.

1787–92
Second Russo–Turkish War.

1789–1807
Reign of Sultan Selim III, nephew of Abdulhamid.

The Treaty

The treaty of Kuchuk Kainarji, signed at Kaynardzha in present-day Bulgaria in 1774, ended the first Russo-Turkish War in favor of the Russians. It ceded several Black Sea ports to Russia, declared the Crimean khanate independent of the new Ottoman sultan Abdulhamid, and gave Russia the right to maintain a fleet on the Black Sea. The Russians were also allowed to represent and protect Greek Orthodox Christians in Ottoman territory.

The Balkan Peninsula

Peter the Great (see page 136) wanted to free the Balkans from Ottoman rule. In 1710 Sultan Ahmed III took his forces into the Northern War against Russia. When the campaign ended in victory for the Ottomans at the River Pruth the following year, the Russians were forced to return Azov to Turkey. War broke out again in 1735, with Russia and Austria allied against the Ottomans. The Russians gained little and agreed not to build a Black Sea fleet.

The Turks Declare War

Sultan Mustafa III declared war on Catherine the Great in 1768 after demanding that Russia stop interfering in the affairs of Poland. Two years later the Russian fleet won a great victory over the Ottomans at the harbor of Chesme on the Aegean Sea. This success inspired great confidence in the Russians among rebels within the Ottoman empire, making military success on land easier.

Above: Catherine the Great had the neo-Gothic Russian Orthodox Church of St. John built at Chesme Palace in St Petersburg in 1780. It commemorated the great naval victory.

Above: This cotton bolster cover embroidered with silk was made in the mid-18th century in the Epirus region of modern Greece. It was an important textile production center.

The Turkish Wars

During the 18th century Russia tried to continue its eastward expansion at the expense of the declining Ottoman Empire. The shores of the Black Sea, which formed an important access to world trade routes, were still in the hands of the Ottoman Turks and their vassals, the khans of Crimea. This situation and a wish by Russia to dominate the Balkan Peninsula, led to two major Russo-Turkish wars. Military victories and territorial gains led to increased Russian and European influence in Ottoman affairs.

Annexation of the Crimea

Under the terms of the 1774 treaty, the territory of the Crimean khanate formed an independent state that was subject to the Ottoman sultan only in religious matters. Nine years later, Catherine annexed the Crimea outright. This led to many Crimean Tartars leaving their homeland, since they preferred to live under Ottoman rule. Their fertile lands were soon colonized by Russians.

Above: These ceremonial horse's knee guards were presented to Catherine the Great by Sultan Abdulhamid.

The Second Turkish War

War broke out again in 1787, with Holy Roman Emperor Joseph II on the side of the Russians. Joseph's army suffered terrible defeat, but Russian successes forced the Ottoman Turks to sign the Treaty of Jassy in 1792. This treaty gave the Russians a large stretch of Black Sea coast to the east of the Dniester River.

Painting of Sultan Selim III, who undertook a program of reform and Westernization within his empire.

Below: Catherine the Great arrives at the Khan's palace in Bakhchisarai, capital of the Crimean khanate, in 1787. She traveled there with a retinue of 2,300 people in order to take possession of her new province.

Denmark and Norway

The Danish-controlled union between Denmark and Norway continued in the 18th century. It developed an important merchant navy as well as a military fleet. In the 1780s the stagnant Danish economy and society were revitalized by land reforms that included the abolition of serfdom. The reforms were a successful expression of "enlightened despotism."

Poland and Scandinavia

Important struggles and battles defined this region early in the 18th century. The Great Northern War, from which Russia emerged victorious, was quickly followed by the War of Polish Succession, in which Russia and Austria played a major part. Sweden was crushed in the Northern War, and later in the century its monarchy was reduced in power by an enlightened parliamentary government. By the end of the period Denmark was introducing reforms, while Poland was divided up by the major powers until it ceased to exist.

SCANDINAVIA 1721

NORTH SEA

KINGDOM OF NORWAY AND DENMARK

SWEDEN

KARELIA

INGRIA

ESTONIA

LIVONIA

BALTIC SEA

- Sweden, 1721
- Kingdom of Norway and Denmark
- Swedish territory lost to Russia, 1721

Sweden
For Sweden the Great Northern War was disastrous, causing the loss of many territories. These included its Baltic provinces of Estonia, Livonia, Ingria, and Karelia. This map shows the situation in 1721. After the war, a new Swedish constitution gave great power to a legislative assembly that allowed parliamentary government, reducing the role of the monarchy.

This Sèvres vase was a gift from Gustav III of Sweden to Catherine II of Russia.

The Northern War
In 1697 Frederick Augustus, Elector of Saxony, was chosen from 18 candidates to be king of Poland. As Augustus II (later known as "the Strong"), he allied Saxony-Poland with Russia and Denmark and started the Great Northern War (1700–21) against Charles XII of Sweden by invading Livonia. Augustus was deposed in 1704 and restored by Russia six years later. By the end of the war, Russia was the major Baltic power.

The "Golden Rider," a gilded statue of Augustus the Strong, erected in Dresden in 1735.

The War of Polish Succession
After the death of Augustus the Strong, Polish nobles elected Stanislaw Leszczynski (father-in-law of Louis XV of France) as their king. But Russia and Austria forced Poland to accept Augustus's son, which led to war. France won territory from Austria, but a peace treaty confirmed Augustus III as king of Poland. Stanislaw was compensated by being made Duke of Lorraine.

After the Great Northern War, Frederik IV of Denmark had a summer palace built beside Lake Esrum. The baroque building was named Fredensborg ("Palace of Peace").

Portrait of Stanislaw II Poniatowski, who reigned from 1764 to 1795 as the last king of independent Poland.

Allegorical illustration of the partition of Poland, showing Catherine the Great, Maria Theresa, Frederick II, and Joseph II dividing up the map.

Below: This painting of the election of Stanislaw II Poniatowski as Polish king in 1764 was completed 14 years later by the celebrated Venetian artist Bernardo Bellotto.

Growth of the Empire

Poland's weakness and disunity led to its being divided and finally completely absorbed by Austria, Prussia, and Russia in three separate partitions (1772, 1793, and 1795). The second partition led to a Polish uprising, but this was quickly put down. Russia received the most territory, but the capital, Warsaw, was taken by Prussia. Maria Theresa opposed the scheme, but Austria accepted its gains. The map shows how Poland was divided among the three invaders.

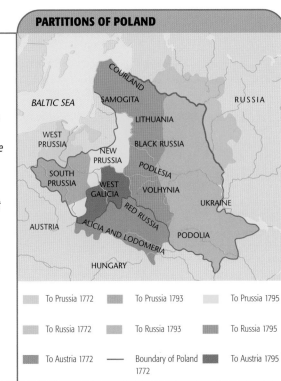

PARTITIONS OF POLAND

- To Prussia 1772
- To Prussia 1793
- To Prussia 1795
- To Russia 1772
- To Russia 1793
- To Russia 1795
- To Austria 1772
- Boundary of Poland 1772
- To Austria 1795

Above: This print shows visitors to the Forum in Rome.

Portrait of Johann Wolfgang von Goethe (1749–1832), the great German writer, who traveled to Italy to study classical art. He later wrote his autobiographical Italian Journey.

The Grand Tour

I t was fashionable during the 18th century for young upper-class Englishmen to undertake a cultural tour of Europe. This Grand Tour was seen as part of a young man's classical education, and he very often took his tutor and a servant with him. Noblemen and artists from other parts of Europe also traveled to pre-revolutionary France and Italy as part of their cultural development. The ultimate goal was Rome, and after 1750 some travelers even went on visit the remains of the ancient cities of Herculaneum and Pompeii.

Travel Accounts

The Grand Tour inspired many journals, travel accounts, and guidebooks. The first was *The Grand Tour, a Journey through the Netherlands, Germany, Italy, and France* by Thomas Nugent, published in 1749. One of the most famous journals was written by James Boswell, the Scottish biographer of Samuel Johnson. Boswell traveled through Europe to Italy in 1763–66. On his travels he met Jean-Jacques Rousseau, who encouraged him to visit Corsica. There he met the Corsican patriot Pasquale Paoli; Boswell wrote *An Account of Corsica*, which made him famous.

Right: Pompeo Batoni was famous for his portraits of tourists among the antiquities of Rome. This is a detail of his study of John Talbot, later 1st Earl Talbot, painted in 1783.

Paris

The culture and beauty of 18th-century Paris were well known. Visitors to the French capital were captivated by the sophistication of its high society. Many also took a trip to Versailles, the home of the French monarchy, where they could marvel at the magnificent palace and gardens. On their journeys many travelers took the opportunity to stay at the homes of their national envoys, who were not in a position to refuse hospitality.

Fashionable clothes were popular with visitors to Paris. This illustration from Diderot's Encyclopédie shows a tailor taking measurements.

Venice

The great attraction of Venice was as a center of pleasure. Many grand tourists made sure they visited the city at carnival time, during the week before Lent. They enjoyed gondola races and masked entertainments. Since the first public casino opened there in 1638, Venice had been known for its gaming houses. The tourist was offered full opportunity to spend (or lose) all his money.

Below: Painting by the Venetian artist Pietro Longhi, who specialized in capturing the extravagant social life of Venice.

Rome

Arriving in Rome was the ultimate aim of many Grand Tourists. This was the center of historical antiquity and classical art. They visited all the famous ancient sites, including the Forum. James Boswell wrote of the Colosseum: "It is hard to tell whether the astonishing massiveness or the exquisite taste of this superb building should be more admired."

Above: This painting by Giovanni Paolo Pannini (1691–1765) shows the walls of the Gallery of Cardinal Silvio Valenti in Rome filled with works of art.

Florence

Florence was visited for its art treasures. On much of their journey, tourists had to gain entry to private collections in order to view classical and Renaissance paintings and sculptures. They were also keen to acquire works for their own collections at home. In Florence they could visit the Uffizi Gallery, as the German-born painter Johann Zoffany did in the 1770s. He was commissioned by George III of England to record the gallery's greatest masterpieces.

Detail of Zoffany's painting of English visitors admiring works in the Uffizi Gallery.

The Low Countries

The region of the Low Countries covers the present-day territory of Belgium, Luxembourg, and the Netherlands. In the 18th century the region of the Dutch republic was governed for the most part by stadholders (chief magistrates or governors) of the House of Orange. During the century there were several revolts against this system of government, as more enlightened groups tried to reform the United Provinces. In 1795 the entire Low Countries fell to an invading French force.

This porcelain cistern was designed for the Dutch East India Company by the Amsterdam artist Cornelis Pronk (1691–1759). It was manufactured in China around 1730 and then taken to Europe for sale.

United Provinces

After the death of William of Orange, there was no stadholder. The Dutch Republic was ruled by a group of hereditary noblemen acting as regents. When this system lost power in 1747 and French troops threatened to invade the republic, William IV, Prince of Orange and Nassau, became stadholder and united all seven provinces under his rule. The office of stadholder was also made hereditary in both male and female lines.

Terracotta bust of William IV (1711–51) wearing the stadholder's ceremonial breastplate and cloak.

War with England

During the American War of Independence (1775–83) the United Provinces saw a trading opportunity for their merchants. They sided with and officially recognized the emerging United States of America. This led to war breaking out against Britain in 1780, but the Dutch navy had been neglected for many years and was overpowered by the British fleet. This disastrous defeat for the Dutch led to a rapid decline in their trading fortunes.

This silver 3-florin piece was issued in 1790, when the southern Netherlands was briefly independent.

THE LOW COUNTRIES

NORTH SEA

UNITED PROVINCES

FRANCE

AUSTRIAN NETHERLANDS

Revolt Against Hapsburg Power

In 1713 the Spanish possessions in the Low Countries—covering the area of modern Belgium and Luxembourg—were transferred to the Austrian branch of the Hapsburgs. The map shows this territory, along with the seven Dutch provinces. In 1789 revolutionaries from Brabant led a revolt against the Holy Roman Emperor and defeated an Austrian force at Turnhout. Imperial authority was re-established in 1790 with little opposition.

☐ United Provinces

▨ Austrian Netherlands

— Boundary of the Holy Roman Empire

The Patriotic Movement

Growing unrest led to the formation of a political movement that was influenced by the ideas and aims of French Enlightenment thinkers, as well as by French and American revolutionaries. The Dutch Patriots opposed the Orangists and stadholder government, and were determined that their policies should benefit the whole nation. In 1787 the Patriots were forced to flee to France.

Below: Patriots rioted in Amsterdam in 1784, attacking the homes of rich burghers.

The Last Stadholder

When William IV died in 1751, his young son succeeded him as stadholder. William V was a conservative and incompetent governor. After losing the war with Britain, the Patriots forced him to leave The Hague. The Prussians restored him, but after the French invasion of 1795 he was dismissed from office and fled to England and later to Nassau.

Portrait of William V (1748–1806) by the German painter Johann Heinrich Wilhelm Tischbein.

Wilhelmina of Prussia, wife of William V, was more strong-willed than her husband. She contributed to restoring the power of the position of stadholder.

Great Britain

After unifying with Scotland in the early 18th century, the Stuart monarchs of England were succeeded by the Hanoverian kings of Great Britain. Three Georges ruled the country from 1714 to the end of the century. This was a period of great economic change, as the Industrial Revolution gathered pace. By mid-century Britain controlled the world's greatest empire, but it sustained a serious loss when its North American colonies broke away in 1783. Ten years later, Britain was again at war with France.

Parliamentary System

The first Hanoverian king, George I, knew little of British politics and did not speak English well. He relied on his council of ministers, and his chief minister Robert Walpole (1676–1745) took control of the council. This was the beginning of the British cabinet system of government. Walpole (*left*) became first lord of the treasury for the second time in 1721, chairing cabinet meetings. He was effectively prime minister (Britain's first), though the title was not used at the time.

GREAT BRITAIN

NORTH SEA

SCOTLAND

IRELAND

ENGLAND

Territory united under the Crown, 1603

Territory united under the Act of Union, 1707

Route of Jacobite forces, 1745–46

Jacobite Invasion / Rebellions

In 1715 and 1745 there were two rebellions in support of James Edward Stuart, son of James II (Stuart king 1685–88). The Catholic supporters of the Stuarts were called Jacobites, from Jacobus, the Latin form of James. The Highland Scots supporting the second rebellion won a victory at Prestonpans in 1745, but were heavily defeated the following year. The map shows Hanoverian unified Britain, with the route taken by Jacobite forces in the second rebellion.

Below: Georgian London was busy, noisy, and full of crime. One of the biggest problems was an enormous consumption of alcohol, especially gin, among the city's poor.

Enlightenment Ideas

English philosopher John Locke was a believer in empiricism, the theory that all human knowledge comes from sense impressions. Locke had great faith in experimental science and confidence in the basic goodness of humanity. Along with the French philosophers, he was a pioneer of Enlightenment ideas. He wrote two treatises on government, which influenced many people's ideas of liberal democracy and civil rights.

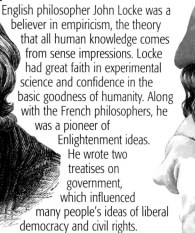
John Locke (1632–1704) was born in the west of England and studied at Oxford University.

London

Eighteenth-century London was the hub of Great Britain. During the century its area more than doubled, and by 1800 it had a million inhabitants and was the largest city in the world. Wealthy Londoners had fashionable houses built around well-designed squares, but the city's poor lived in squalid conditions. Many came to the capital to look for work, but they ended up on the streets or in workhouses.

A bird's-eye view of Grosvenor Square, in London's fashionable Mayfair district, about 1754. The square had been designed about 30 years earlier as the centerpiece of a great family estate.

THE SCIENTIFIC REVOLUTION

1703
Isaac Newton becomes president of the Royal Society of London for the Promotion of Natural Knowledge; two years later he is knighted by Queen Anne.

1720
Edmond Halley (1656–1742) becomes English Astronomer Royal.

1753
Swedish naturalist Carolus Linnaeus (1707–78) classifies plants in his famous Species Plantarum.

1765
First meeting in Birmingham, England, of the Lunar Society, a group of scientists and intellectuals.

1771–78
Carl Scheele of Sweden and Joseph Priestley of England independently discover oxygen.

1781
German-born British astronomer William Herschel (1738–1822) discovers the planet Uranus (which he names the Georgian Star after his patron, King George III).

1785–88
French mathematician and astronomer Pierre-Simon Laplace (1749–1827) publishes five papers demonstrating the stability of the solar system.

1790
The French Academy of Sciences starts work on new universal units of measurement—the metric system.

In 1783 the Montgolfier brothers of France sent two men up in a hot-air balloon. They flew over Paris for 25 minutes.

Studying the Heavens

Many of the astronomical advances of the period were based on an understanding of the law of gravitation. Scientists such as the French mathematician Alexis-Claude Clairaut (1713–65) made great advances in celestial mechanics, especially the motion of the planets and the Moon. By the end of the century astronomers understood that the Sun and planets formed a stable system held together by gravity.

The Scientific Revolution

During the 18th century great advances were made in science, continuing the Scientific Revolution that had begun two centuries earlier. This had its beginnings in astronomy, and following the discoveries of Newton, much knowledge was gained in this period about the motions and especially gravitation of the solar system. An understanding of science was considered essential for any educated person in the Age of Reason. Many enlightened thinkers believed that a similar, methodical approach should be made to social and political issues.

Sir Isaac Newton

The English mathematician, physicist, and astronomer Isaac Newton is known as one of the greatest scientists of all time. His three great discoveries were the law of gravitation, mathematical calculus (invented independently by Gottfried Leibniz) and, in optics, the discovery that light is made up of a spectrum of colors. His great work *Optics* was published in 1704.

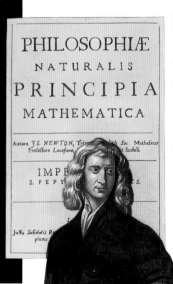

PHILOSOPHIÆ
NATURALIS
PRINCIPIA
MATHEMATICA

Autore JS. NEWTON, Trin... Soc. Matheseos Professore Lucasiano, ...s Sodali.

IMP...
S. PEPY...

Juffu Societatis R... plures...

Left: Isaac Newton (1642–1727) and his great work, Mathematical Principles of Natural Philosophy.

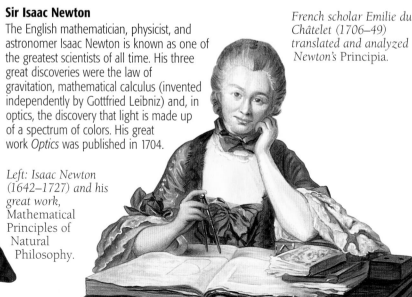

French scholar Emilie du Châtelet (1706–49) translated and analyzed Newton's Principia.

Below: Lavoisier and his wife, from a painting of 1788.

Chemistry

The French chemist Antoine Laurent Lavoisier (1743–94) is known as the founder of modern chemistry. He used his wealth to build a large laboratory, where he discovered in 1778 that air consists of a mixture of two gases, which he called oxygen and nitrogen. He went on to study the role of oxygen in combustion, and published his findings in *Elementary Treatise on Chemistry* (1789), which is regarded as the first chemistry textbook.

Below: Painting of A Philosopher Lecturing on the Orrery by Joseph Wright (1734–97). An orrery was a model of the solar system, often driven by clockwork, which showed the motions of the planets.

Mathematics

The most famous work of the celebrated French mathematician Joseph-Louis Lagrange was *Analytical Mechanics* (1788). Lagrange used algebra to study forces, motions such as planetary orbits, the flow of liquids, and the vibration of strings. Frederick the Great invited "the greatest mathematician in Europe" to his court. Later, Louis XVI gave him apartments in the Louvre. Unlike Lavoisier, Lagrange survived the French Revolution and went on to head the commission that produced the metric system of units.

Below: Portrait of Joseph-Louis Lagrange (1736–1813).

GREAT COMPOSERS

**Baroque Period
(c. 1600–1750)**
*Antonio Vivaldi
(1678–1741), Italian,
composer and violinist who
wrote 811 works, including
more than 450 concertos.*

*Jean-Philippe Rameau
(1683–1764), French, wrote
76 works, including
chamber, keyboard, and
vocal music, and 24
operas.*

*Johann Sebastian Bach
(1685–1750), German,
greatest member of a large
musical family, wrote 972
works, including masses,
cantatas, and the Brandenburg Concertos (1721).*

*George Frederick Handel
(1685–1759), German,
harpsichordist who lived
in England from 1712,
wrote 487 works,
including concertos,
sonatas, and anthems,
many after losing his
sight.*

**Classical Period
(c. 1750–1820)**
*Franz Joseph Haydn
(1732–1809), Austrian,
wrote 1,195 works,
including 104 symphonies,
80 string quartets, sonatas
and operas.*

*Wolfgang Amadeus
Mozart (1756–91),
Austrian, child prodigy
who wrote 655 works,
including 49 symphonies,
25 piano concertos, and
operas.*

*Ludwig van Beethoven
(1770–1827), German,
wrote 398 works,
including 9 symphonies,
32 piano sonatas, and 1
opera (Fidelio,
1805–14), many after
losing his hearing.*

*The closer combination of music and
drama made opera popular with 18th-
century audiences. Mozart was an expert
at developing characterization in his
operatic works.*

Handel and Bach
Baroque music reached its greatest
heights in the work of these two
composers. Much of Bach's work is
religious, including cantatas and
organ compositions for church
services. He combined melodies
and harmonies, but was better
known in his lifetime as an organist
than as a composer. Handel's style
combines the vigor of the late
German Baroque with English and
Italian qualities of clarity and charm.

*Portrait of J.S. Bach, who
wrote masterful works in
almost every musical
form known at the time.*

Eighteenth-Century Music

The first half of the century saw the climax of the
Baroque period in music, which featured elaborate,
expressive forms. Chamber and orchestra music
flourished, and vocal forms such as the oratorio and
cantata were introduced. The Classical period began
around 1750, at a time when public concerts became
more popular with the growing middle class.
Composers began introducing more contrast between
the different movements of a work, increasing the
expression of emotions.

The Opera and the Ballet

Classical opera was greatly influenced by the German composer Christoph Gluck (1714–87), who brought operatic drama and music closer together. Mozart was the greatest exponent of the art. By mid-century ballet was also combining music and dance with the story of a composition. This developing technique was discussed in 1760 by the French choreographer Jean-Georges Noverre in his famous Letters on Dancing and Ballet.

Detail of a painting of the great ballerina Marie Camargo (1710–70), who danced for the Paris Opéra company.

Vivaldi

Antonio Vivaldi was the greatest master of Italian Baroque, and particularly violin music. Ordained a priest in 1703, Vivaldi spent much of his life in Venice. He taught violin at a music conservatory for orphaned girls, and in 1725 composed his most famous works, the violin concertos known as The Four Seasons. He wrote concertos for almost every instrument known at the time in Europe.

Portrait of Vivaldi, who helped standardize the 3-movement form of the concerto.

Mozart

Mozart showed amazing musical talent at a very young age, playing for the Austrian empress at the age of 6. Born in Salzburg, Mozart settled in Vienna as a composer, musician, and teacher. He wrote in almost every musical form, combining a beauty of sound with grace and technical perfection. Poverty and overwork led to his death at the age of 35, possibly from typhus.

The young Mozart performing with his father Leopold, who took him on a musical tour of Europe, and older sister Maria Anna.

Beethoven

Born in Bonn, Beethoven studied in Vienna with Haydn and settled there in 1792. At the age of 30 he started to go deaf, but this not stop him composing. His early masterpieces were influenced by Haydn and Mozart, and his revolutionary compositions crowned the Classical period and led into the following, Romantic era in music.

Left: Portrait of Beethoven, who is recognized as one of the world's greatest composers.

End of the Monarchy

Two months after the approval by the new National Assembly of the Declaration of the Rights of Man and of the Citizen, King Louis XVI and his family were taken forcibly from Versailles. They were made to live under guard in the Tuileries Palace in Paris. A new constitution established a limited monarchy, leaving the king with little authority. In 1791 Louis made a failed attempt to escape from the capital, and then formally accepted the constitution. Sixteen months later he was executed.

Marie Antoinette (1755–93), Louis XVI's wife, encouraged him to oppose revolutionary changes.

The French Revolution

Class conflict and a need for social reform in 18th-century France (see pages 126–127) led to rebellion by the people. The political upheavals that took place between 1789 and 1799 are known as the French Revolution. During this period the monarchy was overthrown and different forms of republican administration were successively introduced. After a brutal Reign of Terror, a Directory government led the republic for the rest of the period.

Storming of the Bastille

The Bastille fortress, where political prisoners were held, was seen by the people as a symbol of the monarchy. On July 14, 1789, a large crowd of Parisians stormed the prison, where they hoped to find weapons to fight the king's army. At the same time there were massive peasant uprisings against nobles and their country estates. The revolution was underway.

The revolutionary crowd overpowered soldiers guarding the Bastille and killed the prison governor. They released the prisoners, who numbered just seven.

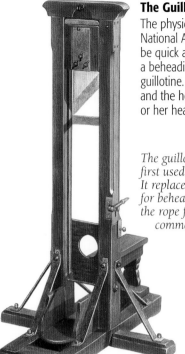

The Guillotine

The physician Joseph-Ignace Guillotin was elected to the National Assembly in 1789. Believing that executions should be quick and painless, he had a law passed that introduced a beheading machine. This came to be known as the guillotine. The victim was placed face down on the bench, and the heavy blade fell between the uprights to cut off his or her head.

The guillotine, which was first used in April, 1792. It replaced the axe used for beheading nobles and the rope for hanging common criminals.

Volunteers from Marseille marched to an army song that became known as the Marseillaise. It was adopted as the national anthem in 1795.

The Republic

The new National Assembly reorganized France's old provinces into 83 departments. They were run by elected councils, but the right to vote was limited to male citizens who paid more than a certain level of taxes. The Assembly seized church lands, which were sold to pay off some of the republic's huge debt, and closed monasteries. The newly elected Legislative Assembly made way for a National Convention that declared France a republic in September 1792.

MARCHE DES MARSEILLOIS

The Reign of Terror

In 1793 a radical political group called the Jacobins gained control of the National Convention. Led by Maximilien Robespierre, they put a Committee of Public Safety in charge of the republic. From June 1973 to July 1974 the Committee acted brutally against anyone who dared go against official policies of the republic. Thousands of suspects were arrested, and many were guillotined.

Portrait of Maximilien Robespierre (1758–94), who made many enemies and was himself executed by order of the Convention.

A Parisian fighter in the long trousers that caused republicans to be called sans-culottes ("without knee breeches").

Sans culotte Parisien.

THE FRENCH REVOLUTION

1789
June: the Estates General adopt the title National Assembly; August: approval of the Declaration of the Rights of Man.

1790
February: suppression of religious orders; June: abolition of noble titles.

1791
September: Louis XVI formally accepts the constitution; October: first meeting of the Legislative Assembly.

1792
September: new republic adopts the slogan "Liberty, Equality, Fraternity."

1793
January: Louis XVI is executed; June: Reign of Terror begins; October: Marie Antoinette executed.

1794
February: the tricolor (blue, white, and red) is adopted as the French flag; July: Robespierre is executed (ending the Reign of Terror).

1795
February: decree separates State from the Church; October: first meeting of the new Directory government (which rules until 1799).

Ink well in the shape of a revolutionary red woolen hat crushing a clergyman.

Revolutionary Wars

The French Revolutionary Wars, fought over a decade from 1792 until 1802, began in an effort to defend the revolution. The conflicts took place between France and several European states, growing into wars of French conquest under the leadership of Napoleon. They are usually divided into wars against a First and Second Coalition of allied countries, during which time France was continuously at war with Britain. Following the uneasy peace of the Treat of Amiens in 1802, the Napoleonic Wars went on for another 13 years.

Coalition Against France

In 1793 Britain, the United Provinces (Netherlands), Sardinia, and Spain joined Austria and Prussia in a First Coalition against France. By 1797 all France's opponents had agreed peace treaties, apart from Britain. In a Second Coalition (1798–1802) Britain was joined by the Ottoman Empire, Naples, Russia, Portugal, and Austria. After victories by Napoleon, Britain at last made peace with France in 1802.

An Austrian soldier in 1798.

Rise of Napoleon

In 1795 the French general, Napoleon Bonaparte, put down a rebellion against the revolutionary National Convention. The following year Napoleon was appointed to command the French army in Italy. In 1799 he overthrew the Directory government and assumed dictatorial power as First Consul. As the people's hero, Napoleon was elected Emperor of France in 1804.

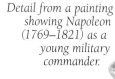

Detail from a painting showing Napoleon (1769–1821) as a young military commander.

This 30-soldi coin of the Cisalpine Republic is dated Year IX in the French Republican Calendar (September 1800–01).

New Republics

After winning great victories, the French revolutionary forces gained the Dutch Republic in 1795 and renamed it the Batavian Republic (see page 146). The following year, Napoleon took command of the poorly equipped French forces in northern Italy. After several victories over the Austrians, Napoleon formed the Cisalpine Republic, with Milan as its capital. French victories also created a new Roman Republic, Parthenopean Republic (Naples), and Helvetic Republic (Switzerland).

The Battle of the Nile

In 1798 Napoleon invaded Egypt in an attempt to destroy British trade with the Middle East and control of India. The French naval forces defeated the Egyptian Mamelukes near Cairo. But just 11 days later, the French fleet of 13 ships of the line and 4 frigates under Admiral Brueys was destroyed in Aboukir Bay by a British fleet commanded by Admiral Horatio Nelson. The victory left the French stranded in Egypt and gave Britain control of the Mediterranean.

FRENCH REPUBLIC AND DEPENDENCIES 1797

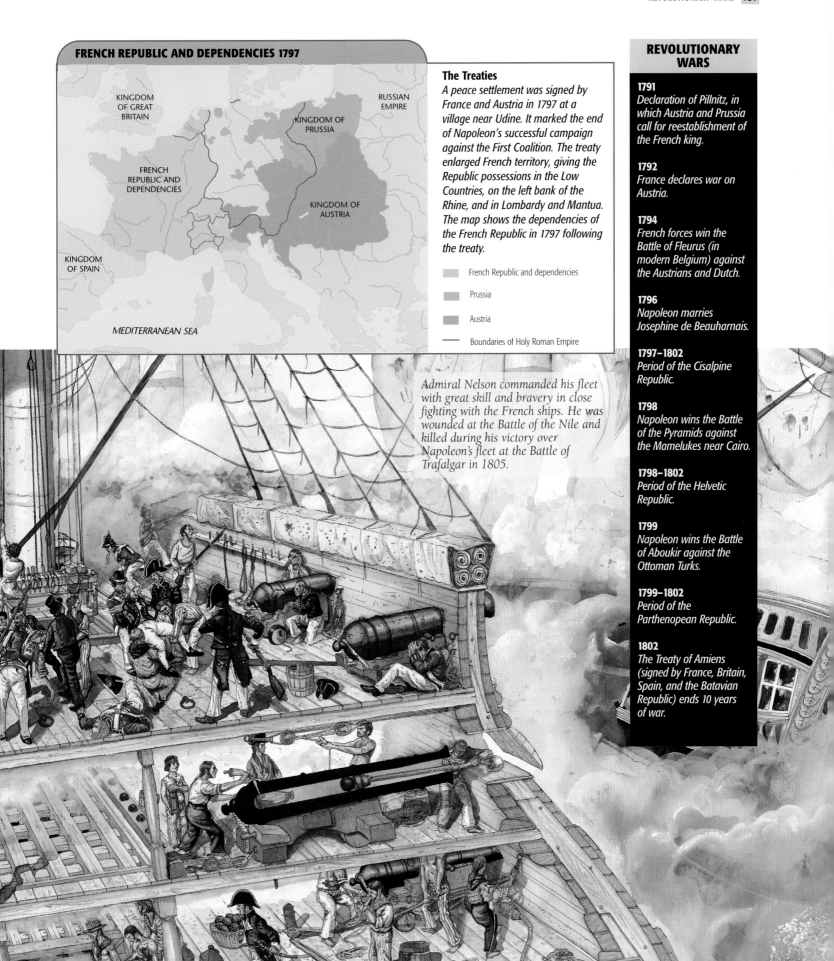

KINGDOM OF GREAT BRITAIN

RUSSIAN EMPIRE

KINGDOM OF PRUSSIA

FRENCH REPUBLIC AND DEPENDENCIES

KINGDOM OF AUSTRIA

KINGDOM OF SPAIN

MEDITERRANEAN SEA

French Republic and dependencies

Prussia

Austria

Boundaries of Holy Roman Empire

The Treaties
A peace settlement was signed by France and Austria in 1797 at a village near Udine. It marked the end of Napoleon's successful campaign against the First Coalition. The treaty enlarged French territory, giving the Republic possessions in the Low Countries, on the left bank of the Rhine, and in Lombardy and Mantua. The map shows the dependencies of the French Republic in 1797 following the treaty.

Admiral Nelson commanded his fleet with great skill and bravery in close fighting with the French ships. He was wounded at the Battle of the Nile and killed during his victory over Napoleon's fleet at the Battle of Trafalgar in 1805.

REVOLUTIONARY WARS

1791
Declaration of Pillnitz, in which Austria and Prussia call for reestablishment of the French king.

1792
France declares war on Austria.

1794
French forces win the Battle of Fleurus (in modern Belgium) against the Austrians and Dutch.

1796
Napoleon marries Josephine de Beauharnais.

1797–1802
Period of the Cisalpine Republic.

1798
Napoleon wins the Battle of the Pyramids against the Mamelukes near Cairo.

1798–1802
Period of the Helvetic Republic.

1799
Napoleon wins the Battle of Aboukir against the Ottoman Turks.

1799–1802
Period of the Parthenopean Republic.

1802
The Treaty of Amiens (signed by France, Britain, Spain, and the Batavian Republic) ends 10 years of war.

The 19th century in Europe was an age of nationalism, when the boundaries of many nations were redrawn after the Napoleonic Wars. Peoples with a shared culture and history tried to form independent states, sometimes with success. Revolution was still in the air in many parts of the continent, as constitutions were drawn up and reforming liberals tried to limit the power of the ruling classes and absolute monarchs. At the same time the Industrial Revolution became widespread, changing many people's way of life from farming to factory work. The Romantic movement responded to these political and social changes, encouraging people of all classes to take an interest in their cultural heritage.

This chapter tells the story of 19th-century Europe. It covers all the major empires and nations, kings and leaders, and wars and peace treaties. It also details developments in science, medicine, technology, art, and architecture, as well as showing how society changed in this dramatic period.

Louis Napoleon, nephew of Napoleon Bonaparte, ruled over the French Second Empire (see pages 168–169). After the European revolutions of 1848, this was a period when reform movements lost power.

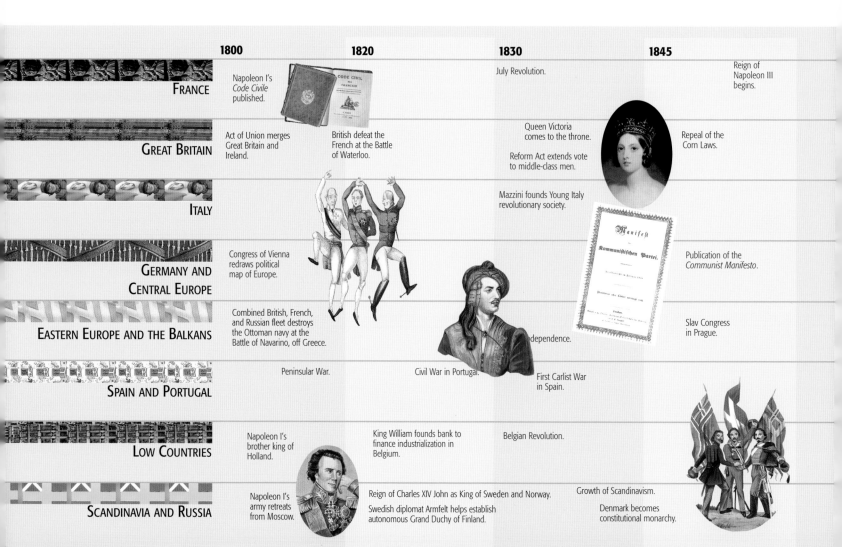

	1800	1820	1830	1845
FRANCE	Napoleon I's *Code Civile* published.		July Revolution.	Reign of Napoleon III begins.
GREAT BRITAIN	Act of Union merges Great Britain and Ireland.	British defeat the French at the Battle of Waterloo.	Queen Victoria comes to the throne. Reform Act extends vote to middle-class men.	Repeal of the Corn Laws.
ITALY			Mazzini founds Young Italy revolutionary society.	
GERMANY AND CENTRAL EUROPE	Congress of Vienna redraws political map of Europe.			Publication of the *Communist Manifesto*.
EASTERN EUROPE AND THE BALKANS	Combined British, French, and Russian fleet destroys the Ottoman navy at the Battle of Navarino, off Greece.		dependence.	Slav Congress in Prague.
SPAIN AND PORTUGAL	Peninsular War.		Civil War in Portugal. First Carlist War in Spain.	
LOW COUNTRIES	Napoleon I's brother king of Holland.	King William founds bank to finance industrialization in Belgium.	Belgian Revolution.	
SCANDINAVIA AND RUSSIA	Napoleon I's army retreats from Moscow.	Reign of Charles XIV John as King of Sweden and Norway. Swedish diplomat Armfelt helps establish autonomous Grand Duchy of Finland.	Growth of Scandinavism. Denmark becomes constitutional monarchy.	

Nationalism and the Romantic Movement

Detail of Liberty Leading the People by Eugène Delacroix (1798–1863), a leading French artist in the Romantic style. The painting commemorates the July Revolution of 1830 (see page 164).

(see page 164)

1860	1870	1880	1890	1900

Treaty of Frankfurt gives Alsace and half of Lorraine to Germany.

Lumière brothers invent cinema.

Reform Bill doubles size of electorate.

Third Reform Bill triples size of electorate.

Unification of Italy proclaimed.

Rome becomes capital city of united Italy.

Long reign of Umberto I, King of Italy.

Dual Monarchy begins in Austria-Hungary.

Franco-Prussian War.

Austria-Hungary joins Italy and Germany in secret Triple Alliance.

Karl Benz invents first automobile.

Herzl publishes Jewish State pamphlet in Vienna.

Suez Canal opens.

First Spanish Republic.

Maria Cristina of Habsburg-Lorena acts as regent for her son Alfonso XIII.

Luxembourg gains independence.

Brussels Exhibition.

Vincent van Gogh paints Postimpressionist paintings in the south of France.

Reformist Tzar Alexander II assassinated.

Leo Tolstoy publishes *War and Peace*.

Nicholas II, last czar of Russia, comes to power.

Nationalism and Romanticism

Nationalism and Romanticism were important movements that helped shape political events in 19th-century Europe. Nationalists felt that their people belonged together as a nation, because they shared culture and history, spoke the same language, and had the same customs and traditions. They wanted to form independent states. Romantics shared many of the same values, since they believed passionately in human feelings and culture. Language was also important to both movements and helped bring many of their followers together in a common cause.

Left: Another medieval German poem inspired Wagner's opera Tristan and Isolde.

Romantic Nationalism

The Romantic movement inspired people's interest in their cultural heritage. This included folklore, myths, and legends. The ideals of Romanticism combined with nationalist feelings to encourage use of local languages and study of literary works that became known as national epics (such as the Finnish *Kalevala*, see opposite). This Romantic nationalism rose from working people, artists, and intellectuals, unlike the loyalty demanded by elite ruling dynasties.

Composer Richard Wagner (1813–83), who was born in Saxony, used themes of German medieval poetry and mythology for his operas. They include his famous four-part series The Ring of the Nibelung *(1869–76).*

Below: Sheet music for Himnusz, *the Hungarian national anthem. Created by poet Ferenc Kölcsey (1790–1838) and composer Ferenc Erkel (1810–93), it was adopted in 1844, when Hungary was still ruled by the Habsburgs.*

National Identity

A sense of national identity was crucial to people struggling for independence. In the 19th century practical expressions of identity, such as national flags and anthems, grew in importance. Revolutionary movements favored patriotic songs and texts, which stirred the loyal feelings of their followers. By the end of the century, many nation states were following this practice.

Towards Liberty and Unity

In 19th century Europe, the greatest moves toward unity were made by the groups of German and Italian states. Both achieved their aim of national unification. Other regions had a sense of nationhood, but did not achieve independence and become separate nation-states. Hungary and Poland, for example, did not become fully independent until 1918.

This Polish nationalist carries a flag with the eagle that had represented Poland since the 13th century. Poles fought for independence from their Russian rulers throughout the century.

PEOPLES AND LANGUAGES OF EUROPE

The map shows the changes in national boundaries over the 19th century. Though frontiers moved, different peoples and their languages remained very much the same. However, national languages became more important around the 1830s and started to be used in newspapers and books, as well as for official purposes. Within the Austrian Empire, these changes applied to Croatian, Czech, and Hungarian, for example. In the German states, some books were published in Latin and French at the start of the century, but almost all were in German by the time of unification.

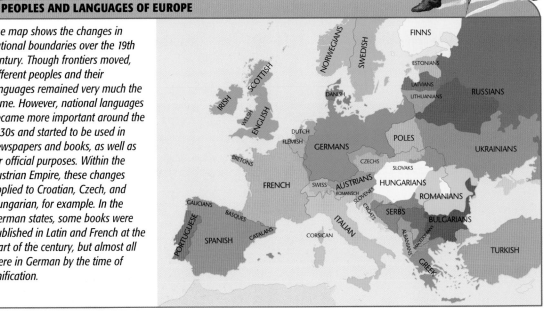

Rise of Finnish Culture

After the Russian conquest had ousted Sweden in 1809, Finland was made a grand duchy ruled by the Russian tsar. There was a strong movement toward self-government among the Finns. It was furthered by the Finnish-language, or Fennoman, movement. In 1835, scholar Elias Lönnrot (1802–84) published his version of the *Kalevala*, the national epic of the Finnish people. But Swedish was still the grand duchy's official language. By 1883, Finnish could be used in official business, but the Finns did not achieve independence from Russia until after the First World War.

The Defense of the Sampo was painted in 1896 by Finnish artist Akseli Gallen-Kallela (1865–1931). The Sampo is a magical artifact in the Kalevala epic. Bringing good fortune, it has been seen as a tree, pillar, compass, or treasure chest.

Napoleon Becomes Emperor

In 1804, Napoleon decided to consolidate his position as First Consul by creating a hereditary empire. The idea was to increase his power and lessen any threat of assassination, since there would be an heir to the imperial throne. Napoleon declared himself emperor in May and was crowned seven months later. At the lavish ceremony, he took the crown from Pope Pius VII and put it on his own head.

Napoleon's Europe

The French military and political leader Napoleon Bonaparte (1769–1821) became Emperor Napoleon I in 1804. The Corsican-born general made such an enormous impact on the history of Europe that the first 15 years of the 19th century are commonly known as the Napoleonic Era. During this time he was the French people's hero, as their empire grew in importance. At the end of the era, however, Napoleon was exiled and France became a monarchy once again.

In 1804 Napoleon combined all the French civil laws into one code. It soon became known as the Code Napoléon.

This detail of a painting by Jacques-Louis David shows the coronation ceremony in the Cathedral of Notre Dame in Paris on 2 December 1804. Empress Joséphine kneels before her husband.

Legal Reforms

Napoleon's new Civil Code was drawn up by legal experts over a period of four years. The *Code Napoléon* included ideas of the French Revolution, giving more individual liberty to the people, as well as freedom of work and conscience. But it protected property ownership and inheritance, and granted only limited rights to women. Napoleon applied the Code to all his territories, and it was influential throughout continental Europe.

NAPOLEONIC EUROPE

NORTH SEA

SWEDEN

BALTIC SEA

Moscow •

• Borodino, 1812

GREAT BRITAIN
LONDON

PRUSSIA

Beresina, 1812

Friedland, 1807
Eylau, 1807

RUSSIAN EMPIRE

Waterloo, 1815

Leipzig, 1813

ATLANTIC OCEAN

• Paris

Jena, 1806

AUSTRIA

FRANCE

Ulm, 1805

Austerlitz, 1800

• Vienna

BLACK SEA

Marengo, 1800

ITALY

OTTOMAN EMPIRE

SPAIN

CORSICA

Ajaccio

• Rome

ELBA

MEDITERRANEAN SEA

Trafalgar, 1805

☐ French Empire (1812) ☐ States ruled by Napoleon's family (1812) ☐ Other dependent states (1812)
• Battle

The Napoleonic Wars lasted from 1794 to 1815. At the height of his power in 1812, Napoleon had succeeded in gaining control of most of Europe. The map shows French territory ruled directly from Paris, states dependent on France, from Spain in the west to Warsaw in the east, and French allies, including Austria, Denmark-Norway, and Prussia.

The eagle standard of the French 105th Infantry Regiment was lost to the enemy at the Battle of Waterloo.

The Congress of Vienna

After Napoleon abdicated in 1814, the Congress of Vienna re-drew the political map of Europe. Attended by five monarchs and the heads of 216 princely families, the congress went on from September 1814 to June 1815. The restored French king Louis XVIII sent Talleyrand, a former supporter of Napoleon, who represented France with great skill. In general, Austria, Britain, and France opposed Prussia and Russia at the congress.

A contemporary cartoon shows delighted allied monarchs dancing together at the Congress of Vienna.

Escape and Final Defeat

While Napoleon's victors were planning the future of Europe in Vienna, Napoleon left exile and sailed for France. He made a triumphant return to Paris and began a second reign as emperor. This time, his rule lasted just a hundred days. His army was crushed at Waterloo, and the emperor was forced to abdicate again. Exiled to the British island of St. Helena, in the South Atlantic, Napoleon died in 1821.

In this cartoon, little Johnny Bull (symbol of England) dares oppose the great Napoleon as he tries to take over the world.

Left: The Vendôme Column, in Paris, is decorated with bronze reliefs showing the victory at (1805). It is topped by a statue of Napoleon.

1805–1815

1805
Austria, Russia, and Sweden join Britain to form the Third Coalition against France; October: French defeat by the British at the Battle of Trafalgar; December: victory over Austria and Russia at Austerlitz.

1806
Napoleon replaces the Holy Roman Empire with the Confederation of the Rhine.

1807
French victory over Russia at Friedland.

1808
Charles IV of Spain is forced to abdicate in favor of Napoleon's brother Joseph.

1808–14
The Peninsular War, by the end of which French forces are driven from the Iberian peninsula.

1809
Napoleon defeats the Austrians at Wagram.

1810
Napoleon divorces Joséphine de Beauharnais and two months later marries Marie Louise of Austria (by whom he has a son, Napoleon II).

1812
Napoleon's army retreats from Moscow.

1814
France's allied opponents take Paris, Napoleon abdicates and is exiled to the island of Elba; Louis XVIII, the "Restoration King," comes to the French throne.

1815
Napoleon's army is defeated by the Duke of Wellington's British forces at the Battle of Waterloo.

This caricature of Louis XVIII shows him losing control of a shaky French crown.

The Restoration King

It suited the allied powers that had defeated Napoleon to restore the French monarchy. Louis XVIII (1755–1824), the younger brother of Louis XVI who had been in exile since 1791, returned the Bourbon Dynasty to the throne. He followed a middle course between liberal and reactionary factions, and between former revolutionaries and the social elite, introducing moderate policies and a constitutional charter.

MONARCHY TO REPUBLIC

1814–24
Reign of Louis XVIII as King of France (interrupted by Napoleon's Hundred Days in 1815).

1820
Assassination of Louis XVIII's nephew, the Duc de Berry, leads to more repressive controls by the king.

1824–30
Reign of Charles X as King of France.

1830
July 27–29: three days of fighting between workers and royalist troops during the July Revolution.

1830–48
Reign of Louis-Philippe as King of France, a period known as the July Monarchy, ended by the February Revolution.

1847
French troops invade northern Algeria and consolidate lands originally taken in 1830.

1848–52
The Second Republic.

1851
Louis Napoleon declares himself president for a further ten years (and emperor the following year).

Bourbon Rule to the Second Republic

Napoleon's downfall as emperor led to the restoration of the Bourbon Dynasty of monarchs, which had ruled France from 1589 to 1792. During the first half of the 19th century (1814–48), three kings ruled France with varying degrees of authority. Their rule provoked and was interrupted by further revolutions, despite constitutional changes and some liberal moves. The third king, Louis-Philippe, was finally replaced by a president in the person of Napoleon's nephew.

Head of Charles X on a 20-franc coin of 1828.

Charles X

On Louis's death, the French crown passed to his brother Charles (1757–1836). The new King Charles X aimed to restore more power to the throne, as well as increase the authority of the aristocracy and the clergy. Not surprisingly, the king's conservative measures were increasingly opposed by French liberals, who saw the policies as a return to pre-revolutionary days.

July Revolution of 1830

In July 1830 Charles X dissolved a newly elected Chamber of Deputies before it had even met, reduced the number of people eligible to vote, and introduced censorship of the press. The new measures led to protests, demonstrations, and three days of fighting during what became known as the July Revolution. Charles was forced to flee and then abdicate.

Fighting at the Porte St. Denis, in Paris, during the July Revolution.

Louis-Philippe was caricatured as a pear, probably because the French word poire *(pear) can mean a fool who is easily deceived.*

The "Citizen King"

Following the July Revolution, the son of the Duke of Orléans (a junior branch of the Bourbon Dynasty) was proclaimed King of the French (rather than King of France). Known as the "Citizen King," Louis-Philippe (1773–1850) tried to stay in the middle between right-wing Legitimists, who supported the senior Bourbon line, and left-wing republicans, socialists, and Bonapartists. He strengthened France's position in Europe, but was forced to abdicate in 1848.

Symbolizing the end of the French monarchy, Louis-Philippe's throne is burned on a bonfire.

This was the scene at the Paris Hôtel de Ville (Town Hall) on 28 July 1830. The Revolutionary tricolor flag, which had been replaced by the Bourbon white flag, was restored and adopted by Louis-Philippe.

The Second Republic

A republic was proclaimed following Louis-Philippe's abdication, with a provisional government. All French men (but not women) were given the right to vote, and in December 1848 they elected Louis-Napoleon Bonaparte, who had just returned from British exile, as their president. The new leader was given a four-year term of office, by the end of which time he had declared himself emperor.

Louis Napoleon (1808–73), nephew of Napoleon I, became Emperor Napoleon III in 1852.

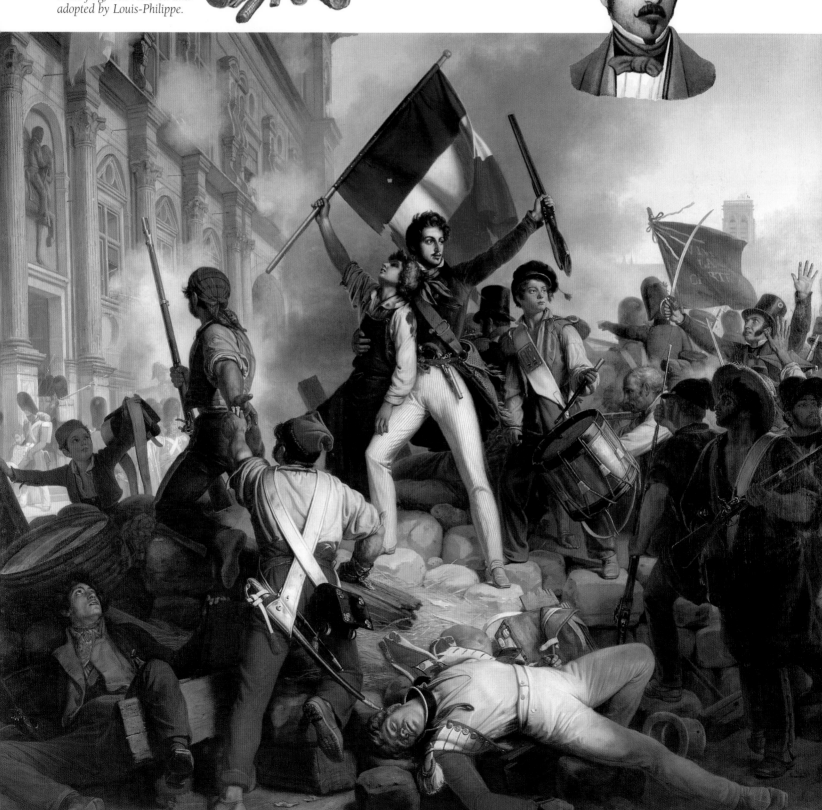

KEY EVENTS

January
Demonstrations in Milan against Austrian rule. Revolution in Sicily and Naples against Bourbon King Ferdinand I.

February
Demonstrations in Paris; Louis-Philippe abdicates.

March
Rebellion in Venice leads to Venetian Republic. Piedmont fights Austria (and is defeated in July). Riots in Vienna (Austria) and Berlin (Prussia). Hungarian parliament abolishes serfdom.

April
Constituent Assembly is elected in France.

May
New parliament meets in the free imperial city of Frankfurt.

June
Slav Congress opens in Prague (Bohemia, Austrian Empire).

August
Emperor Ferdinand returns to Vienna.

October
Vienna is recaptured by the Austrian imperial army.

December
Louis Napoleon is elected President of France. New Prussian constitution. Austrian emperor Ferdinand abdicates in favor of Franz Josef.

Pope Pius IX fled Rome in November 1848, but with French help was able to return in 1850.

The Year 1848

In Europe, 1848 became known as the "year of revolution." Throughout most of the continent there were protests, revolts, and riots against traditional monarchies and existing political systems. People wanted social and economic improvements, more democracy, and national freedom. The uprisings were strongest in the Austrian Empire, France, and the German and Italian states. Some led to more liberal parliamentary government, but many hard-fought revolutionary successes were short-lived.

Lajos Kossuth (1802–94) led the Hungarian rebellion but was forced to flee to Turkey in 1849.

The title page of the original German Manifesto includes the words, "Proletarians of all countries, unite."

Austrian Empire

Riots in Vienna were enough to make Austrian foreign minister Klemens von Metternich resign and flee to England. Even the Habsburg Emperor Ferdinand I left his court and fled to Innsbruck, but the revolutions were soon put down. Stronger demands were made in Bohemia and Hungary. A revolutionary Hungarian government was formed, but the country soon came under Habsburg rule again.

Italian States

People of the Italian regions rose up against the three main ruling powers—Austria in the north, the Papal States in the center, and the Kingdom of Two Sicilies in the south. Constitutions were granted in many regions, Venice declared itself a republic, and Piedmont fought the Austrians. The independent gains were short-lived, however, as the Austrians overcame the revolutionaries and re-established control the following year.

German Confederation

In Berlin, the capital of Prussia, a popular uprising caused King Frederick William IV to promise a constitution. There were similar rebellions in Cologne (in Prussia), Frankfurt (a free imperial city), and Munich (capital of Bavaria), where many people wanted to turn the Confederation of German states into a closer union. By the end of the year disagreements were destroying unity among the rebels, and in 1849 the Confederation was re-established.

Communist Manifesto

The *Manifesto of the Communist Party*, written for the Communist League by the German radicals Karl Marx and Friedrich Engels, was published in February 1848. It called for a proletarian revolution to overthrow capitalism and the ruling class and bring about a workers' society by abolishing private property. The pamphlet had an immediate effect and became a famous political statement throughout Europe.

EUROPE IN 1848

Revolutionary Movements

The events of 1848 are often called the "Springtime of the Peoples." This political map of Europe shows how the centers of unrest spread right across the continent. They stretched from Paris in western Europe to Bucharest in the east, and from Berlin in the north to Palermo in the south. In addition, there were Chartist protests in Britain, republican uprisings in Ireland, and peaceful reforms in the Low Countries and Denmark.

KINGDOM OF SWEDEN

HOLLAND KINGDOM OF DENMARK

RUSSIAN EMPIRE

GREAT BRITAIN AND IRELAND

KINGDOM OF PRUSSIA

KINGDOM OF BELGIUM

GERMAN CONFEDERATION

AUSTRIAN EMPIRE

FRANCE

SWITZERLAND

KINGDOM OF PORTUGAL

KINGDOM OF SPAIN

KINGDOM OF SARDINIA

PAPAL STATES

KINGDOM OF THE TWO SICILIES

OTTOMAN EMPIRE

KINGDOM OF GREECE

In Berlin workers and students manned barricades. The Prussian king ordered these to be cleared, which led to violent clashes between protesters and royal troops.

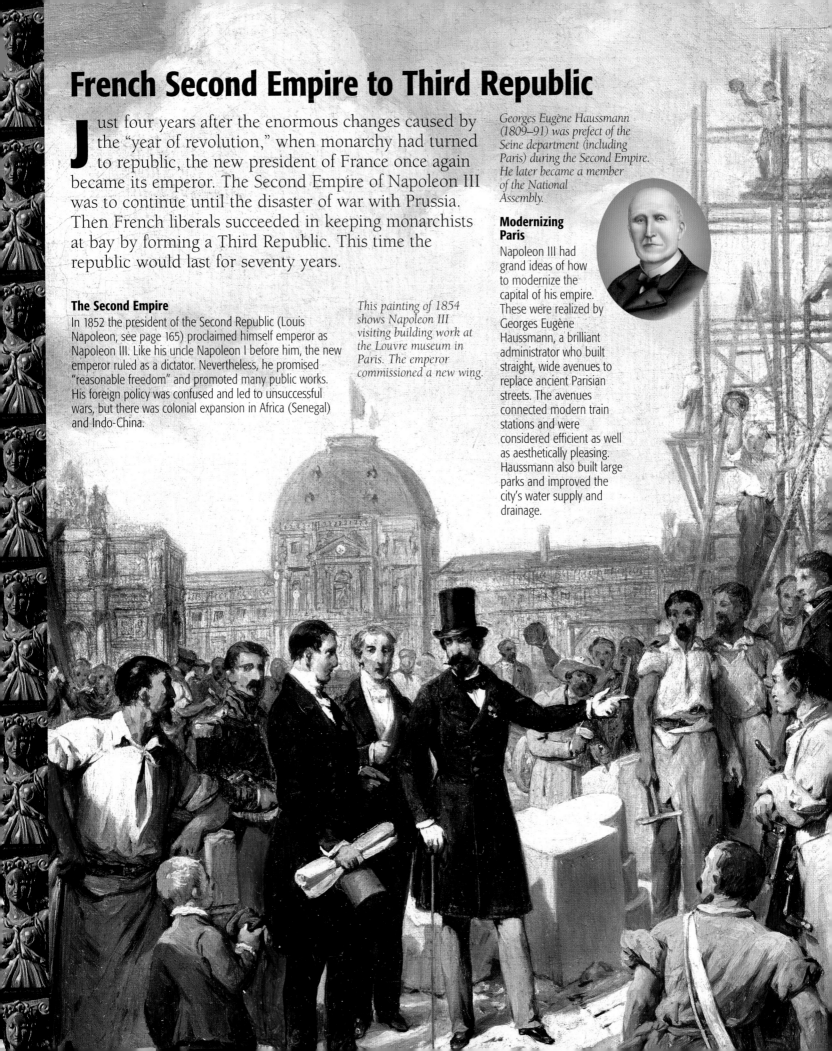

French Second Empire to Third Republic

Just four years after the enormous changes caused by the "year of revolution," when monarchy had turned to republic, the new president of France once again became its emperor. The Second Empire of Napoleon III was to continue until the disaster of war with Prussia. Then French liberals succeeded in keeping monarchists at bay by forming a Third Republic. This time the republic would last for seventy years.

The Second Empire

In 1852 the president of the Second Republic (Louis Napoleon, see page 165) proclaimed himself emperor as Napoleon III. Like his uncle Napoleon I before him, the new emperor ruled as a dictator. Nevertheless, he promised "reasonable freedom" and promoted many public works. His foreign policy was confused and led to unsuccessful wars, but there was colonial expansion in Africa (Senegal) and Indo-China.

This painting of 1854 shows Napoleon III visiting building work at the Louvre museum in Paris. The emperor commissioned a new wing.

Georges Eugène Haussmann (1809–91) was prefect of the Seine department (including Paris) during the Second Empire. He later became a member of the National Assembly.

Modernizing Paris

Napoleon III had grand ideas of how to modernize the capital of his empire. These were realized by Georges Eugène Haussmann, a brilliant administrator who built straight, wide avenues to replace ancient Parisian streets. The avenues connected modern train stations and were considered efficient as well as aesthetically pleasing. Haussmann also built large parks and improved the city's water supply and drainage.

This French coin was countermarked by the Prussians to remind the French of their defeat at Sedan.

Franco-Prussian War

In 1870 French troops entered into a disastrous war with Prussia, led by prime minister Otto von Bismarck and supported by the other German states. The Prussians were much better prepared for war and there were crushing defeats for France at Sedan and Metz. When the news reached Paris, the emperor was deposed and Parisians prepared to defend the capital.

Cartoon showing the revolutionary artist Gustave Courbet (1819–77) pushing down the Vendôme Column (see page 163), a symbol of imperial rule.

Paris Commune

In March 1871 the new Versailles-based government, which was conservative and supported a return to monarchy, tried to disarm the National Guard in republican Paris. This led to an uprising and the formation of a Parisian revolutionary council, or Commune. Two months later, government troops entered an undefended part of the city, broke down barricades, and ended the Commune with huge loss of life.

Third Republic

Despite the efforts of royalist sympathizers, the new regime that had replaced Napoleon III established itself as the Third Republic. A new constitution included a seven-year term for the president of the republic, elected by the two houses of the Senate and Chamber of Deputies. Despite difficulties, the Third Republic survived to the end of the century (and continued until 1940). Railroads and public education were expanded during the 1880s, followed by industry in the following decade.

The Dreyfus Affair

Alfred Dreyfus (1859–1935) was a Jewish French army officer. In 1894 he was charged with spying for Germany, court-martialled, and transported to French Guiana. However, many people thought Dreyfus was innocent and he became a symbol of republican liberties to many socialists and liberals. They were opposed by monarchists and militarists. The case was tried again in 1899, when Dreyfus was found guilty but pardoned. A civilian court finally declared him innocent in 1906.

On this poster, the "defenders of law, justice and truth" declare Dreyfus innocent, praise France, the republic and the army, but denounce the "traitors."

A cast-iron Wallace fountain in Paris. More than 70 such fountains were donated to the city in the 1870s by the English art collector Sir Richard Wallace.

Below: Brighton Pavilion is a classic example of extravagant Romantic architecture. Designed by John Nash, it looks Indian from the outside, a tribute to Britain's huge 19th century Empire.

Great Britain

Compared to its European neighbors, Great Britain enjoyed a time of relative peace and prosperity during the 19th century. Industry continued to flourish at home, the British navy ruled the seas, and the overseas Empire expanded in Africa, Asia, India, and the Pacific. The population increased dramatically, from about 8 million people in 1800 to almost 40 million in 1900.

Parliamentary Reforms

Wide-ranging reforms were passed during the 19th century, extending the right to vote to working men, removing corrupt electoral practises, and repealing acts of parliament that made everyday foodstuffs more expensive. The Reform Act of 1832 extended the vote to many men of the middle classes. The Reform Bill of 1867 made much more sweeping changes. It almost doubled the number of people who could vote, extending the right to many working men in the towns and cities. The Third Reform Bill of 1885 tripled the size of the electorate and gave the right to vote to many agricultural workers. The hated Corn Laws, which kept the price of grain artificially high, were finally repealed in 1846.

Left: The Clock Tower at the northern end of the Houses of Parliament in London houses a 13-ton bell popularly known as Big Ben. The tower was built in the mid-19th century.

Entertainment

Theater, music, opera, and the arts were enjoyed by the wealthier classes. Publishing flourished and a newly literate public eagerly read novels, many of which were published in weekly installments. Gambling at cards became wildly popular, as did hypnotism and ghost conjuring (calling up the dead).

Above: Frankenstein; Mary Shelley wrote her famous novel in 1818.

Ireland

In 1801, by a new Act of Union, Ireland was officially merged with Great Britain to form the United Kingdom of Great Britain and Ireland. But the Irish were never given the right to vote and sit in parliament. Demand for independence, or Home Rule, grew during the 19th century and there were many rebellions and uprisings.

Potatoes were a staple food crop for Irish peasants. In 1848–49 a blight struck and there was a great famine. Many people starved to death while others—as shown here (right)— gathered their meager possessions and emigrated. The population of Ireland dropped from more than 8 million at the start of the famine to about 4.4 million in 1911.

*Right:
A portrait of
Queen Victoria
in 1843. She
reigned for almost
64 years, from
June 1837 until
January 1901.*

The Victorian Era

The Victorian era is sometimes known as the *Pax Britannica* (Latin for "British Peace"), although this is not strictly true as Britain was at war somewhere on the planet in every year of Victoria's reign. The peace was also often disrupted at home as factory workers demanded better conditions and pay while others sought the right to vote. Trade unions grew stronger and in 1859 a strike among workers in the building trade led to the introduction of a nine-hour working day. Trade flourished and London became the financial capital of the world.

GREAT BRITAIN

1801
Act of Union merges the Kingdom of Great Britain and the Kingdom of Ireland.

1807
Great Britain outlaws the slave trade.

1832
Reform Act extends vote to middle class males.

1837
Victoria is crowned Queen.

1840
Queen Victoria and Prince Albert marry.

1845–49
Irish potato famine.

1846
Repeal of Corn Laws.

1851
Great Exhibition, the first World's Fair, opens in London.

1861
Death of Prince Albert (Queen Victoria's husband).

1867
Reform Bill doubles the electorate.

1881
Jack the Ripper murders prostitutes in London.

1885
Third Reform Bill triples the size of the electorate.

FORMING A KINGDOM

1831
The Carbonari secret society causes revolts in Bologna, Modena, and Parma; Giuseppe Mazzini founds the Young Italy revolutionary society.

1836–48
Giuseppe Garibaldi is exiled to South America.

1848
Uprisings form the First War of Italian Independence.

1852
Count Cavour becomes prime minister of Piedmont.

1859
Piedmont leads the drive toward Italian unification; the Second War of Independence.

1861–78
Reign of Victor Emmanuel II (1820–78) as first King of Italy.

1866
Third War of Independence coincides with the Austro-Prussian War.

1871
Rome becomes the capital of united Italy.

1873
Giuseppe Verdi composes his Requiem in honor of the great Milanese poet and novelist Alessandro Manzoni (1785–1873).

1878–1900
Reign of Umberto I, son of Victor Emmanuel II, as King of Italy.

UNIFICATION OF ITALY 1859–70

Kingdom of Sardinia in 1815 — Lost to France, 1860

Territories annexed by:
1859 — Nov. 1860 — 1866
March 1860 — Nov. 1860 — 1870

Unification, 1859–70
After Lombardy was gained by Piedmont in 1859, all the northern states, except Venetia, were joined to Piedmont-Sardinia to form a kingdom of northern Italy. The following year, the Kingdom of the Two Sicilies (Sicily and Naples) fell to the forces of Garibaldi (see opposite). The unified kingdom of Italy was proclaimed in 1861, with Victor Emmanuel II at its head.

Rise of Piedmont

The region of Piedmont, in northwestern Italy, was part of the Kingdom of Piedmont-Sardinia ruled by the house of Savoy. During the 1850s Prime Minister Cavour gained France as an ally and provoked war against the Austrians, who ruled neighboring Lombardy. Victory brought Piedmont territory and a position as the most powerful Italian state. Many nationalists decided that the best hope for Italian unification lay with Piedmont.

The Unification of Italy

During the first half of the 19th century, the Italian movement toward unification and independence became more powerful. The Risorgimento (Italian for "revival") came about largely through the diplomatic and military efforts of the northern state of Piedmont. By 1861 the Piedmontese had united most of Italy under the rule of their own king. During the next decade the new kingdom succeeded in completing unification of the peninsula under a constitutional monarchy.

The Piedmontese statesman Count Camillo di Cavour (1810–61) was born in Turin when it belonged to France. By the time of his death, it was an Italian city.

The Genoese republican revolutionary Giuseppe Mazzini (1805–72) championed Italian unity.

Above: 2nd September 1870: Italian troops take possession of Rome, the last phase in the Unification of Italy.

Right: 2nd October 1870: At a plebiscite, Romans voted overwhelmingly to join the Kingdom of Italy.

Rome and Venice

In 1866, Victor Emmanuel supported Prussia in a war against Austria. When this was successful, Italy gained the state of Venetia, including the city of Venice. Four years later, the Franco-Prussian War took French troops away from their protection of the pope and Rome. This gave the Italians their chance, and Rome was gained, while the pope withdrew to the Vatican palace. United Italy was complete.

Garibaldi's Expedition

In 1860 the revolutionary soldier Giuseppe Garibaldi (1807–82) set out with a thousand men on a campaign that came to be known as the Expedition of the Thousand. The army of red-shirted volunteers sailed from Genoa to Sicily, where support from local rebels against Bourbon rule helped Garibaldi seize control of the island. He then crossed to the mainland, where victories secured more territory, including Naples.

When he met Victor Emmanuel (on the left) in October 1860, Giuseppe Garibaldi was able to hand over the whole of southern Italy to the king.

Viva Verdi!

The composer Giuseppe Verdi was a strong supporter of Italian independence. Those who agreed with him realized that the letters of his surname also stood for "Vittorio Emanuele Re d'Italia" ("Victor Emmanuel, King of Italy"), so they would write "Viva Verdi!" ("Long live Verdi") on walls. The authorities thought they were supporting the composer rather than the king. In 1860 Count Cavour persuaded Verdi to stand for the Italian chamber of deputies.

Giuseppe Verdi (1813–1901) was born a French citizen in the duchy of Parma. He composed 27 operas.

The magnificent Milanese theater La Scala, during a performance.

The Austro-Hungarian Empire

Nineteen years after the revolutionary events of 1848 (see page 166), the Austrian Empire gave status to Hungary and transformed itself into a Dual Monarchy. The Austro-Hungarian Empire of 1867 was made up of many nationalities and language groups in the territories that had been acquired by the Habsburgs over the centuries. German-speaking Austrians and Hungarian Magyars dominated others in their respective parts of the empire. Despite internal problems, the Dual Monarchy was to continue into the 20th century.

1848–96

1848–1916
Reign of Franz Josef as Emperor of Austria.

1867
Fundamental Laws grant all people of the Dual Monarchy equality before the law.

1867–1916
Reign of Franz Josef as King of Hungary.

1873
Austria-Hungary joins the Three Emperors' League with Germany and Russia.

1878
The Congress of Berlin gives control of Bosnia-Herzegovina and the Serb region of Novi Pazar to Austria-Hungary.

1882
Austria-Hungary joins Germany and Italy in a secret Triple Alliance.

1883
Austria-Hungary makes a secret treaty with Romania.

1892
The Krone replaces the Gulden as the official Austro-Hungarian currency.

1896
Theodor Herzl's pamphlet The Jewish State is published in Vienna, discussing a "political world question."

Dual Monarchy

In 1867 Austrian emperor Franz Josef made a compromise with rebellious Hungary. He gave Hungary equal status with Austria by agreeing to the creation of the Dual Monarchy of Austria-Hungary. This constitutional arrangement allowed him to remain as Habsburg emperor of Austria and become king of Hungary, which in theory was allowed to run its own internal affairs. Foreign and financial policy remained with the imperial government.

Left: Habsburg emperor Franz (or Francis) Joseph (1830–1916) was the grandson of Holy Roman Emperor Francis I.

Above: Johann Strauss the Younger (1825–99) lived in Vienna. His most famous waltz is The Blue Danube. Right: The Court Ball in Vienna.

HABSBURG TERRITORIES, 1878

Nationalities in Austria-Hungary

The territory of the empire was occupied by many different ethnic groups. Languages officially recognized by the empire were Croatian, Czech, German, Hungarian, Italian, Lithuanian, Polish, Romanian, Ruthenian, Serbian, Slovak, Slovene, Turkish, and Ukrainian. There was no common citizenship of the state, but the constitution officially allowed for equality between nationalities. Each ethnic group had the right to preserve its own nationality and use its own language in schools and public administration.

Right: The Széchenyi Chain Bridge was opened in 1849. It was the first bridge to span the Danube River between the separate towns of Buda and Pest. They combined to form the city of Budapest in 1873, taking over from Pest as the capital of the Kingdom of Hungary.

Composers and Poets

In both parts of Austria-Hungary, talented artists helped create a sense of national identity. In Austria Johann Strauss II, who became known as the "Waltz King," had sided with the revolutionaries of 1848. Later, however, the famous composer directed the imperial court's balls and dedicated patriotic marches to the emperor. In Hungary, many writers used their works to discuss and promote the idea of national freedom.

Revolutionary Hungarian poet Sandor Petofi (1823–49) was of Serb and Slovak descent. He wrote an anthem for the 1848 rebellion called "Rise, Hungarian," but disappeared a year later.

Theodor Herzl (1860–1904) is here flanked by fellow Zionists, Hungarian Max Nordau, and Russian Max Mandelstamm. Herzl became the first president of the World Zionist Organization in 1897.

Jewish Movement

Some nationalists in the Austrian Empire were hostile to non-German groups, especially the Jews. Anti-Semitism led some thinkers to consider the possibility of a Jewish state. Theodor Herzl was born in Pest and moved as a young man to Vienna, where he studied law. There he founded a political form of Zionism, a movement dedicated to developing a Jewish nation in Palestine.

The Unification of Germany

The German Confederation of 39 states was formed in 1815. By 1864, Prussia had become the most powerful state by far. It proved this by winning three wars in the next seven years, with victories over Denmark, Austria (the previous Habsburg powerhouse), and France (gaining Alsace and Lorraine). The Prussian king and chancellor then united with all the other states to form the German Empire. Prussia occupied more than three-fifths of the empire and made up about three-fifths of its population.

Intellectual Influence

In 19th-century Germany, the Romantic movement in literature and other artistic fields had great influence on intellectual life. Romanticism created fervent feelings of nationalism by drawing attention to cultural origins through the collection of folklore, ballads, and poetry. Poets such as Heinrich Heine were critical of the political establishment, and from the middle of the century, German writers and philosophers focused even more on national culture and the political situation.

Bismarck

Otto von Bismarck was a conservative, patriotic Prussian from the noble, land-owning class. He studied law before going into the army and then politics. As chancellor, his main aim was to establish Prussia as the leading power among the German states. When this was achieved, the "Iron Chancellor" achieved even more status as the head of government of the new German Empire.

Heinrich Heine (1797–1856) belonged to a group of politically radical writers called the "Young Germans." He moved to Paris in 1831.

Otto von Bismarck (1815–98) remained chancellor of the German Empire until 1890.

Above: The castle dominates the skyline of Heidelberg, a center of German Romanticism. The city's famous university was founded in 1386.

This gilded bronze statue of Victoria, goddess of victory, was put up in Berlin in 1873 to commemorate Prussian military success.

The Expansion of Prussia
After the failed revolutions and collapse of the Frankfurt Parliament in 1848, liberal nationalists in the German states gave more support to Prussia. Victory over Austria in the Seven Weeks' War gave the Prussians more power, and the following year a North German Confederation replaced the previous German Confederation. The new group was totally controlled by the Prussians, who had the military power and political confidence to press on toward an even larger Prussian-led empire.

GERMANY 1848–71

NORTH SEA
DENMARK
BALTIC SEA
SCHLESWIG
HOLSTEIN
OLDENBURG
MECKLENBURG
POMERANIA
WEST PRUSSIA
EAST PRUSSIA
NETHERLANDS
WESTPHALIA
BRUNSWICK
ANHALT
BRANDENBURG
POSEN
RUSSIA
RHEINISCH PRUSSIA
NASSAU
SAXONY
WETZLAR
THURINGIA
SILESIA
HESSE
BOHEMIA
PALATINATE
LORRAINE
BAVARIA
ALSACE
WÜRTTEMBERG
FRANCE
BADEN
SWITZERLAND
AUSTRIA

Prussia in 1815
Acquired by Prussia 1815–66
Imperial territory of Alsace-Lorraine 1871
German Empire 1871

This French cartoon was titled "The modern Charlemagne enters Paris." It shows the humiliation of France after the Franco-Prussian War. Bismarck leads Emperor Wilhelm down the Champs Elysée on a pig (Napoleon III).

German Empire

After victory in the Franco-Prussian War of 1870–71 (see page 168), the southern German states (Baden, Bavaria, Hesse, and Württemberg) agreed to join the North German Confederation in a united empire. Bismarck had made clear that the new German Empire of 26 member states was to be led by Prussia. Its constitution created a two-house parliament, one elected by the people and the other by state governments, with the chancellor appointed by the emperor.

King Wilhelm I of Prussia was proclaimed German Emperor in the Palace of Versailles on 18 January 1871. In this painting, Wilhelm stands in the middle on the podium, flanked by his son Friedrich (left) and Grand Duke Friedrich of Baden (right). Bismarck is in white uniform.

Mehmet Ali was Ottoman viceroy of Egypt from 1805 to 1849. During his rule he improved Egyptian agriculture.

Waning of the Ottoman Empire

The Ottoman Empire lost power and size during the course of the 19th century. Ruling sultans made efforts to reform the old-fashioned state, but they were met by internal opposition. Government corruption added to the decline of the empire, which was threatened by expansionist Russia. After forceful rebellions, many former Ottoman territories gained independence. From 1878 until the end of the century the sultan succeeded in preserving his reduced empire.

Egypt and the Suez Canal

Napoleon had investigated a canal across northeast Egypt, to connect the Mediterranean and Red Seas. Further surveys were made later, and in 1854 the Ottoman viceroy Said Pasha gave a French diplomat permission to survey the region. The resulting Suez Canal, which opened in 1869, was owned jointly by France and the Ottomans. But the British bought the Ottoman shares from Said's successor Ismail Pasha in 1875.

The Ottoman Turks tried three times to invade the Peloponnesus and retake land from the Greek rebels. After fierce fighting, the Greeks held out. From 1822 they fought under their new blue-and-white flag.

Greek War of Independence

The Greeks rebelled against Ottoman rule in 1821. The Egyptians helped the Ottomans fight the Greek nationalists, and in 1827 Britain, France, and Russia entered the conflict on behalf of independent Greece. Peace negotiations began in 1829, and Greek independence was declared three years later. The European powers agreed to make Prince Otto of Bavaria the new King of Greece.

English poet Lord Byron (1788–1824) supported the Greek cause. He traveled to Greece, but fell ill and died there of a fever.

The Crimean War

Britain and France joined the Ottomans in their concern about Russian expansion in the Black Sea region and elsewhere. The war of 1853–56 was fought on the Crimean Peninsula (in present-day Ukraine). Battle conditions were appalling, and the armies were poorly led and equipped. The result was that each side lost more than a quarter of a million men, before Russia accepted peace terms.

Breakaway Nations

A series of wars between the growing Russian and the declining Ottoman empires helped a number of Balkan peoples liberate themselves from Turkish rule. In 1878 Bosnia-Herzegovina came under Austrian administration; Bulgaria was given limited self-rule; and Montenegro, Romania, and Serbia became independent. The emergence of the Balkan nations weakened the Ottomans even further.

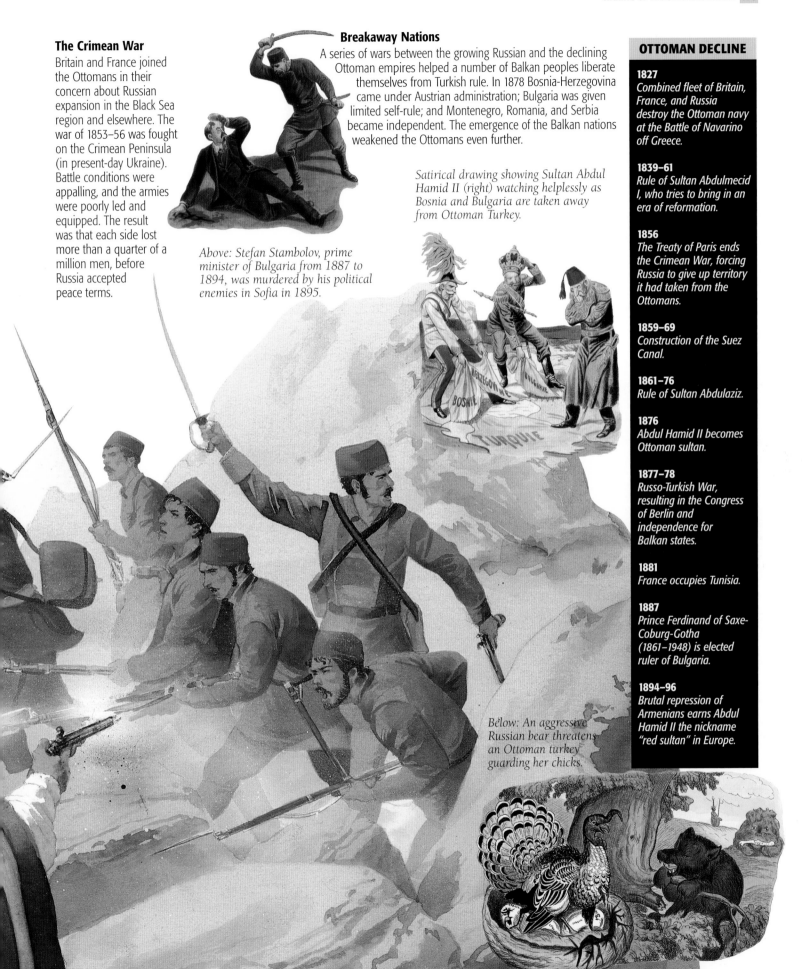

Above: Stefan Stambolov, prime minister of Bulgaria from 1887 to 1894, was murdered by his political enemies in Sofia in 1895.

Satirical drawing showing Sultan Abdul Hamid II (right) watching helplessly as Bosnia and Bulgaria are taken away from Ottoman Turkey.

Below: An aggressive Russian bear threatens an Ottoman turkey guarding her chicks.

OTTOMAN DECLINE

1827
Combined fleet of Britain, France, and Russia destroy the Ottoman navy at the Battle of Navarino off Greece.

1839–61
Rule of Sultan Abdulmecid I, who tries to bring in an era of reformation.

1856
The Treaty of Paris ends the Crimean War, forcing Russia to give up territory it had taken from the Ottomans.

1859–69
Construction of the Suez Canal.

1861–76
Rule of Sultan Abdulaziz.

1876
Abdul Hamid II becomes Ottoman sultan.

1877–78
Russo-Turkish War, resulting in the Congress of Berlin and independence for Balkan states.

1881
France occupies Tunisia.

1887
Prince Ferdinand of Saxe-Coburg-Gotha (1861–1948) is elected ruler of Bulgaria.

1894–96
Brutal repression of Armenians earns Abdul Hamid II the nickname "red sultan" in Europe.

Spain and Portugal

I t took time for the two nations of the Iberian peninsula to recover from French rule early in the century. The return to constitutional monarchy left many republicans and nationalists unhappy at the lack of liberal reforms, leading to revolution in 1820. In Spain there was a brief republican period in the 1870s, but there was no one force to unite different factions. In both countries, monarchies remained in power through the turn of the 20th century, as the strength of governments and political parties increased.

Below: Francisco Goya painted The Third of May 1808 *six years after the event depicted. It shows the execution of Spanish defenders of Madrid by French riflemen. Its brutal subject and bold, dramatic use of light have led to it being known as a revolutionary image in the history of art.*

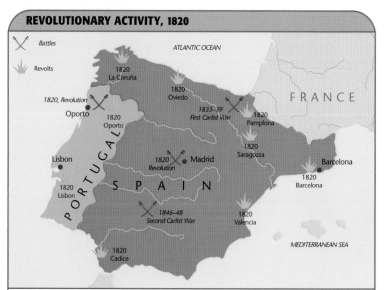

REVOLUTIONARY ACTIVITY, 1820

Battles

Revolts

ATLANTIC OCEAN

1820
La Coruña

1820
Oviedo

1820, Revolution

FRANCE

1833–39
First Carlist War

1820
Pamplona

Oporto

1820
Oporto

1820
Saragozza

Lisbon

1820
Revolution

Madrid

Barcelona

1820
Lisbon

S P A I N

1820
Barcelona

P O R T U G A L

1846–48
Second Carlist War

1820
Valencia

MEDITERRANEAN SEA

1820
Cadice

Civil Unrest in Iberia
There was rebellion throughout Spain and Portugal in 1820. Ferdinand VII had annulled the liberal constitution of 1812 on his return to power, which was the main cause of an army revolt and popular revolution. The revolutionaries succeeded in re-establishing the constitution and bringing in further liberal laws. In Portugal, unrest in the absence of King John VI led to the formation of a liberal assembly in Lisbon.

Peninsular War

Known by the Spanish as the War of Independence, the Peninsular War started as e revolt in 1808 against Napoleon's brother Joseph Bonaparte being made King of Spain. The Spanish were joined by British and Portuguese troops, and the Duke of Wellington (Arthur Wellesley, 1769–1852) secured a base in Portugal before slowly driving the French from the peninsula. The Spanish and Portuguese cause was helped by Napoleon withdrawing troops for his Russian campaign in 1812.

Portugal

Portuguese King John VI fled to Brazil during the French occupation, returning in 1821. By then, many Portuguese wanted a more representative, liberal form of government. After Civil War, Maria II reigned for 19 years, and was succeeded by her son, Pedro V. The monarchy and Portuguese government were relatively stable throughout the century, until the rise of republicanism in 1890.

Right: Maria II was the daughter of the first Emperor of Brazil, Peter IV. She was just 15 when she came to the throne.

Spanish Nationalism

After Ferdinand VII (known in Spain as "the Desired") was returned to the Spanish throne, he abolished the constitution and began persecuting liberals. In 1833, Ferdinand was succeeded by his daughter, Isabella, who was supported by the liberals. Her reign was opposed by the Carlists, who wanted Ferdinand's brother, Don Carlos, to be king. This weakened Isabella's reign, and in 1868 army officers rebelled and overthrew the queen.

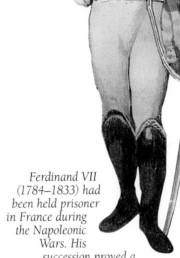

Ferdinand VII (1784–1833) had been held prisoner in France during the Napoleonic Wars. His succession proved a problem because he had no son from four marriages.

First Republic and Restoration

The First Spanish Republic (1873–74) began with a presidential system, which was opposed by provincial federalists. The Republican Party was not strong enough to keep Spain united, and there was civil war between the liberals and Carlists. In December 1874 the army restored the monarchy by bringing Isabella's son Alfonso XII to power.

Gaudí's Casa Batllo, in Barcelona, was built in 1877 and remodelled in 1905. The building is decorated with broken ceramic tiles.

Representation of the First Spanish Republic published in a satirical journal. The Republic lasted less than two years.

Antoni Gaudí

Antoni Gaudí (1852–1926) was born in Catalonia and became most famous for the modernist buildings he designed in Barcelona. Gaudí supported the Catalan independence movement, which became a serious force toward the end of the century.

Art and Architecture

Neoclassical and Romantic art dominated the first half of the 19th century. They were completely opposed in style and feeling. Neoclassicism was inspired by ancient Greek and Roman art and the perceived virtues of classical times, such as intellectual rigueur, discipline, and patriotism. In outright contrast to this, Romanticism championed mood, passion, spirituality, and the mysteries of the unknown. By mid-century industrialization and the rapid growth of cities and the middle classes had brought profound changes to Europe and a new generation of artists had appeared. These were the Realists, and they tried to paint the world just as they saw it, sometimes with warts and all. The Pre-Raphaelites were another mid-century art group; their style was elaborate, detailed, and often sentimental. In the 1860s the Impressionists burst onto the art stage. They changed ideas about art quite radically.

Romanticism
This painting, entitled *The Wanderer Above the Sea Fog*, by Casper David Friedrich, captures the majesty of nature and the solitude of the artist in true Romantic style. Romantic painters often portrayed contemporary events and they were much involved in promoting rebellion and the causes of the common people against the tyranny of corrupt monarchies and the ruling classes.

Neoclassicism
Neoclassical artists observed the work of ancient Greek and Roman artists that were being uncovered at excavations in Italy. Their outlook suited the new rulers of revolutionary Europe and Napoleon was particularly fond of the style.

Realism
Realist artists painted the everyday world. This was a new direction in art with the artists often showing a strong sympathy with the hardships of daily life of working people. This painting by the French artist Jean-François Millet, called *The Gleaners*, shows women at the backbreaking task of collecting grain that has fallen on the ground during the harvest.

St. Isaac's Cathedral in St. Petersburg was commissioned by Alexander I in 1818 and took more than three decades to complete.

Impressionism

The Impressionists were also realists, but they were not interested in grim reality. Instead, they wanted to paint the aspects of the modern world that appealed to them, and to capture the fleeting moment of the present. To do this they painted outdoors, working quickly, using rapid brushstrokes and dabs of unmixed color. Critics complained that their paintings looked unfinished—that they were just "impressions." In the past, it had not been easy to do oil painting outdoors: The paints and equipment were just too cumbersome. But in the 1840s, paint manufacturers learned how to put oil paint into small tubes, which were easy to carry around. Suddenly the possibility of painting outdoors became practical. The Impressionists realized that they could catch the immediate, spontaneous sense of weather in a landscape—and the effect of light at different moments of the day—only by painting the finished work on the spot, outdoors.

The Pre-Raphaelite Brotherhood

In 1848 a group of English artists formed the Pre-Raphaelite Brotherhood, claiming that art had gone wrong since the time of the Renaissance artist Raphael. Many Pre-Raphaelites were inspired by the delicacy and preciousness of the Florentine early Renaissance artists Filippino Lippi and Botticelli. Others admired the precision of Jan van Eyck. From this they evolved a distinctive style of their own: elaborate, detailed, and highly colored. The founders were William Holman Hunt (1825–1910), Dante Gabriel Rossetti (1828–82), and John Everett Millais (1829–96). They shared a romantic belief in the virtues of the medieval world and the horrors of industrialization.

Above: Persephone, by Rossetti, was modelled on the artist's beautiful wife, Jane. The Pre-Raphaelites often depicted mythological subjects.

Right: One of Monet's many Waterlilies canvases. Monet was an experimental artist during his entire career, often creating series of paintings of a single subject and showing it throughout the day as the light changed.

The Low Countries

The Low Countries began the century as the Batavian Republic, controlled and named by the French after an ancient tribe of the region. At the end of the Napoleonic Wars, the region became a kingdom, with great cultural differences between north and south. Rebellion led to independence for Belgium from the Netherlands, and later in the century Luxembourg also became autonomous. Great efforts were made throughout the Low Countries to solve social, religious, and language differences.

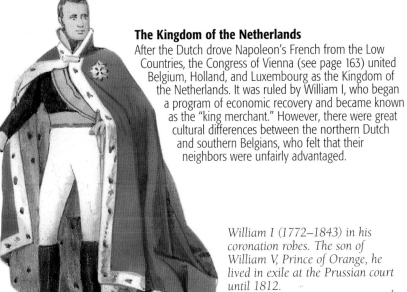

The Kingdom of the Netherlands

After the Dutch drove Napoleon's French from the Low Countries, the Congress of Vienna (see page 163) united Belgium, Holland, and Luxembourg as the Kingdom of the Netherlands. It was ruled by William I, who began a program of economic recovery and became known as the "king merchant." However, there were great cultural differences between the northern Dutch and southern Belgians, who felt that their neighbors were unfairly advantaged.

William I (1772–1843) in his coronation robes. The son of William V, Prince of Orange, he lived in exile at the Prussian court until 1812.

The Belgian Revolution

Just a month after the July Revolution in Paris (see page 164), opposition to the Dutch government and the king led to rebellion in Belgium. Industrialists and liberals tried to reduce the monarch's personal power. They also wanted more freedom and influence for French-speakers and Catholics, who they believed did not have enough representation. This led swiftly to a wish for complete independence for the southern region.

In 1830 riots in Brussels (above façades on the Grand Place) ignited the Belgian Revolution.

At the Conference of London (1830–39) the great powers of Austria, Britain, France, Prussia, and Russia ordered an armistice and agreed on independence for Belgium. Belgium's neutrality was guaranteed on a scrap of paper. This satirical illustration suggests that the powerful nations had more pressing matters, such as Russia's suppression of a revolution in Poland.

BELGIAN INDEPENDENCE

- Belgium
- Holland

FRESIA, GRONINGEN, DRENTHE, HANNOVER, NORTHERN HOLLAND, OVERIJSEL, GELDERLAND, SOUTHERN HOLLAND, UTRECHT, NORTHERN BRABANTE, ZEELAND, ANTWERPEN, PRUSSIA, WEST FLANDERS, EAST FLANDERS, LIMBURG, DUCHY OF LIMBURG, BRABANTE, HAINAULT, NAMUR, LIEGE, LUXEMBOURG

New Kingdom Proclaimed

The map shows the boundaries of the new state of Belgium, which the National Congress decided should be a monarchy. The Belgians decided on Prince Leopold of Saxe-Coburg, who was also acceptable to both Britain and France (and who had declined the Greek crown a year earlier). The French-speaking part of the grand duchy of Luxembourg became a province of Belgium, while the rest remained Dutch. William I was not happy with this, but was forced to accept it.

Pillars of Society

From 1850, people in Belgium and the Netherlands were organized into parallel social groups (or "pillars") with their own hierarchy. The pillars were based on religions and ideologies, such as Protestant, Catholic, social-democratic, and liberal. Each group had its own churches, political parties, universities, schools, trade unions, and newspapers. Members of different pillars lived close to each other and spoke the same language, but they rarely socialized or intermarried.

Political Reform

In the Netherlands, William II accepted a constitution that was more like the Belgian model. The monarch became responsible to his government rather than master of it. William III allowed the introduction of more liberal ideas and greater democracy. In Belgium, where there was religious freedom, the liberal party tried to limit the growing power of the church. It was opposed by the Catholic conservative party.

Economic Growth and Cultural Revival

Belgium was one of the earliest industrialized countries. There were strong coal and steel industries in the south, while the north was mainly agricultural. The government encouraged free enterprise and did little to regulate industry. Throughout the Low Countries, socialists pushed for new labor laws, protection of the right to strike, and other welfare measures. Throughout the region, painting, literature, music, and science all flourished in the 1880s and 1890s.

The Brussels Exhibition of 1880, commemorating the 50th anniversary of the independence of Belgium from Dutch rule.

Dutch painter Vincent van Gogh (1853–90) was born near Breda. He moved to France in 1886. His work is considered to have had a strong influence on the development of 20th-century art.

This portrait by Swiss artist Felix Valloton shows Emile Verhaeren (1855–1916), a Belgian poet who wrote in the French language and was one of the chief founders of the school of Symbolism.

Engraving of the Frederiksborg Palace, near Copenhagen, where the Danish national constitutional assembly was held in 1848.

Scandinavia

The histories of Denmark, Norway, and Sweden had always been bound together, and had included Finland for many centuries. The situation changed early in the 19th century, following the Napoleonic Wars, when Norway left Denmark and joined Sweden, which had lost Finland to Russia. The new political arrangements lasted through the century, despite growing nationalism in the individual regions and the expansion of the German and Russian empires.

Representing Scandinavism, Norwegian (left), Danish, and Swedish soldiers (right) join hands.

Scandinavism

A movement for Scandinavian political and cultural unity, called Scandinavism, arose during the Schleswig War of 1848–50 between Denmark and Prussia. Swedish and Norwegian volunteers, concerned at the expansion of the Russian empire and Prussian power, joined the Danes in their unsuccessful struggle. The movement weakened in the 1860s, remaining strong only among the Swedish minority in Finland.

The Grand Duchy of Finland

From 1809 the autonomous Grand Duchy of Finland was effectively under the control of Russia. Many Finns rebelled against being part of the Russian Empire, and nationalism grew (see page 161). This resulted in some concessions by the Russian tsar. Finland had its own monetary system from 1865; a legislative assembly met regularly from 1869; and a conscription law laying foundations for a Finnish army was passed in 1878.

Left: Swedish diplomat Gustaf Mauritz Armfelt (1757–1814) helped establish the autonomy of the grand duchy. He is regarded as a father of the Finnish nation.

Denmark

The treaty of 1814 allowed Denmark to keep the old Norwegian colonies of Greenland, Iceland, and the Faroe Islands. But in the Danish homeland there were constant problems with the duchies of Schleswig and Holstein, which were the cause of wars with the German Confederation and were eventually lost to the Prussians. In 1849 King Frederick VII signed a liberal constitution that ended absolute monarchy.

Map of Norway and Sweden, 1847. The flag is a naval ensign of the United Kingdoms.

United Kingdom of Norway and Sweden

Union with Sweden was forced on Norway, which also had to accept the Swedish king. Norwegians were proud of their history and culture, and there was a growing sense of nationalism throughout the century. Though foreign policy was joint, Norway was allowed some self-government in rural districts. Its constitutional approach also encouraged Swedish radicals to demand more parliamentary democracy.

Alfred Nobel

Swedish chemist Alfred Nobel (1833–96) was born in Stockholm and educated in St. Petersburg. He was a great innovator and is most famous for inventing dynamite. He and his brothers also had interests in the oil fields of Baku (in modern Azerbaijan), and Alfred made his fortune from explosives and oil. He left much of this in trust to establish the Nobel Prizes, which are still important today.

Alfred Nobel at work in his laboratory. As well as inventing dynamite (by combining nitroglycerin with another substance), he researched the preparation of artificial forms of rubber and leather.

Russia

Russia has always been a land of contrasts. In 1800, it was backward in every way compared with the countries of Western Europe. Yet it was also a great European power. In the previous century the population had increased nearly four times, largely due to Russian expansion and the acquisition of new territories. Over 95 percent of the people lived in the country, and the majority were serfs. The number of educated people was tiny. Russia continued to expand in the 19th century, especially to the south, where it gained many more non-Russian peoples. Great progress was made in modernizing society: the number of town-dwellers tripled, modern industry was established, and serfdom was abolished. But Russia still lagged behind the West in economic development and in education. Although the arts, especially literature and music, flourished, 75 percent of the people could not read or write in 1900.

Reform

Alexander II introduced real and far-reaching reforms. He overhauled law and order, banned the worst forms of torture, reduced censorship, and allowed elected assemblies at local level. Above all, he carried out the emancipation of the serfs, a step that earlier rulers had avoided because of the huge practical difficulties. In fact, it did little to improve the condition of the peasants, who were still dominated by landowners, and criticism of the government actually increased.

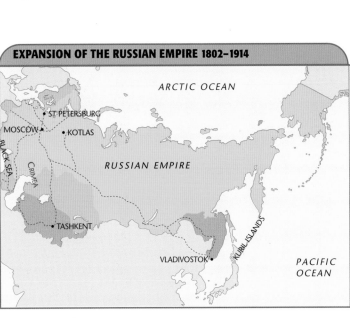

Below: Four previous attempts to assassinate Tzar Alexander II had failed but a fifth attack on March 13, 1861 succeeded. His murder was a setback for reform and his plans to establish an elected Duma (parliament) were trashed by his successor Alexander III.

EXPANSION OF THE RUSSIAN EMPIRE 1802–1914

ARCTIC OCEAN

ST PETERSBURG
MOSCOW
KOTLAS
BLACK SEA
CRIMEA

RUSSIAN EMPIRE

TASHKENT

KURIL ISLANDS

VLADIVOSTOK

PACIFIC OCEAN

☐ Russian Empire 1802

TERRITORIAL GAINS

☐ 1809–55
☐ 1855–1914

Growth of the Empire

The Russian Empire continued to grow in the 19th century. Finland was taken from Sweden in 1809; Bessarabia (northwest of the Black Sea) from the Ottoman Turks in 1812; central Poland was gained in 1815; the Caucasus (Georgia, Armenia, Azerbaijan) by 1859; the Amur region by 1860; and the Uzbek khanates by 1900.

Rebellions

A large empire, with people of different cultures, was difficult to govern, especially in a time of growing nationalism. Old enemies, such as the Finns and Poles, resented Russian dominance. The small Polish Kingdom established in 1815 was supposed to be self-governing—but its king was the tzar! In 1830 the Poles launched a major rebellion, which took a year to crush. Greater repression followed, as the Polish constitution was abolished. After further outbreaks in 1848 and 1863, Poland was reduced to a Russian province.

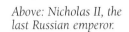

Nicholas II

The last Russian emperor, Nicholas II (reigned 1894–1917), was well-meaning but weak and stubborn, a poor leader of 120 million subjects. A conservative, like his father Alexander III (reigned 1881–94), he believed that it was his religious duty to maintain Russian autocracy. Meanwhile, the activities of revolutionaries and government agents (sometimes the same people!) threatened to destroy all government authority. Nicholas's failure to keep Russia out of costly and unsuccessful wars hastened the revolution of 1917.

Above: Nicholas II, the last Russian emperor.

Writers and Artists

Few writers and artists of world class appeared in Russia before the 18th century, but by 1900, Russian literature, of which the poet Pushkin (1799–1837) is called the founder, stood on equal footing with that of France or England. The Russian novel achieved unique status in the works of Dostoyevsky, Tolstoy (left), and Turgenev; and Russian theater in the works of playwrights Chekhov and Gorky. Russian artists included Kandinsky, founder of abstract painting, and Chagall.

KEY EVENTS

1801
Alexander I takes power (dies 1825).

1812
French troops under Napoleon invade Russia and are defeated.

1825
Nicholas I takes power (dies 1855); Decembrists' revolt.

1830
Polish rebellion.

1853–56
Crimean War.

1855
Alexander II takes power.

1860–70
Russian expansion into Turkestan.

1861
Serfdom abolished.

1877
Russia invades Balkans.

1878
Congress of Berlin.

1881
Alexander II assassinated. Alexander III takes power; Pogroms in Russia hit Jewish people hard.

1891
Trans-Siberian railroad begun (completed 1916).

1894
The last czar, Nicholas II, takes power (abdicates 1917; assassinated 1918).

Joseph Lister's antiseptic steam spray dispenser was known as "Puffing Billy.".

Science and Medicine

There were pioneering developments in scientific medicine in 19th-century Europe. The workings of the human body were well understood by 1800, but further discoveries were made in physiology. Most importantly, the role of microbes in transmitting disease was realized, allowing preventive measures to be introduced. On a practical level, anesthesia caused a major advance in surgery, and the use of antiseptics helped sanitation in hospitals and elsewhere.

Germ Theory

French chemist Louis Pasteur proved that microscopic living organisms, called bacteria or microbes, caused and spread disease. He discovered a method to treat food to kill these germs, which came to be known as "pasteurization" and is still used today. German physician Robert Koch (1843–1910) succeeded in identifying the bacteria that cause individual diseases, such as anthrax and tuberculosis.

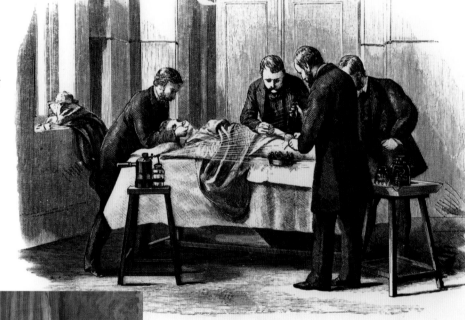

By the 1860s antiseptics were being used during surgery, as well as anesthesia, making operations less painful and hazardous.

Louis Pasteur (1822–95) investigates a flask containing the spinal cord of a rabies-infected rabbit.

Anesthetics and Surgery

In 1846 the American dentist William Thomas Morton (1819–68) demonstrated the use of ether as a general anaesthetic to a group of physicians. News of this advance quickly reached Europe, and general anesthesia was soon used during surgery. The following year, Scottish professor James Simpson (1811–70) tried using chloroform in the same way, with great success.

Sanitation

Discoveries about germs led medical experts to realize the vital importance of basic hygiene in medicine and surgery. Doctors and surgeons began washing their hands in a lime solution to stop infection from spreading. When the nursing pioneer Florence Nightingale arrived at the Crimean War in 1854, her first request was for scrubbing brushes, soap, clean bandages, and fresh towels.

Florence Nightingale (1820–1910) founded the nursing profession. Known to wounded soldiers as the "Lady with the Lamp," she introduced sanitary measures that improved conditions enormously.

X-ray photography soon became a basic procedure in hospitals, especially for investigating patients' bones.

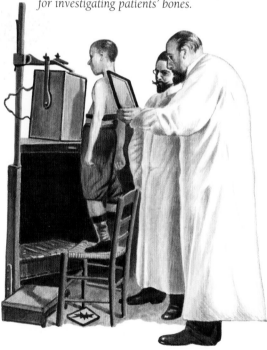

X-Rays

The German physicist Wilhelm Conrad Röntgen (1845–1923) discovered X-rays in 1895. He called them X because he did not understand what this form of radiation was. However, its usefulness was soon clear, since X-ray images allowed doctors to see inside the body. Röntgen took the first X-ray photographs, including a famous photo of the bones in his wife's hand. For his discovery, he received the first Nobel Prize for Physics in 1901.

Charles Darwin and Evolution

The British naturalist Charles Darwin developed his theory of evolution from his world travels aboard the ship HMS Beagle. Darwin believed that all species of plants and animals had evolved over millions of years from a small number of common ancestors. He said that the main evolutionary mechanism was a process called natural selection (which others have called "survival of the fittest").

Charles Darwin (1809–82) (right) discusses his theories with geologist Charles Lyell (1797–1875) (standing) and botanist Joseph Hooker (1817–1911).

Darwin studied finches and noted that their beaks varied depending on the food available where they lived. They had evolved according to their environment.

Why the Controversy?

Darwin's theories caused bitter controversy among scientists, religious believers, and the general public. Many people objected to the idea that humans were descended from apes, and some saw a conflict with their religious faith. Some Christians saw evolutionary theory as being opposed to the idea of divine creation and the teachings of the Bible. Most scientists came to accept Darwin's ideas.

This scornful caricature of Darwin as an ape appeared in a journal in 1871.

An Age of Invention

The 19th century was an era of rapid technological progress. In many ways innovation was driven by the industrial revolution as inventors and industrialists sought ways to improve factories, mines, and transportation to increase their output and sales and to maximize profits. Combined with important scientific discoveries, these advances overcame distances and improved peoples' everyday lives in many ways.

Alessandro Volta, inventor of the electric battery and an early type of generator.

Michael Faraday's dynamo was the world's first electrical generator.

Electricity

In about 1800, Italian inventor Alessandro Volta found that a wire connecting two different metals placed in salt water carried an electric current. By connecting many cells together he made the first electric battery. The decisive step in putting electricity to use was made by Englishman Michael Faraday, who showed that a magnet can produce electricity—the principle of electromagnetic induction. This led to the first electric generator. Faraday also invented the electric motor in 1821, and the dynamo and transformer in 1831. Electric lighting for houses needed an incandescent bulb (one that produced white heat). One of the earliest successful ones was developed by American inventor Thomas Edison in 1879; it burned for 40 hours continuously.

Communication

Telecommunications began with the telegraph, which sent messages along a cable carrying an electric current. The messages were encoded, usually in Samuel Morse's code of dots and dashes. In 1837 two Englishmen, Charles Wheatstone and William Cooke, were granted a patent for an electric telegraph system which made the telegraph available to the public. It was widely used by the fast-growing railroads and the military. The telephone, in which actual speech was carried by the cable, was invented in 1876 by Alexander Graham Bell. Telephone lines soons spread across much of Europe and the United States. At the end of the 19th century Italian inventor Guglielmo Marconi came up with a telegraph system that could transmit without wires using radio waves instead.

Wheatstone and Cooke's telegraph had five needles which, powered by electrical impulses transmitted along a cable, could be moved to indicate letters or numbers on an inbuilt panel.

Transportation

Throughout history the fastest way to travel on land was on horseback, but that changed forever in the 19th century, with the invention first of steam engines and railways, then automobiles, followed—on the cusp of the 20th century—by airplanes.

The first bicycle was invented by a Scottish blacksmith, Kirkpatrick Macmillan, in 1839. The "penny-farthing," (right) named after very large and very small British coins, was popular in the 1870s.

The first automobile—a wooden three-wheeler with a small gas engine and a tiller for steering—was invented by the German engineer Karl Benz in 1885.

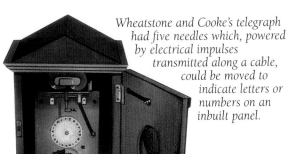

Thomas Edison was a prolific inventor and was granted more than 1000 patents during his lifetime.

An early telephone with mouthpiece and earpiece connected by a cord.

Left: Photograph of the internationally famous French actress Sarah Bernhardt, also known as "The Divine Sarah," snapped in about 1860.

Above: In 1901 the East Kodak Company began selling the "Box Brownie," the first camera for a mass market.

Below: The Horse in Motion (1878), by Eadweard J. Muybridge (1830–1904), the English photographer who tried to capture motion with cameras of his own invention, hence pioneering motion pictures.

Photography and Cinema

The principle of making a picture with light was known by Frenchman Joseph Nièpce in 1816, but he was unable to print positive impressions from his negatives. In 1839 several French and British pioneers found ways to make photographs. The process spread rapidly, and improvements came thick and fast. Photographers knew that moving pictures were possible, too. In 1895 the French brothers Louis and Auguste Lumière invented their cinematograph. The movies had arrived.

Above: A poster advertising the Lumière brothers' new invention – the cinema.

Right: This scene is a still from what is regarded by many as the first movie in history, "La Sortie des usines Lumiere" (Workers the Lumière Factory) by Auguste and Louis Lumière.

Leaving Europe

In the 19th century the population of Europe more than doubled to about 420 million. During the course of the century many people began to feel that they could make a better life for themselves on another continent and decided to emigrate. Some did so because they were persecuted as a result of their religious or political beliefs, while others simply felt that life was so difficult that they and their families had nothing to lose by leaving. In the first half of the century most European emigrants came from Britain and Germany; later they were joined by others from Italy, Scandinavia, and the Balkans. In the USA the flood of immigrants rose so sharply that the authorities felt they had to try and stem it.

The US government began using Ellis Island (above) in New York Harbor as a reception center for immigrants in 1892. All newcomers were questioned in the main building on the island and examined by doctors. Altogether more than 12 million people first entered the United States via Ellis Island, which was conveniently close to the Statue of Liberty—first unveiled in 1886.

The United States

About one person in ten left Europe between 1850 and 1914. It was the largest population movement of all time, involving more than 50 million people. A few emigrants went to Australia and New Zealand, but the vast majority ended up in the Americas. The first wave of mass European emigration—mainly of Germans and Irish—to the USA occurred between 1840 and 1850. It was caused by economic hardship, and in the case of Ireland, by the potato famine (see page 170). In the last 20 years of the 19th century, more than nine million people entered the United States.

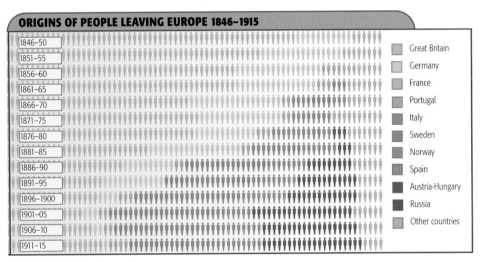

ORIGINS OF PEOPLE LEAVING EUROPE 1846–1915

1846–50	
1851–55	
1856–60	
1861–65	
1866–70	
1871–75	
1876–80	
1881–85	
1886–90	
1891–95	
1896–1900	
1901–05	
1906–10	
1911–15	

Great Britain
Germany
France
Portugal
Italy
Sweden
Norway
Spain
Austria-Hungary
Russia
Other countries

Right: European immigrants sail past the Statue of Liberty as they enter New York Harbor.

Left: Bronze statue of Annie Moore, a 15-year-old Irish girl, and the first person to be processed at Ellis Island on January 1, 1892.

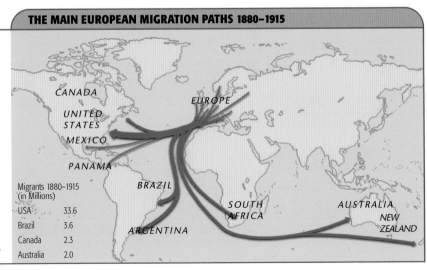

THE MAIN EUROPEAN MIGRATION PATHS 1880–1915

Mass Migration
The main incentives for Europeans, especially Britons, to emigrate to Australia and New Zealand were the cheap fares offered by shipping lines and the expected high standard of living when they arrived. In Victorian Britain, some wealthy liberals and charities helped poor people move to British colonies.

CANADA
UNITED STATES
MEXICO
PANAMA
BRAZIL
SOUTH AFRICA
ARGENTINA
EUROPE
AUSTRALIA
NEW ZEALAND

Migrants 1880–1915
(in Millions)

USA	33.6
Brazil	3.6
Canada	2.3
Australia	2.0

During the 19th century European countries greatly expanded their overseas empires. The industrial revolution was in full swing in Europe and countries there sought raw materials for their factories just as they were also looking for new markets to sell their products.

Famine, poverty, and political revolt, combined with large increases in population caused a lot of Europeans to look for new homes overseas and many emigrated to places like Australia and Argentina. But while countries such as Britain, France, and Holland were enlarging their empires in Africa, Asia, and the Pacific, Spain and Portugal were losing theirs in Latin America. By 1830 most of the countries in Central and South America had thrown off their colonial overlords. In this chapter we look at all the various parts of the world during the century that is often called, like this chapter, "the Age of Empire."

Britain built an empire on which "the sun never sank." Queen Victoria, shown here in a statue by a Yoruba artist from Africa, was the monarch who oversaw its creation.

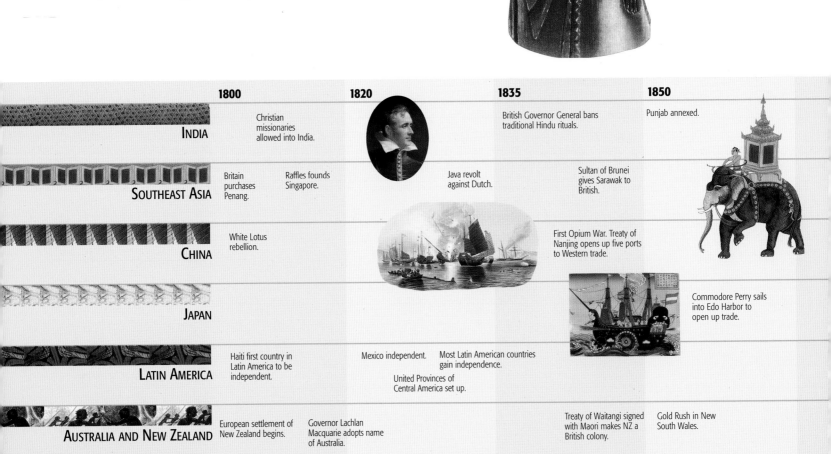

	1800	1820	1835	1850
INDIA	Christian missionaries allowed into India.		British Governor General bans traditional Hindu rituals.	Punjab annexed.
SOUTHEAST ASIA	Britain purchases Penang.	Raffles founds Singapore.	Java revolt against Dutch. / Sultan of Brunei gives Sarawak to British.	
CHINA	White Lotus rebellion.		First Opium War. Treaty of Nanjing opens up five ports to Western trade.	
JAPAN				Commodore Perry sails into Edo Harbor to open up trade.
LATIN AMERICA	Haiti first country in Latin America to be independent.	Mexico independent. / United Provinces of Central America set up.	Most Latin American countries gain independence.	
AUSTRALIA AND NEW ZEALAND	European settlement of New Zealand begins.	Governor Lachlan Macquarie adopts name of Australia.	Treaty of Waitangi signed with Maori makes NZ a British colony.	Gold Rush in New South Wales.
AFRICA	Britain acquires Cape Colony.		French invade Algeria. / Boers begin the Great Trek.	David Livingstone explores central and southern Africa.
CULTURAL AND ECONOMIC MILESTONES	Britain abolishes slave trade.	Gold standard established.	Slavery abolished throughout the British Empire.	

The Age of Empire

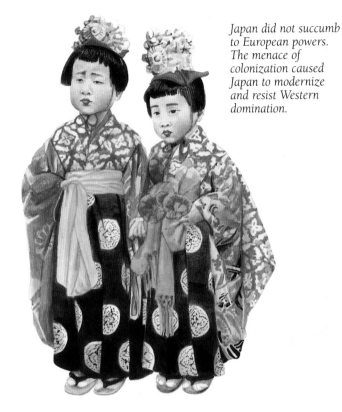

Japan did not succumb to European powers. The menace of colonization caused Japan to modernize and resist Western domination.

1860	1870	1880	1890	1900
Indian Mutiny.	East India Company dissolved. India now run by British government.	Indian National Congress founded.		Muslim League formed in Dhaka.
French capture Saigon.	Dutch attack Aceh sultanate.	France creates Indo-Chinese union.		Spanish-American War. US rules the Philippines.
Taiping rebellion. Second Opium War.			Sino-Japanese War. China loses Taiwan.	Boxer rebellion against foreign interests in China.
	Civil war. Emperor Meiji takes over from shogun.		Japan defeats China in Sino-Japanese War.	Japan defeats Russia in Russo-Japanese War.
Honduras becomes British colony. Jamaica independent.		Costa Rica grants land to Minor C. Keith, founder of Untied Fruit Company.	Cuba independent.	Panama independent.
	Wellington becomes capital of NZ. 		New Zealand first country in the world to grant the vote to women.	British colonial rule over Australia ends.
Suez Canal opens.		Scramble for Africa begins. Gold discovered in Transvaal.		Foshoda incident brings Britain and France to the brink of war over Africa.
	United States abolishes slavery.	Frozen meat shipped from Argentina.	Brazil abolishes slavery.	

Right: Poster advertising chocolate made from cocoa imported from the colonies.

Markets and Materials

There were many reasons why the imperial powers were interested in expanding their empires. One was strategic: to keep their rivals from becoming too powerful. Another was to increase trade. As Western powers industrialized, they needed to look further afield for raw materials and markets. Many of the colonies had excellent climates for growing products such as sugar, tea, coffee, fruit, and cocoa, and were rich in natural resources.

Afghans Resist Britain

During the late 19th century, both Britain and Russia wanted to control Afghanistan. The competition between the two imperial powers was called the Great Game and resulted in two wars: the First Anglo-Afghan War of 1839–42 and the Second Anglo-Afghan War of 1878–80. The Afghan tribesmen, who were fiercely independent, managed to resist the British, and the British finally signed a border agreement and an agreement to recognize Afghanistan's independence. Afghanistan became a buffer between the British and Russian empires.

Afridis tribesmen from Afghanistan, who showed fierce resistance to the British.

Japanese Colonialism

By adopting Western-style government, military, and technology, Japan was able to avoid colonization and become a major colonial power itself. Successful wars against China 1894–95 and Russia 1904–05 resulted in Japan gaining control of Korea, Taiwan, southern Manchuria, and half of Sakhalin.

Colonialism

Colonialism is the extension of a nation's government over territory beyond its borders. Colonial powers either send settlers to take over the colony, or set up a local government to exploit the indigenous people and their wealth. During the 19th century several European countries built up such vast overseas colonies that they were called empires. Britain, for example, gained power over a quarter of the world's land surface and controlled roughly the same percentage of the world's population. France, Germany, Italy, Belgium, Portugal, as well as the United States and Japan claimed territories across the world. Although the imperial powers developed many of their colonies, bringing international trade and infrastructure (railroads, for example), the colonists often treated indigenous peoples badly, seizing their land and depriving them of some of their most basic human rights.

Emperor Meiji came to power in 1868. he modernized Japan, preparing its path to become a world power.

THE PEAK OF EMPIRE 1912

CANADA

RUSSIA

BRITAIN

UNITED STATES OF AMERICA

CHINA

JAPAN

INDIA

AUSTRALIA

- British
- Italian
- Portuguese
- Belgian
- French
- Russian
- Japanese
- American
- German
- Dutch
- Spanish
- Danish

A European Free For All

From 1870 European powers rushed to expand their empires. During this time two major continents, Africa and Asia, were almost completely carved up. Missionaries, traders, and military officers all saw enormous potential in these areas and pressed their countries for imperial advances. Britain and France, as well as emerging powers such as Germany and Italy, concerned about the strategic advances of their rivals, scrambled to seize new territories. They also raced to claim areas rich in natural resources for the new wave of industrialization. Britain made the greatest gains to its empire during this time, seizing lands all over Africa as well as strategic points in the Pacific.

Map showing the British Empire in about 1886.

"Anglobalization"

In 1897, in the year of her Diamond Jubilee, Queen Victoria of Great Britain reigned over the largest empire the world has ever seen. The British Empire was three times larger than the French empire and ten times larger than the German empire. Some 445 million people lived under some form of British rule. Britain led the scramble for Africa, as well as gobbling up huge territories in Asia and Oceania.

In this cartoon an evil serpent, symbolizing imperialist Britain, squeezes the globe, squashing traditional cultures.

The Scramble for Africa

After British explorers traveled inland in Africa, claiming new areas for the queen, Britain began to colonize vast areas of the continent. Between 1880 and 1914 the British gained Egypt, the Sudan, Uganda, Kenya, Nigeria, and Northern and Southern Rhodesia. They also consolidated their rule of South Africa with their victory in the Second Boer War of 1899–1902.

This cartoon of Cecil Rhodes (1853–1902), the British statesman and businessman, shows his desire to see Britain bestriding Africa. Rhodes made a fortune in the diamond industry. Rhodesia (now Zambia and Zimbabwe) was named after him.

Right: In Indochina a group called the Black Flags, led by De Tham (top right), resisted French domination.

European Explorers

European explorers traveled extensively in Africa before it was colonized. On returning to Europe, many encouraged their governments to begin colonization. In the words of British-American explorer Henry Morton Stanley, it was their duty "to put the civilization of Europe into the barbarism of Africa."

Asia gets Carved Up

Britain controlled the Indian subcontinent, Burma, Malaysia, Singapore and many other parts of Southeast Asia. The French gradually took over Indo-China, while the Dutch maintained their extensive empire in Southeast Asia, or the East Indies, as the region was known then.

Left: French explorer Count Pierre Savorgnan de Brazza sold photographs of himself to help finance expeditions north of the Congo River in the 1880s.

India and the East India Company

After the British East India Company virtually annexed the state of Bengal in 1765, it began to change from a trading company to a military and political institution. In the India Act of 1784 the British government had declared that territorial expansion was against "the honor and policy of this nation." However, territorial expansion did occur, and by the middle of the 19th century the British effectively ruled India. Early governors believed that British rule would be brief. Then the idea arose that their rule was a great benefit to the Indian people, a "sacred trust." At first the British treated Indians as equals and did not interfere with local customs, but once the "sacred trust" idea took hold, they began to enforce reforms, many of which were strongly resented by some groups of Indians.

Ram Mohun Roy (1772–1833) was a Hindu liberal reformer who opposed the caste system and adopted aspects of Christianity. He founded the Brahmo Samaj (Society of God, 1828) and the Hindu College in Calcutta (1817), and had great influence on the British as well as Hindus.

Hindu Reformers

The British could not have ruled India without the co-operation, active or passive, of most Indians. While Muslims in general kept themselves apart from Western influences, a growing number of Hindus identified with them. They spoke English (the official language) and studied European history and literature. Many government reforms were brought about by pressure from Hindus.

Before a bridge was built, this locomotive was ferried across the Indus River.

Making block-printed cotton cloth. The collapse of India's cotton trade brought severe hardship.

Roads and Transportation

No roads existed before 1830. The famous Grand Trunk Road between Calcutta and Delhi was begun in 1839. The first railroad was constructed from Bombay in 1853. The British governor-general's plan was to develop trade routes connecting the seaports of Bombay, Calcutta, and Madras. This involved tremendous feats of civil engineering, including crossing mountain ranges and the great Ganges and Indus rivers. Nearly 40,000 (70,000 km) of railroad track were working by 1914.

The British

In the early days, many of those employed by the East India Company retired to England with huge fortunes. This profiteering was later stopped, but life in India, though it had drawbacks, was very comfortable for the ruling British. A young nobody in London, sent out as a clerk for the Company, found himself with a large house and 20 servants. Some Britons came to love and understand Indian ways and chose to stay on after retirement, but others were bored, superior, and increasingly racist.

A "memsahib" (meaning "the lady of a sahib," a man of high status) with her servants.

Trade and Industry

The British saw India as a market for its booming industry and did not invest in Indian industry, which might compete. The industrial revolution was a disaster for India's cotton workers (as it had been earlier for Britain's own hand-weavers). Hindu ritual and the caste system also hindered technological progress. However, India was brought into the world capitalist system, with great benefits for the merchants and bankers of the growing middle classes, who became closely identified with British rule.

The Princely States

One third of British India was made up of nominally independent states. The British recognized the value of maintaining the Indian princedoms, and until 1858 many areas experienced little contact with Europeans. But British reluctance to interfere was combined with reforming zeal. (The custom of killing baby girls, for example, was unacceptable, so the British made it a capital crime, yet failed to end it entirely.) After 1858, under the rule of the Crown, the princes felt more secure. They generally remained firm allies of Britain.

Below: Procession with Maratha ruler Serfoji II, Rajah of Tanjore in southern India from 1787. Soon after gaining power, he was deposed by his uncle and regent Amarsingh who seized the throne for himself. With the help of the British, Serfoji recovered the throne in 1798. A subsequent treaty forced him to hand over the real power in the kingdom to the British East India Company. Serfoji remained until 1832.

Territorial Expansion

In 1780 the British were confronted with three major enemies: the Marathas, the Nizam of Hyderabad, and Tipu Sultan of Mysore. It took three wars to defeat the Marathas and establish British supremacy, while other campaigns resulted in British authority stretching, in the east, from Bengal to Ceylon (Sri Lanka). Other states were taken over when the ruler died without – according to the British, but not Hindu, interpretation – leaving a direct heir.

After the death of Ranjit Singh (1839), the Punjab fell into disorder. Invasion of British territory resulted in war and annexation under Ranjit's successor, Duleep Singh (left).

INDIA 1784–1857

1784
The India Act says British will not expand further.

1798
Ceylon (modern Sri Lanka) becomes British colony.

1799
Tipu Sultan is defeated by British Governor General Cornwallis and killed.

1813
Christian missionaries are allowed to preach in India.

1815
Around 40 million Indians under British rule.

1818
Final defeat of Marathas.

1828–35
British Governor General Bentinck bans traditional Hindu rituals, including suttee, thuggee and infanticide.

1835
English becomes the official language in schools in India.

1836
Large road-building program begins.

1839–42
First Afghan War. Ends with humiliating British defeat.

1849
Punjab annexed.

1853
First railroad in operation.

1856
Oudh annexed.

India after the Mutiny

Increasing hostility to British rule led to a widespread rebellion, known as the Indian Mutiny, across north and central India in 1857–8. It took 14 months of bitter fighting to put it down. At the end of the rebellion the British government took over from the East India Company, and from that point on India was governed by a tiny minority of British civil servants. The Indians, forbidden to participate in the government of their own country, began to organize themselves to regain their independence.

BRITISH INDIA 1914

AFGHANISTAN · KASHMIR · CHINA · PUNJAB · TIBET · DELHI · NEPAL · OUDH · ASSAM · SIND · MEWAR · BENGAL · BURMA · ARABIAN SEA · HYDERABAD · ORISSA · CALCUTTA · BOMBAY · BAY OF BENGAL · GOA · MYSORE · MADRAS · CEYLON

☐ Possessions 1858 ☐ Acquired 1858–1914 ☐ Dependent Indian states

British Territories and Spheres of Influence
By 1914 Britain effectively controlled the entire Indian subcontinent, either by direct rule or through the rule of dependent princely states and protectorates. Beyond India, they gradually took over Burma to the east. In the west, they failed to absorb Afghanistan into the Indian Empire. Fierce Afghani tribesmen repelled the British twice and Afghanistan remained an independent buffer between the British and Russian empires.

The Mutiny
New practises introduced in the army offended the Company's Indian soldiers (called "sepoys"), both Hindu and Muslim. In 1857 several regiments mutinied against their British officers. The rebellion spread across much of northern India, fuelled by hostility to British rule. Delhi was captured and fighting was fierce (above). Horrible atrocities were committed by both sides. The Mutiny was ruthlessly crushed in 1858; many civilians were executed without trial.

Law and Administration
In theory, Indians were to be part of the civil service that ruled India after the mutiny but in practise hardly any Indians were recruited. Often, an inexperienced British district officer would be in charge of an area containing a million people. Excluded from the administration of their own country, many Indians turned to nationalism.

Meaning of the Mutiny
The rebellion was more than a mutiny, but it was not a nationalist rising. Few Indians yet thought of an all-Indian "nation," and no great leader emerged to unite resistance to the British. The motives of the rebels were conservative. They feared that modernization was destroying their ancient culture.

Left: Rebel sepoys from Bengal.

The End of East India Company Rule
The mutiny ended the rule of the East India Company. After 1858 India was placed directly under the British government, with a viceroy and a council, responsible to the government in London. Indian involvement in government was increased by later acts, but the concessions were minor (though resented by many British).

Below: British Queen Victoria was crowned Empress of India in 1876.

Left: British officer ruling over a court in the Punjab.

Famine

Famine was a continual curse in India. It could wipe out half the people in a town or region. Relief usually arrived too late. The 1866 famine in Bengal, with over a million dead, was made worse by monsoon rain preventing transportation and merchants hoarding grain. In 1883 the government set up an elaborate plan, the Famine Code, to deal with the problem. It was an unusually large social-welfare program for the time, and brought improvement, but did not stop famines.

The National Congress and the Muslim League

The Indian National Congress was founded by educated Hindus and Muslims in 1885. Its original object was to press the government for a greater share of power for Indians; national independence was not part of the agenda. A more extreme wing soon emerged and gained control of the party. It advocated self-government for India as a dominion of the British Empire, like Canada or Australia. Muslims in the Congress feared that, in a more democratic India, they would be swamped by the Hindu majority. They founded the separate Muslim League in 1906, which reached an agreement with Congress (the Lucknow Pact) for certain seats to be reserved for Muslims in future elections. Members of the League took part in the non-cooperation movement and some Muslims remained members of Congress.

Right: B. G. Tilak (1856–1920) led the extreme wing of Congress. He first had the idea of opposing the British by massive civil disobedience, or non-cooperation, the policy later adopted by Gandhi.

Below: The Delhi Durbar was a large assembly held at Delhi to celebrate the coronation of a new British king or queen (who were also emperor and empress of India). The Delhi Durbar of 1903 included two weeks of dazzling celebrations planned by British Governor General Lord Curzon. King Edward VII and Queen Alexandra did not attend.

French Indo-China

The French fought long and hard to gain control of Indo-China. During the Tonkin campaign (right), they battled against the Vietnamese and various Chinese armies. Like the other European powers in the region, the French wanted access to valuable local produce, including rubber, rice, silk, and tea. They concentrated on modernizing their colonies and maximizing profits. Peasants were encouraged to sell their land and take jobs in the salt mines or opium factories.

Indo-China

French traders and missionaries had been interested in Indo-China since the 17th century, but it wasn't until Napoleon III's troops captured Saigon in 1858–59 that French influence took hold in the region. From the 1820s the British gradually took control of the western half of mainland Southeast Asia, including the Malay Peninsula. Siam (modern Thailand) lay between the French- and British-controlled territories, creating a buffer and never becoming a colony itself.

The Malay Peninsula

Britain gradually colonized the Malay Peninsula, beginning with the purchase of the island of Penang in 1796. British Malaya was never united under a single administration; even so, as the world's largest producer of tin and rubber, it was one of the most profitable of British colonies.

Right: Detail of a Burmese painting showing the royal elephant carrying the king in an elaborate enclosed basket.

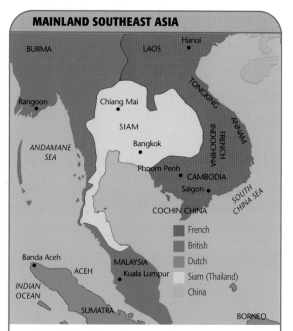

MAINLAND SOUTHEAST ASIA

The British and French in Mainland Southeast Asia
To protect India's borders, Britain annexed Burma in three separate wars between 1824 and 1886. Burma was administered as part of British India. The French captured Saigon in 1858–59 and then gradually acquired other territories. By 1887, after several years of undeclared war against China, they had successfully merged Cochin China, Cambodia, Annam, and Tongking into the Indo-Chinese Union. Laos was added in 1893.

Thailand

Thailand, known as Siam, was ruled by the Chakri Dynasty of kings in the 19th century. The first Chakri king, Rama I (reigned 1782–1809), moved the capital to Bangkok in 1782. He and his successors became increasingly worried as they saw neighboring countries being absorbed into European empires. However, they were able rulers and by studying English and learning European ways were able to keep their country independent.

Below: Rama IV (reigned 1851–68) was interested in astronomy. In 1868 he correctly predicted an eclipse of the sun and invited his doubting courtiers and members of the foreign community in Bangkok to accompany him to Sam Roi Yod to view the eclipse.

Island Southeast Asia

B y 1890 all the islands of Southeast Asia were under European rule. The Dutch East Indies covered almost all of what is now Indonesia, the Spanish controlled the Philippines, the British had Sarawak, Brunei, Borneo, and Papua (as well as Singapore), while the Germans and Portuguese held German New Guinea and East Timor, respectively. The Europeans met with fierce resistance as local rulers sought to protect their valuable lands and exports. Nationalist movements gathered force and there were frequent uprisings.

Below: A Wayang shadow puppet from Indonesia. Traditional culture was not strongly affected by Dutch rule.

Left: Raffles realized immediately that Singapore, with its deep natural harbor, abundant supplies of fresh water and timber, plus its position near the Straits of Malacca was exactly what he needed.

The Dutch

The Dutch consolidated their hold on fertile Java in the bitterly fought Java War of 1825–30. Dutch colonial authority rested on a tiny percentage of the overall population—there were just 42,000 Dutch troops and armed police to rule over a combined population of 62 million in Indonesia.

Singapore

Sir Stamford Raffles landed at Singapore in 1819. He negotiated a treaty with a local leader to develop the southern part of the island for the British East India Company. A free port was established which attracted Chinese, Arab, and Malay traders who were happy to avoid local Dutch levies. The settlement grew rapidly and the whole island became a British colony in 1824. Although the Dutch government protested, Singapore remained a British colony and continued to flourish throughout the 19th century.

Below: A view of Singapore from Government Hill in 1830.

ISLAND SOUTHEAST ASIA 1800–1900

1811
Dutch give up Java to British invasion.

1814–16
Dutch regain Java.

1819
British administrator Sir Stamford Raffles founds Singapore.

1825–30
Revolt against Dutch rule of Java.

1841
Sultan of Brunei gives Sarawak to the British to repay help in putting down rebellion.

1859
Dutch and Portuguese agree to partition island of Timor.

1873
Dutch attack the Aceh sultanate.

1884
Germany annexes northern New Guinea and the Bismarck Archipelago. Southern part of the island to Britain.

1898–99
Spanish-American War. The US take control of the Philippines.

Above: An American soldier sitting on a church statue during the Spanish-American War of 1898.

The Spanish in the Philippines

The Philippines had been a Spanish colony since the 16th century. The archipelago was administered from Mexico until 1821 and then directly from Madrid. The Spanish built towns, introduced new crops and livestock, and encouraged trade. Missionaries converted the population to Christianity and founded schools, universities, and hospitals. In 1896 a revolution against Spain ended with the establishment of the First Philippine Republic. However, the Treaty of Paris, at the end of the Spanish-American War, gave control of the Philippines to the United States.

Valuable Trade

Southeast Asia had been a sources of spices for European traders for centuries. At the end of the 19th century, rubber began to be commercially grown in Malaya and Indonesia from plants imported from South America. Rubber became an important crop, along with traditional exports such as rice, tin, copra, and oil.

Right: Indigenous peoples of New Guinea photographed in 1885 by a Danish explorer.

New Colonial Players

Germany was slow in developing its colonial interests in Southeast Asia but in 1884 it laid claim to the eastern part of the island of New Guinea. It was partly blocked by Australia, and then Britain, and its presence was limited to the northern part of New Guinea and the Bismarck Archipelago.

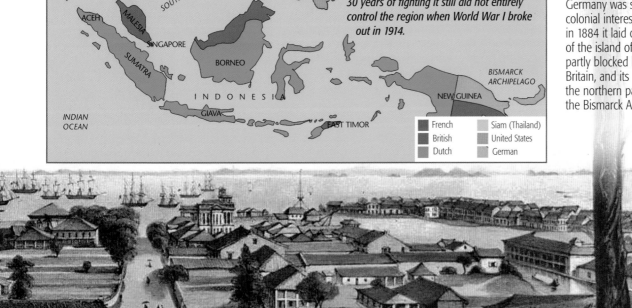

ISLAND SOUTHEAST ASIA 1800–1914

BURMA
TONKINO
LAOS
SIAM
ANNAM
FRENCH INDOCINA
CAMBODIA
COCINCINA
PHILIPPINES
SOUTH CHINA SEA
ACEH
MALESIA
SINGAPORE
SUMATRA
BORNEO
INDONESIA
GIAVA
EAST TIMOR
INDIAN OCEAN
BISMARCK ARCHIPELAGO
NEW GUINEA

French	Siam (Thailand)
British	United States
Dutch	German

A Time of Empire

The British traded Benkulen and other claims on Sumatra in exchange for Dutch recognition of their authority in Penang, Singapore, and the Straits of Malacca. The Sultanate of Aceh, on the northern tip of Sumatra, strongly opposed Dutch rule. In 1873 the Dutch declared war, but even after 30 years of fighting it still did not entirely control the region when World War I broke out in 1914.

China

China had enjoyed a long period of prosperity and growth under its Manchu rulers in the 18th century. The emperor Qianlong reigned for 60 years, abdicating in 1796 in order not to rule longer than his grandfather, Kangxi. In contrast, the 19th century would prove to be much more difficult. Despite efforts to keep them out, "barbarian" Western traders and businessmen gained ever larger footholds in China. British imports of opium from India led to two so-called Opium Wars. China lost both wars and was forced to concede even more trading rights to Western powers. To add to their problems, the Manchu also had to deal with internal corruption, high taxation, and frequent rebellions.

A painted fan decorated with a scene of Guangzhou, where the flags of different European trading nations are flying.

The Opium Wars

To stop the outflow of silver, which the Chinese paid to traders in return for opium smuggled in from India, and to fight the spread of drug addiction, in 1800 the Chinese banned the production and import of opium. In 1813 smoking the drug was made illegal, but smuggled quantities kept increasing. Finally, in 1839 Chinese officials seized 20,000 chests of opium from British merchants in Guangzhou, and the first of two Opium Wars broke out.

The wooden junks of the Chinese forces were no match for the iron steamships of the British in the Opium Wars.

Chinese workers packing crates of porcelain bound for Europe.

Trade with Europe

During the 19th century cotton goods became a major Chinese export, along with traditional silk. Europeans were keen to buy Chinese porcelain, furniture, and lacquer ware, and sales of tea to Britain soared. Goods were paid for in silver, but since China bought few goods in return, European merchants increasingly smuggled in opium from India to earn some of the silver back.

CHINA IN THE 19TH CENTURY

MONGOLIA
MANCHURIA
DZUNGARIA
XINJIANG
Beijing
KOREA
QINGHAI
JAPAN
TIBET
HENAN
GUIZHOU
TAIWAN
Hong Kong

Manchu China

The map shows the border of China in 1800. The Manchu lost territory steadily throughout the 19th century, including Hong Kong (to Britain), Macau (to Portugal), Taiwan and the Pescadores (to Japan), northwestern Xinjiang and Outer Manchuria (to Russia), as well as tributaries such as Indo-China (to France), Burma (to Britain), and Korea and the Ryukyu Islands (to Japan). At the end of the first Opium War, the Treaty of Nanjing forced the opening of five treaty ports to the British. By the terms of the treaty the island of Hong Kong was also handed over, and the mainland peninsula of Kowloon was added in 1860. In 1898 the New Territories were granted to Britain on a 99-year lease.

Right: This satirical drawing shows—from left—Queen Victoria (from Great Britain), Kaiser Wilhelm (from Germany), Tzar Nicholas (from Russia), Marianne (from France), and Emperor Mutsuhito (from Japan), as they are about to cut up China, as though it were a cake to be shared among them.

China Resists European Colonization

Although China never became a colony of any Western power, its economy was dominated by Europeans who created enclaves, such as Shanghai, and treated the Chinese with contempt. This led to frequent nationalist uprisings against foreigners.

Chinese government officials at the end of the 19th century.

The Taiping Rebellion

The Taiping rebellion consisted of a series of uprisings between 1851 and 1864. The rebellion's leader, Hong Xiuquan, was convinced by a dream that he was Jesus Christ's brother and the savior of China. His preaching gained him many followers, who combined Christian beliefs with communist ideals. They captured Nanking in 1853 and introduced many socialist policies, such as the abolition of private property. After Hong's death, the Manchus crushed the rebellion, in which about 20 million people had been killed.

Hong Xiuquan (1814–64) had failed to get a place in the Chinese civil service before he declared himself "Heavenly King of the Great Peace."

Commander Perry Arrives in Japan

In 1853 Commodore Perry steamed into Edo (Tokyo) Bay and presented a treaty of friendship and commerce to the emperor's representatives, implying that he would use power if the Japanese did not comply. He returned in 1854 with an even more powerful fleet of ships and the government signed the Treaty of Kanagawa, which opened up two ports to US trade.

Right: Until Perry arrived the Japanese had never seen a steamship. As this contemporary Japanese illustration shows, many thought it was a devilish machine.

Left: A samurai warrior's suit of armor, from the 1870s. It was during this time that the Japanese government officially abolished the samurai class of professional warriors.

Japanese pistol used during the civil war of 1867–68.

Japan

The military government established at the beginning of the 17th century stayed in power until the mid-19th century. Under this system, political power lay with the shogun at Kyoto, who controlled the local barons. All contact with foreigners was shunned, and despite repeated attempts by Russia and America to trade, Japan maintained its isolationist position. During the 1850s American ships tried to force trading contacts, which led to conflict. Anti-foreign feelings eventually caused a civil war in Japan (1867–68) and the overthrow of the shogun. He was replaced by the emperor. Under the emperor, Japan decided to compete with the West and began a rapid program of industrialization. It also built a powerful army and navy and set out to dominate East Asia. In wars against China and Russia, it gained more territories, including Taiwan (1895) and Korea (1910).

End of the Tokugawa Dynasty

Even before Perry's arrival, many of the great clans resented the Tokugawa government and supported the emperor in Kyoto. After Japanese ports were opened up to trade, the presence of foreign ships enraged these clans even further. Young samurai attacked the ships, but their attacks were quelled by a multinational force in 1863–64. Civil war followed in 1867–68, further weakening the shogunate. Tokugawa Yoshinobu, the last shogun, resigned in 1868, and Emperor Mutsuhito began the Meiji government.

JAPANESE EXPANSION 1895–1910

Japan

Territory acquired by 1910

SAKHALIN

KURIL ISLANDS

JAPAN

KOREA

• PORT ARTHUR

EDO •

KYOTO •

RYUKYU ISLANDS

TAIWAN

PACIFIC OCEAN

Left: Statue of a geisha from the 19th century.

Japan Dominates East Asia

Japan transformed itself from an isolated, conservative country to a great economic and military nation in just over 30 years. From acquiring its surrounding islands, it went on to fight modern wars to gain a mainland empire. In 1910 Japan extended its empire by formally annexing Korea, which it renamed Chosen. Japan continued to expand its realm and by the end of World War I gained commercial rights in Mongolia and Manchuria.

The Meiji Restoration

Prince Mutsuhito's accession to the throne marked the beginning of what is called the Meiji restoration. Influential Japanese and Westerners helped to strengthen the government and unify the country. Meiji abolished the feudal system of shoguns, daimyos, and samurais. New political, economic, and social systems were established and Western-style systems of law, administration, and taxation were introduced.

KEY EVENTS

1853
Commodore Matthew Perry arrives in Japan.

1854
Perry forces Japan to begin trading with the United States.

1863–64
Western naval force bombards Kagoshima and Shimonoseki in response to attacks on Western shipping.

1867–68
Civil war after Choshu and Satsuma clans oppose shogun.

1868
Emperor Meiji takes power from the last shogun; the capital is moved from Kyoto to Edo (modern Tokyo); the feudal system is abolished.

1879
Japan takes over the Ryukyu Islands.

1889
Western-style constitution and parliament are introduced.

1894–95
Japan defeats China in the Sino-Japanese War.

1904–05
Japan defeats Russia in the Russo-Japanese War

1910
Japan annexes Korea.

Japan Industrializes

Japan was one of the few Asian countries not colonized by the West. This was mainly due to industrialization, which began in 1873 when the Meiji government formally abolished the old feudal system. The Japanese government invited Western industrialists and engineers to advise Japan on how to modernize. Japanese businessmen set up coal mines, steel mills, shipyards, and factories.

Increasing Trade

The Japanese realized that they must increase trade in order to avoid European domination. A new central bank financed the building of railroads, factories and telegraph lines. Businessmen opened mines and factories to produce silk, textiles, metals, wood, and ships, all using modern Western technologies. In just over 30 years Japan became a strong economic power and foreign trade increased dramatically.

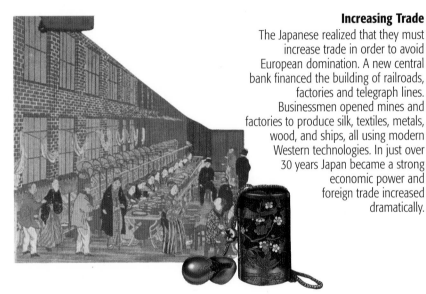

Army Reforms

Japan reorganized and modernized its military in order to compete with Western powers. In 1872 the emperor decreed a universal military service. The Japanese government brought in French officers to remodel the army and British seamen to help create a new navy equipped with modern ships. With its stronger military, Japan was able to look for new territories to colonize.

Well-equipped and organized Japanese troops fend off the Chinese during the Sino-Japanese War of 1894–95.

A Japanese cartoon showing a Japanese emperor baiting a Russian bear.

Sino-Japanese War

In 1894 a growing economic crisis in Korea prompted the Tonghak revolt. China and Japan intervened, but then began a struggle themselves for domination of the area. The Japanese navy crushed the Chinese at the Battle of the Yellow Sea, while the army defeated the Chinese in Manchuria. Under the Treaty of Shimonoseki, Japan gained Taiwan and the Pescadores, while Korea became briefly independent. Japan was also awarded the Liaodong Peninsula in southern Manchuria, but Russia, France, and Germany forced Japan to accept a payment instead.

Relations with Russia

In 1898 Japan and Russia signed a treaty pledging Korean independence. In 1900, however, Russian armies began to enter northern Korea. They attacked the Russian-controlled Port Arthur in southern Manchuria, starting the Russo-Japanese War. The Japanese defeated the Russians in less than 18 months. In the treaty of 1905, Japan was awarded the Liaodong Peninsula and the southern half of Sakhalin. Russia was also forced to recognize the predominant interests of Japan in Korea.

Central America and the Caribbean

The Spanish and Portuguese colonial powers were ousted from all of Latin America in a remarkably short period of time, from 1818 to 1828, leaving only some colonies in the Caribbean. Independence was gained through a combination of local rebellions and events in Europe. Mexico began its revolt in 1810, led by the Catholic priest Miguel Hidalgo y Costilla. The initial revolt failed, and Mexico did not gain its independence until 1821. Central Americans won freedom in the same year, with Costa Rica, El Salvador, Guatemala, Honduras, and Nicaragua becoming part of Mexico in 1822. The following year they broke away again and formed the United Provinces of Central America. By 1847 each of the five states was an independent republic. Panama was a Colombian province until 1903, when it rebelled with the help of the United States and became independent. British Honduras (present-day Belize) became a British colony in 1862 and only gained independence in 1981.

Economy

In 1884 the President of Costa Rica, Oreamuno, gave the American businessman Minor C. Keith huge tracts of land in exchange for building railroads. Keith grew bananas there and throughout Central America and the Caribbean. His company, United Fruit, became the largest employer in Central America and built one of the largest merchant navies in the world. However, the profits from United Fruit and other US companies did not go to ordinary people; they were paid to corrupt local politicians or exported north with the produce.

Justo Rufino Barrios, president of Guatemala (1873–1885), was known for his liberal reforms and attempts to reunify Central America.

A locally made vase shows the three constituents of the Latin American population: indigenous, Spanish, and African.

Unity in Central America

The United Provinces of Central America, formed in 1823, consisted of Guatemala, El Salvador, Honduras, Nicaragua, and Costa Rica. It dissolved in civil war between 1838 and 1840. Various attempts were made to reunite it, but none succeeded for any length of time. Guatemalan President Justo Rufino Barrios tried in the 1880s and was killed in the process. A union of Honduras, Nicaragua, and El Salvador as the Greater Republic of Central America lasted from 1896–98.

A Creole overseer on a banana plantation in Central America. Once slavery was abolished, the backbreaking work was carried out by local inhabitants, including freed slaves.

CENTRAL AMERICA AND THE CARIBBEAN

UNITED STATES OF AMERICA

ATLANTIC
OCEAN

MEXICO
1821

MEXICAN
GULF

BAHAMAS
1973

CUBA
(INDIP. DA SPAGNA)
1902

DOMINICAN REPUBLIC
(INDI. FROM HAITI)
1844

HAITI
1804

GIAMAICA
1862

PUERTO RICO
(FROM SPAIN TO U.S.A.)
1898

UNITED PROVINCES
OF CENTRAL
AMERICA
1823

CARIBBEAN
SEA

PANAMA
(IND. FROM COLOMBIA)
1903

GREAT COLOMBIA

Fighting for Freedom

Spanish and Portuguese colonies in Central America and the Caribbean gained their independence during the 19th century. The map shows the dates when countries became independent. Haiti was the first country to free itself from foreign rule in 1804 as the result of a slave revolt against plantation owners that began in 1791. The revolt was led by a slave named François Toussant L'Ouverture. Despite help from the British and French, independence was finally proclaimed on January 1, 1804.

South America

Spain and Portugal were greatly weakened by events in Europe, especially Napoleon's invasion of the Iberian Peninsula in 1807. Simón Bolívar and other American liberators quickly took the opportunity to rise up against and defeat the Europeans. But the newly liberated Latin Americans did not find it easy to make their new republics work efficiently and peacefully, and ambitious military leaders or wealthy landowners often seized power. Although slaves were freed by the end of the 19th century, independence did not bring much economic benefit to most ordinary people.

Peru

Peru declared its independence in 1821. The Spanish were defeated by General Sucre's troops three years later. Caudillos, or "military leaders," fought for control of the new nation, and stability was only achieved when General Ramón Castilla became president in 1845.

Right: Peruvian patriot José Olaya.

Chile

The Chileans began their revolt in 1810, when a provisional republic was declared. General Bernardo O'Higgins led the fight for independence. In 1814 he joined forces with the army of the Argentinian liberator, José de San Martin. The two men led the "Army of the Andes" from Argentina over the Andes into Chile, and in 1817 defeated the Spanish. Chile gained independence in 1818, and O'Higgins served as "supreme director" until 1823. He made sweeping reforms, but was forced to resign after revolts in the provinces.

Chileans rejoice beneath their new flag.

Brazil

Brazil declared independence in 1822, and Pedro I (1798–1834), son of John VI of Portugal, became emperor. He was forced to resign in 1831 and left his throne to his five-year-old son, Pedro II (1826–91), who ruled from 1840 for more than 50 years. Despite wars against Argentina and Paraguay, Brazil prospered; agriculture and industry expanded, railroads were built, and between 1870 and 1888 slavery was abolished. Brazil became a republic in 1889.

LATIN AMERICA

PANAMA 1903
CARIBBEAN SEA
VENEZUELA 1821
GUYANA IND. FROM BRITAIN 1966
NUOVA GRANADA 1831
SURINAME IND. FROM HOLLAND 1975
GREAT COLOMBIA
FRENCH GUYANA
ECUADOR 1830
BRAZILIAN EMPIRE
PERU 1824
BOLIVIA 1825
PARAGUAY 1811
CHILE 1818
PACIFIC OCEAN
UNITED PROVINCES OF RIO DELLA PLATA (ARGENTINA) 1816
URUGUAY 1828
ATLANTIC OCEAN

Latin America with Dates of Independence

The map shows the countries of Latin America with the date by which independence was gained. The largest country in South America, Brazil, won its freedom from Portugal without bloodshed. The Portuguese court had moved to Brazil during the Napoleonic Wars, and in 1815 the colony was made a kingdom. In 1822 independence was declared by Pedro I (1798–1834), who became emperor.

Simón Bolívar

Bolívar was South America's greatest general. Known as "the Liberator," he gained independence for Bolivia, Colombia, Ecuador, Peru, and Venezuela. Bolívar became president of Gran Colombia in 1819, and the area formerly known as Upper Peru took the name Bolivia in his honor. Rather than creating many independent nations, Bolívar had hoped to form a united Andean republic. But his dream was never realized and he became disillusioned by the political disagreements that put paid to unity.

Below: This detail from a fresco in the Simon Bolivar Amphitheatre in Mexico, shows the American creole soldier and statesman fighting Spanish royalist troops.

Below: Antonio José de Sucre (1795–1830) was born in Venezuela. He was the most able of Simón Bolívar's generals and helped to liberate Ecuador, Peru, and Bolivia. He served as president of Bolivia. The nation's legal capital, Sucre, is named after him.

Von Humboldt

In 1799 the German scientist Alexander von Humboldt (1769–1859, right) set out for Central and South America. He spent five years studying the geology and biology of Latin America, collecting a vast number of samples. On his return to Europe in 1804 he met Simón Bolívar, and it is said that he told Bolívar that South America was ripe for revolution.

Ending Slavery

Ideas about slavery changed markedly between the 18th and 19th centuries. In 1750 almost no one seriously questioned the existence of slavery, but by 1888 it had been abolished from the Americas and Europe. The ideas of Enlightenment thinkers such as Locke and Montesquieu led people to reflect carefully about equality and some began to think that slavery was unacceptable. In America, a radical Protestant group called the Quakers were among the first to mount organized opposition to slavery and by 1787 it had been eliminated from the northern states.

Great Britain

The international antislavery movement was largely organized by the British. During the 1780s antislavery reformers had decided to work first to end the trading of slaves (rather then the abolition of slavery itself which they felt would come naturally once the sale of slaves had been abolished). By 1807 the British parliament had voted to eliminate the slave trade throughout the British Empire. They also sent ships to the coast of Africa to arrest any slaving ships. By 1865 an estimated 150,000 slaves had been emancipated in this way. These people were often sent to Sierra Leone or Liberia, two African states founded by Britain and the United States, respectively, as homes for freed slaves.

Left: William Wilberforce was the founder of the Society for the Abolition of the Slave Trade. A British politician, he introduced a bill into parliament each year calling for the end of the slave trade; he was finally successful in 1808.

Below: A procession in Wiltshire, England, on February 3, 1808, after the slave trade was outlawed in the British Empire.

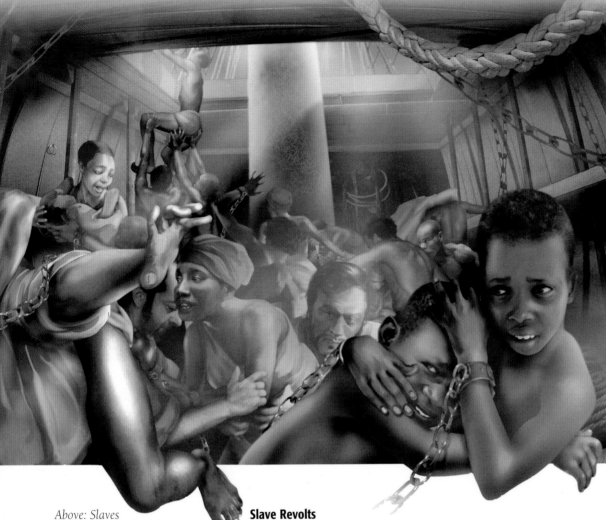

Above: Slaves were transported from Africa to the Americas in dreadful conditions and many died during the long journey.

Resurgence of Slavery

Despite the advances made in ending slavery there were some setbacks in the early years of the 19th century. World demand for products such as cotton, coffee, and sugar, led plantation owners in the southern United States, Brazil, and Cuba to actually increase their demand for slaves and many more Africans were transported across the Atlantic. Slavery did not end in the US until after the Civil War and it continued in Cuba until 1886 and in Brazil until 1888.

Right: Slaves harvesting coffee in Brazil. Between 1800 and 1855 about two million Africans were brought to Brazil.

Slave Revolts

Slaves also often tried to take the matter into their own hands by organizing revolts against their owners. A revolt in Haiti was successful in ending slavery and in freeing the colony from its Spanish overlords. Other revolts in the Caribbean during the 1820s and 1830s were brutally repressed.

Abolition of Slavery

Slavery was gradually abolished in Latin America as the various countries achieved independence. In the 1820s, British antislavery reformers abandoned the goal of gradually emancipating slaves and began to demand a complete and immediate end to slavery. They were successful in 1833 when their parliament abolished the right of British subjects to hold slaves. The other European colonial powers gradually followed suit, until slavery no longer existed.

1843
Argentina abolishes slavery.

1845
36 British Navy ships are assigned to the Anti-Slavery Squadron, making it one of the largest fleets in the world.

1847
Sweden abolishes slavery.

1848
Denmark abolishes slavery.

1851
Brazil ends slave trade.

1854
Peru abolishes slavery.

1854
Venezuela abolishes slavery.

1862
Cuba abolishes slave trade.

1863
Slavery abolished in Dutch colonies.

1865
United States abolishes slavery.

1873
Puerto Rico abolishes slavery.

1886
Cuba abolishes slavery.

1888
Brazil abolishes slavery.

1890
Brussels Act: Treaty granting anti-slavery powers the right to stop and search ships for slaves.

1896
France abolishes slavery in Madagascar.

1897
Zanzibar abolishes slavery.

World Trade

During the 19th century world trade was dominated by the industrialized nations of Europe and the United States. They traded manufactured goods and food among themselves and, increasingly, with countries in Asia, Latin America, and Africa. The infrastructure, such as railroads, roads and ports, that was required to support global trade was built by the industrialized nations in many parts of the world. However, economies in traditional societies were often destroyed by the demands of the Europeans and any opposition to them was usually brutally repressed. Large gold rushes in California, Australia, South Africa, and Canada increased the supply of money available and helped sustain international trade.

Gold standard

Increasing global trade required an international standard for currencies. Britain adopted the gold standard in 1821, by which different country's currencies were convertible into gold at a fixed rate and international debts were met in gold. If a country had a trade deficit, there would be an outflow of gold, reducing its money supply. This would lead to lower prices, which would encourage exports.

1 Local people in the Niger Delta extract oil from palms using traditional methods.

2 British merchants collect the palm oil and ship it back to Britain.

Global Trading

Industrialized countries in Europe imported raw materials from their colonies, turned them into manufactured goods in their factories, and then either sold them at home or re-exported them back to the colonies. The series of illustrations above shows how the British imported palm oil from the Niger Delta, in Africa, and used it to manufacture soap, which was then exported all over the world.

WORLD SHIPPING ROUTES AND COALING STATIONS

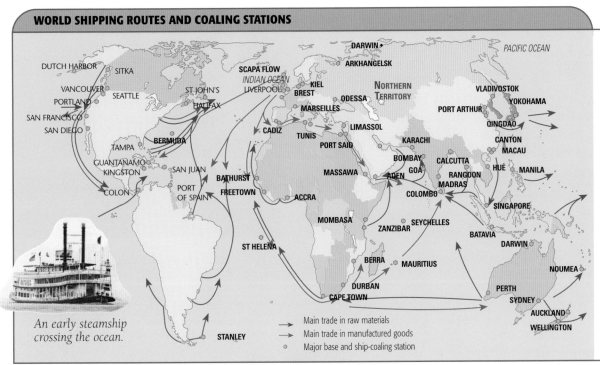

DUTCH HARBOR · SITKA · VANCOUVER · PORTLAND · SEATTLE · SAN FRANCISCO · SAN DIEGO · TAMPA · BERMUDA · GUANTANAMO · KINGSTON · SAN JUAN · COLON · PORT OF SPAIN · ST JOHN'S · HALIFAX · BATHURST · FREETOWN · ACCRA · ST HELENA · STANLEY

SCAPA FLOW · LIVERPOOL · KIEL · BREST · MARSEILLES · CADIZ · TUNIS · PORT SAID · ODESSA · LIMASSOL · MASSAWA · MOMBASA · ZANZIBAR · BERRA · DURBAN · CAPE TOWN · SEYCHELLES · MAURITIUS

DARWIN · ARKHANGELSK · NORTHERN TERRITORY · VLADIVOSTOK · PORT ARTHUR · YOKOHAMA · QINGDAO · CANTON · MACAU · KARACHI · BOMBAY · CALCUTTA · HUÉ · GOA · ADEN · RANGOON · MADRAS · MANILA · COLOMBO · SINGAPORE · BATAVIA · DARWIN · PERTH · SYDNEY · NOUMEA · AUCKLAND · WELLINGTON

INDIAN OCEAN

PACIFIC OCEAN

→ Main trade in raw materials
→ Main trade in manufactured goods
● Major base and ship-coaling station

An early steamship crossing the ocean.

Increased Trade

The canals opened at Suez (1869) and Panama (1914) cut voyage times around Africa and South America, and between 1850 and 1914 the world's merchant fleet expanded almost fourfold. Fast and efficient sea routes, combined with the opening up of fertile lands in Canada, the United States, Australia, Russia, and Argentina, brought down the price of wheat and other staple foods in industrialized nations.

3 *The palm oil is manufactured into soap in British factories ready for consumption at home or re-export.*

4 *Families in Africa, where the raw material originated, buy imported British soap. Soap was marketed as a "civilizing" product.*

Ship Design

The introduction of steam had a great impact on trade. The first Mississippi steamboat left New Orleans in 1812, and seven years later the American-built Savannah became the first steamship to cross the Atlantic. By 1835 paddle-steamers were making regular transatlantic crossings. Ports were modernized and enlarged to handle the new, bigger ships and larger cargoes. Clippers were still the fastest ships, however, speeding to Europe with wool from Australia and tea from China.

Gold Fever

Gold has been known and highly valued since ancient times, but in 1821 when Great Britain introduced the gold standard (see page 218), it became a truly global currency. As new territories opened up in Canada, Australia, New Zealand, South Africa, and many other places too, gold was often discovered and a great "gold rush" would follow. The many gold rushes of the 19th century contributed to the political and economic growth of the surrounding regions, helping to develop and enlarge new colonies. The discovery of gold usually led to the construction of railroads and telegraph lines as well as cities with banks, roads, businesses, and bustling social activities.

Right: Prospectors arriving in the Klondike region. Many of the miners, who were mainly men (although there were some women too), carried everything they owned on their backs.

The Klondike

The discovery of gold along the Klondike River, near Dawson, in Yukon, Canada, in 1896 led to the last great gold rush of the 19th century. News of the strike spread fast and thousands of prospectors had arrived by 1898. The population of the once tiny town of Klondike swelled to more than 40,000, almost causing a famine since there was barely enough food to go around. People from all walks of life headed for the Yukon from as far away as New York, Britain, and Australia. Surprisingly, a large proportion were professionals, such as teachers and doctors, who gave up respectable careers to make the journey. Most of them knew that their chances of finding significant amounts of gold were slim, but they went anyway, just for the adventure. As with other gold rushes, the arrival of many adventurous souls in search of fortune contributed greatly to the economic development of the entire region.

Below: There were several gold rushes in Australia. The scene below shows the early stages of the gold rush in Victoria in 1851. This was the biggest of the Australian rushes and contributed greatly to the political and economic development of Victoria and the city of Melbourne.

Above: Chinese gold miners during the gold rush in California. The Chinese had a good knowledge of minefields and the best technology to extract gold efficiently. Chinese workers migrated to many of the gold rush areas. Many stayed on, creating the beginnings of a multicultural society in some parts of the New World.

GOLD RUSHES

1829
Georgia Gold Rush, in the Appalachians, USA.

1848–52
California Gold Rush, in the Sierra Nevada, USA.

1851
Victoria Gold Rush, in Australia.

1851
Queen Charlotte's Gold Rush, is the first of several gold rushes in British Columbia, Canada.

1861–63
Central Otago Gold Rush, in New Zealand.

1880s onward
Tierra del Fuego, in Argentina.

1886
Witwatersrand Gold Rush, in South Africa, leads to the founding of Johannesburg.

1893
Kalgoorlie Gold Rush, in Western Australia.

1898–99
Klondike Gold Rush, in the Yukon, Canada.

Australia

The British explorer James Cook claimed New South Wales in Australia for Britain. The arrival of the British in Sydney Cove resulted in catastrophic changes for the Aboriginal people who had been living in Australia for at least 40,000 years. The British claimed New South Wales was unoccupied, largely based on Cook's incorrect reports that the Aboriginals were not settled there. New South Wales was established by the British as a penal settlement. Western Australia and Queensland were also founded as penal colonies, but free settlers colonized South Australia and Victoria. Convicts built roads, churches, and government buildings until as late as 1868, even as growing numbers of immigrants arrived from 1830 onward. They were attracted by the opening up of grazing land for merino sheep and beef cattle, and later by the gold rush.

Exploration

By 1804, Matthew Flinders in his sloop "Investigator" had circumnavigated Australia and proved it was an island continent. In 1813, explorers crossed the Blue Mountains west of Sydney and found land suitable for crops and cattle. Between 1820 and 1850, inland explorers discovered more pastoral land in eastern Australia as well as large rivers such as the Murray and the Darling. Others discovered hot, arid regions, unsuitable for farming. Burke and Wills (above), with their camels and horses, first crossed the continent in 1860–61.

Above: A view of Sydney from the North Shore.

Below: An entire British family arrives in Adelaide. Australia was an expensive, six-week-long sea voyage from Europe. Immigrants leaving Britain knew that they would not see home again.

AUSTRALIA

1770
James Cook lands at Botany Bay.

1778
First British convicts arrive on the First Fleet.

1801–03
Flinders circumnavigates Australia.

1813
Blue Mountains crossed.

1817
Governor Lachlan Macquarie formally adopts the name "Australia" for the Colony.

1825
Tasmania secedes from New South Wales.

1829–36
Free colonies established in Australia.

1851
Gold rush in New South Wales and Victoria.

1901
British colonial rule of Australia ends.

Aborigines

The Australian colony's first Governor, Arthur Phillip, treated the Aborigines with respect, but most of his successors did not. There was much violent conflict. In their search for farming country, the Europeans invaded Aboriginal food-gathering and hunting territories, and forcibly occupied their lands. The Aborigines had no choice but to give up their traditional way of life. Infectious European diseases such as influenza and measles, as well as extreme poverty, caused the deaths of many Aborigines.

LAND USE IN AUSTRALIA

INDIAN OCEAN

PACIFIC OCEAN

• DARWIN

NORTHERN TERRITORY

AUSTRALIA

WESTERN AUSTRALIA

QUEENSLAND

SOUTH AUSTRALIA

BRISBANE •

• PERTH

NEW SOUTH WALES

SOUTHERN OCEAN

• ADELAIDE

CANBERRA •
VICTORIA   • SYDNEY

• MELBOURNE

By 1845   By 1900

By 1860   Since 1900

By 1880   Not used

TASMANIA

The Search for "Fresh Pastures"

When Charles Darwin visited New South Wales in 1836, he observed that the settlers were obsessed with money and sheep. Darwin also noted the continual push for "fresh pastures." Successive colonial governors failed to control the grab for land. However, by 1850 these so-called "squatters" had seized millions of acres of land. For most of the 19th century, the Australian colonies existed separately. Gradually, however, the colonials came to see themselves as Australians rather than as Victorians or Queenslanders. As no single colony could produce a defense force, protecting the coastline required a national strategy. In 1898 a new constitution was agreed, with the British monarch retained as head of state. British colonial rule ended in 1901 when Edmund Barton became prime minister of the Commonwealth of Australia with its new capital in Canberra.

WAITANGI

Territory purchased from
Ngai Tahu 1844–64

AUCKLAND

Center of Maori King
Movement 1858

NORTH ISLAND

Maori land confiscated
by Government 1864–67

TASMAN SEA

WELLINGTON

CHRISTCHURCH

SOUTH ISLAND

*PACIFIC
OCEAN*

DUNEDIN

STEWART ISLAND

*The New Zealand Wars, also known as the
Land Wars, were fought between 1845 and
1872 mainly over land ownership issues.
The Treaty of Waitangi was supposed to
guarantee Maori ownership of land and
fishing rights, but large tracts of land were
confiscated by the government in 1863.*

New Zealand

The first Europeans to reach New Zealand were the Dutch explorer Abel Tasman and his crew in 1642. No Europeans returned until British explorer James Cook's voyage of 1768–71. Cook reached New Zealand in 1769 and mapped almost the entire coastline. After that, New Zealand was visited by whaling, sealing, and trading ships from Europe and North America. They traded food and goods, especially metal tools and weapons, with the Maori in exchange for timber, food, artifacts and water. From the early 19th century, Christian missionaries began to settle in New Zealand, eventually converting most of the Maori population.

*Above: Settlers introduced
sheep which flourished on
the good agricultural land.*

*Below: Maori warriors
prepare for war by
dancing the Haka.*

Settlers and the Maori

At first, most Maori welcomed the new arrivals, trading their decorative wooden carvings, food, flax mats, and shrunken human heads for metal products such as nails, axes, and guns, as well as rum. In the 1820s some Maori chiefs, including Hongi Hika, traded goods for muskets, with which they attacked and killed their tribal enemies. Musket use spread south, in a series of tribal wars that disrupted the traditional Maori way of life.

Treaty Of Waitangi

In 1840, the Treaty of Waitangi appointed Queen Victoria as the supreme ruler, or sovereign, of New Zealand. In return, Maori chiefs were promised protection and possession of their property and fishing grounds if they agreed to sell land only to the Crown. However, such transactions created problems, as Maori land was held communally rather than individually owned, and some chiefs refused to sign the Treaty. Under the Treaty, the Maori people became British subjects.

Below: View of Queen Street, Auckland, toward the end of the 19th century. Auckland grew quickly around its port after 1840.

The Treaty of Waitangi was signed in the Bay of Islands on February 6, 1840. Because the English and Maori language versions of the Treaty differed significantly, there is no consensus as to exactly what was agreed.

KEY DATES

1769
James Cook maps NZ coastline.

1800
European settlement begins.

1814
British missionary Samuel Marsden founds mission in the Bay of Islands.

1840
Treaty of Waitangi.

1845–72
Land Wars.

1854
Parliament meets for first time.

1856
Colony becomes self-governing.

1865
Wellington becomes the capital.

1890s
Refrigerated shipping allows NZ to base economy on export of meat and dairy products to Britain.

1893
NZ is the first country in the world to grant women the right to vote.

1907
New Zealand becomes a Dominion of the British Empire.

A Farming Economy

More and more settlers came after 1840, mainly from Great Britain and Ireland. By 1859 they outnumbered the original Maori inhabitants, many of whom died of European diseases to which they had no resistance. Farming became the economic backbone of the country with meat, wool, and dairy products exported mainly to Great Britain.

Africa Before Colonization

During the first part of the 19th century most of Africa, then known to Europeans as the "Dark Continent," was free from outside imperialist powers. During the course of the century explorers, adventurers, and Christian missionaries journeyed widely through the continent, including the northern deserts and central rainforests. The Europeans became aware that there were vast, untapped resources in Africa, including diamonds and gold.

Early colonization

Before 1880 only two African regions were colonized by Europeans on a large scale. Northern Algeria was invaded by the French in 1830, and in southern Africa the original Dutch Cape Colony had been seized by the British. Then came the formation of the Afrikaner states of Transvaal and Orange Free State. Apart from this, there were Portuguese territories in Angola and on the east coast, as well as Spanish, British, and French trading stations and those slaving ports that still existed.

African Empires

African leaders continued to build their empires after the arrival of Europeans. As European countries developed more of a demand for Africa's resources, including slaves, they began to claim more power in the continent. Despite this, during the 18th century and early part of the 19th century the majority of African leaders managed to retain political control of their kingdoms.

Exploration

The best-known African explorers were David Livingstone and Henry Morton Stanley (1841–1904), a British-American journalist. Livingstone first crossed the continent in the 1850s. In 1871 an American newspaper hired Stanley to look for Livingstone, of whom nothing had been heard for some time. When he met Livingstone on the shores of Lake Tanganyika, Stanley greeted him with the famous words: "Dr Livingstone, I presume?"

Below: Scottish missionary and explorer David Livingstone traveled through Africa in 1850 with his wife and four small children.

The Great Trek

The Dutch East India Company founded the Cape Colony in modern South Africa as a supply station in 1652. The British seized the Cape Colony from the Dutch in 1806. The British and Dutch settlers did not get along well; they fought over land, protection from attack by indigenous peoples, and the fact that the British had abolished slavery, among other things. Starting in 1836, some 6,000 Boer (Dutch) families, together with large numbers of Khoikhoi and black servants, gathered up their belongings and traveled by ox-wagon up into the Highveld interior to the north of the eastern Cape frontier. Fewer Boer families migrated from the western Cape, where they were more prosperous on their grain farms and vineyards and therefore less concerned about land shortages and frontier pressures. The exodus from the Cape was not organized in a single movement, but it became known as the Great Trek, and those who took part were called Voortrekkers (pioneers).

Above: The Voortrekkers on their long journey north.

The Partition of Africa

In the 1860s Europeans became aware that there were large, untapped resources in Africa, including diamonds and gold. During the last quarter of the century they sent armed expeditions to claim exclusive rights over vast territories. Many African peoples resisted, but the Europeans used their advantage of superior weapons to dominate and divide up the continent. By the end of the century most of Africa was under European control.

Mineral Wealth

Two discoveries changed the European attitude to southern Africa: in 1866 diamonds were discovered on the banks of the Orange River, and in 1886 prospectors struck gold near Pretoria. Fortune hunters descended on the region, including Englishman Cecil Rhodes, who gained control of the diamond mines and became prime minister of Cape Colony.

Left: French diplomat Paul Cambon and British prime minister Lord Salisbury discussing Africa in 1899.

Below: This illustration celebrates the Ethiopian victory over the Italians at the battle of Adwa in 1896.

Above: South Africa had some of the richest diamond-bearing territories on the planet. It all began in 1866 on a farm near Hopetown, when a young shepherd named Erasmus Jacobs found a small white pebble on the bank of the Orange River. It was passed on to a neighboring farmer who sent it to Grahamstown to be identified. The pebble turned out to be a 21.25 carat diamond, which came to be known as the "Eureka."

The Berlin Conference

In 1884–85 representatives of 15 European nations met in Berlin to discuss how they would proceed in Africa. The Conference did not give specific territories to specific countries, but it did establish guidelines as to how the Europeans could take over certain areas. This led to rapid, piecemeal, and violent colonization of the entire African continent. Some countries worked through trading ventures such as the German South West and East Africa Companies or the British South Africa Company.

Resistance

Some African states collaborated with the invaders, but most opposed them fiercely. The Mahdist revolt in Sudan and defiance by the Asante proved difficult for the Europeans to quell, but other uprisings were quickly put down. Ethiopia was the only state that successfully opposed an invading colonial army, in this case from Italy. The Italians were definitively beaten at the battle of Adwa in 1896 and forced to withdraw. This defeat of a colonial power and the ensuing recognition of African sovereignty became rallying points for later African nationalists.

AFRICA IN 1913

- French
- British
- German
- Portuguese
- Belgian
- Spanish
- Italian
- Anglo-Egyptian

Map labels: RIO DE ORO, MOROCCO, ALGERIA, LIBYA, EGYPT, FRENCH WEST AFRICA, FRENCH EQUATORIAL AFRICA, SUDAN, ERITREA, GOLD COAST, NIGERIA, ETHIOPIA, CAMEROON, UGANDA, KENYA, ITALIAN SOMALILAND, GABON, BELGIAN CONGO, GERMAN EAST AFRICA, ANGOLA, NORTHERN RHODESIA, SOUTHERN RHODESIA, MOZAMBIQUE, MADAGASCAR, GERMAN SOUTH WEST AFRICA, UNION OF SOUTH AFRICA

Slicing it Up

France and Britain were the major players in Africa. The French occupied most of north western Africa, Gabon, and the island of Madagascar in the south. The British controlled most of southern Africa, Kenya, Uganda, Egypt, Nigeria, and other territories. Germany had South West Africa, East Africa, and the Cameroon, while the Italians took Libya, Eritrea, and part of Somaliland. Belgium ruled the Congo and the Portuguese had Angola and Mozambique. Only Ethiopia and Liberia stayed free.

Taken by Force

The imperial powers usually had well organized armies and modern technology to take their colonies by force. With their modern weapons, European armies were able defeat armies that far outnumbered them. The invention of the machine gun in 1884, for example, enabled 320 French troops to overpower 12,000 African soldiers in Chad during a battle in 1899.

KEY DATES

1866
Diamonds found on the Orange River, in South Africa.

1883
French begin conquest of Madagascar.

1884–85
The Berlin Conference.

1885
King Leopold of Belgium establishes Congo Free State.

1886
Gold discovered near Pretoria, in South Africa.

1885
British save Khartoum from Mahdist siege.

1889
Italy establishes first colony in Eritrea.

1890
First Nama rebellion against Germans in South West Africa.

1892
France defeats the Tukulor empire in modern Mali.

1893
France defeat Fon warriors in Dahomey.

1894
Britain occupies Uganda.

1896
Ethiopian victory over Italians at Battle of Adwa.

1898
Kitchener defeats Mahdists at Omdurman.

1900
Britain finally defeats the Asante in West Africa.

Northern Africa

The British and French ruled most of northern Africa, with the Italians controlling parts of Libya and Eritrea and the Spanish parts of what is now Morocco. The French invaded Algeria in 1830–31 and gradually spread until they controlled most of West Africa. The British made Egypt a protectorate in 1882 then spread south into Sudan. Rivalry between the two colonial powers came to a head in 1898 at Foshoda when British forces found the French flag flying over territories they regarded as their own. The French withdrew but the incident led to the *Entente Cordiale* of 1904 which calmed French and British disputes in Africa.

Top: Traditional costumes of people in Algeria in the 1880s.

The raising of the French flag in Timbuktu (modern Mali), in 1894.

Left: This Yoruba statue from West Africa shows a Catholic missionary travelling on a donkey.

Missionaries and Religion

There were Christian missionaries all over Africa throughout the 19th century. They were especially important in opposing and helping to end the slave trade. Many people in northern Africa were Muslim while others maintained traditional beliefs. Opposition to the colonial powers sometimes coalesced into religious opposition too, for example when Muhammad Ahmed (the Mahdi) rebelled against Anglo-Egyptian rule and founded a strict Islamic state in Sudan.

Right: Behanzin, the king of Dahomey (modern Benin). The French had a trade agreement with Dahomey, but war broke out in 1892 and the kingdom became part of French West Africa.

Imperial Power

The colonial powers roughly imposed Western ways and methods of trade and taxation. They abolished local currencies, replacing them with European coinage. To pay the new taxes, many Africans became wage laborers on the large sugar, cocoa, and rubber estates that sprang up, worked in the mines, or helped build infrastructure, such as the railroads. Many aspects of the local cultures were destroyed and the people were resentful and looking for ways to revolt.

Above: The Suez Canal was a vital shipping route for Britain as it greatly shortened the sea journey to its colonies in India, Australia and New Zealand.

Above: European tourists in front of the Sphinx at Giza, Egypt.

Right: A European woman meets local women in Algiers.

Egypt and the Suez Canal

The Suez Canal, opened in 1869, was largely financed by the French and had been designed and built by a Frenchman (Ferdinand de Lesseps). But when the Egyptian ruler had financial difficulties in 1875 he sold most of his shares to the British government. In 1879 the Egyptian ruler refused to honor his foreign debt and Britain and France forced him to abdicate. Despite rebellion, Britain then took control of Egypt and slowly moved its sphere of influence south through the Sudan and British East Africa.

Below: Leopold II (1835–1909) greatly expanded the Belgian presence in Africa. He made a fortune from rubber and ivory.

The Belgian Congo

In 1879–84 King Leopold II of Belgium hired Henry Morton Stanley, who had extensively explored the Congo River region, to set up Belgian outposts along the river. In 1885 the region became Leopold's personal colony, named Congo Free State. The king's harsh rule brought protests, however, and the Belgian government took control in 1908, renaming the colony the Belgian Congo.

Left: A French soldier plants the tricolor in Madagascar.

Other Colonial Powers in Southern Africa

France claimed the island of Madagascar and the Portuguese ruled over Angola and Mozambique. Germany had control of German South West Africa. German settlers were encouraged to settle on land belonging to the Herero and Nama tribes. In 1903–04 the Herero and Nama people rebelled against the colony. Their rebellion was brutally put down; more than 80 percent of the Herero lost their lives.

SOUTHERN AFRICA

1814
Britain acquires the cape Colony.

1820
20,00 new British settlers arrive at the Cape Colony.

1834
Britain abolishes slavery in its empire.

1835–37
Boers make the Great Trek north to Natal.

1843
Britain annexes Natal.

1852–54
Britain recognizes independence of Transvaal and Orange Free State.

1871
Diamonds found at Kimberley.

1877–78
British annex Transvaal.

1881
First Boer War.

1886
Gold found in Transvaal.

1889–1902
Second Boer War.

1910
Union of South Africa formed.

Southern Africa

In 1800 there were already 15,000 Boer (Afrikaans or Dutch) farmers living in the Cape Colony. Britain annexed the region early in the 19th century and subsequent friction with the Boers caused many to emigrate north in the Great Trek (see page 227). In 1843 the British annexed Natal and the Boers moved further north again to form the Orange Free State and the Transvaal. When diamonds and gold were discovered there in the 1860s and 1880s, respectively, the British again annexed Boer territories. This led to the Boer Wars and the ultimate defeat of the Boers.

Left: Boers soldiers in the Second Boer War of 1899–1902.

The Boer Wars

Beginning in 1880, the British and the Boers (from the Dutch for "farmers") fought a series of wars for control of southern Africa. In the first Boer War (1881) the Boers rebelled against British rule and regained the Afrikaner state of Transvaal. In the second Boer War (1899–1902), the Boers were successful at first, besieging Ladysmith, Mafeking, and Kimberley. The British, under Lord Kitchener and Lord Roberts, brought in many more troops and finally defeated the Boers. The two Afrikaner states became British colonies.

Below: German colonial troops attacking the Herero people in 1904.

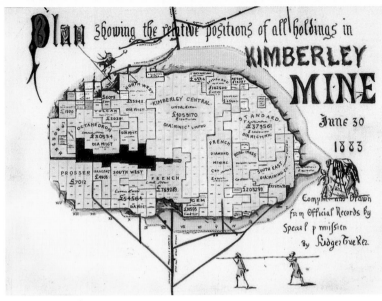

South African Gold

The gold rush in South Africa started in 1886 after gold was found in Witwatersrand. People from as far away as Britain and India poured into the Transvaal and the region quickly became the world's largest goldfield. Growth was spectacular, with new roads and railroads transforming the countryside, and foreign investment and expertise quickly creating a modern nation of the whole area. To protect their interests in the area the British annexed the Transvaal and invaded Zululand.

Below: A Zulu shield and spears. The Zulus developed a new kind of spear, called an assegai, that was not thrown at enemies in battle but used to stab them.

The Zulu People

The kingdom of the Zulus, a Bantu people, was formed in the early 19th century. The Zulus clashed with the Boers in 1838, and won a great battle at Isandlhwana against the British in 1879. They were finally defeated by the British at Ulundi. The Zulu king was exiled and former Zululand was divided into 13 chieftaincies. The end of the Zulu military threat encouraged the Boers to shake off British power in Transvaal and led to the first Boer War (1881).

Below: A Zulu village. Zulu society was well organized, with clearly defined roles for men and women. Women worked in the fields and carried out domestic chores, including the weaving of baskets. Zulu homes were dome-shaped and had spartan furnishings. Millet was a staple crop and it was ground into a flour then cooked into a thick porridge. Zulu men married quite late, when they were in their mid-30s, while women were usually 10 to 15 years younger. Some wealthy men had more than one wife.

Glossary

Absolute monarchy A form of government where a king or queen has complete, or absolute, control over every aspect of the lives of his or her subjects. Absolute monarchs may claim to be accountable to God alone.

Anthrax An often lethal disease in humans and other animals caused by bacteria.

Anti-semitism A prejudice or bias against Jewish people.

Aristocracy A ruling class of people, usually families or dynasties, who inherit power, land, and wealth.

Armistice An agreement between warring armies to stop fighting, at least temporarily, usually so that they can discuss terms for permanent peace.

Ascetics People who live very simply and deny themselves worldly comforts and pleasures, usually for religious reasons.

Autocracy A form of government in which the political power is held by a single, self-appointed ruler, known as an "autocrat."

Bourgeoisie A term used to describe a social class of merchants, or wealthy middle class people.

Buccaneer A pirate, especially one preying on Spanish settlements in the West Indies during the 17th century.

Buddhism A religion based on the teachings of Buddha (c. 566–480 BCE). Buddhists believe that human beings face endless reincarnations (rebirths and deaths) unless they gain release through wisdom and peace.

Bushido The Japanese samurai's code of honor. The main rule was to be willing to die in the service of one's lord.

Caravan A company of traders traveling together, usually with a train of camels, through the desert or along the Silk Road.

Caravel A small Spanish or Portuguese ship of the 15th and 16th centuries. It had a broad bow and triangular sails.

Castes The hereditary classes that make up the social divisions of Hindu society in India.

Censorship When a government controls what is printed in books or newspapers, removing information it does not want to be made public.

Ceramic A hard, breakable material made by firing clay in an oven.

Cholera An infectious disease that humans catch by eating food or drinking water that is contaminated with cholera bacteria.

City-states Independent cities that govern themselves through a council or a ruling family.

Civil war Armed conflict between different groups of people from the same country.

Clan A group of people belonging to the same tribe who are related or share a common mythical ancestor.

Clergy the official religious leaders of a given religion. Priests, nuns, and bishops are some examples of the clergy in most Christian churches.

Cobbler A person who makes or repairs shoes.

Colonization The process by which settlers not only settled but completely took over the lands of the first indigenous inhabitants.

Communism A political system or philosophy that seeks to establish an egalitarian (equal for all) society where there are no social classes and property is owned equally by all.

Concerto A musical term that usually refers to a three-part musical work in which one solo instrument is accompanied by an orchestra.

Confederation A permanent union of sovereign states for common action in relation to other states.

Conglomerate A large company made up of many sections all carrying out different kinds of business.

Constitution A system for government, often written down, that establishes the rules and principles of a country.

Coptic An Afro-Asiatic language, written in the Greek alphabet. Also, anything that relates to the Coptic Church, an ancient Christian Church in Egypt.

Creole A term originally used to describe people born in European colonies in the Americas and other parts of the world. Later it came to refer to the languages they spoke, which were often a mix of European, African, and local languages.

Customs duties A tariff or tax paid when goods are imported or exported from one country or region to another.

Decentralize To move decision-making and/or government from large, central groups to smaller, local groups.

Deism The belief that a supreme God exists who created the physical universe, and that religious truths can be arrived at by the application of reason and observation of the natural world.

Despotism A form of rule where all power is in the hands of one person or a small group of people. A despot is someone who rules this way.

Diplomacy The art of managing international relations with other countries through negotiation rather than by warfare.

Divine right of kings A political and religious system where the king or queen is not controlled by a parliament, aristocracy, or any other group but is believed to rule directly under God.

Doubloon A gold coin used in Spain and Spanish America.

Dynasty A line of rulers coming from the same family, or a period during which they reign.

Economy The wealth and resources of a country or a region.

Empire All of the land controlled by a ruler or government, including overseas territories.

Empiricism In philosophy, a theory which says that knowledge comes from experience and evidence rather than from innate ideas.

Enclosure A process by which commonly owned land becomes privately owned.

Entrepreneur A person who owns a company and is responsible for the risks and general outcome.

Envoy A messenger sent by a government on a special mission and who acts as a representative of the government or state.

Exile The condition of having been forced to leave one's homeland.

Figurine A small statue.

Fluyt A Dutch cargo ship from the 17th century.

Folklore All of the tales, music, dance, legends, oral history, proverbs, jokes, popular beliefs, and customs, shared by a people.

Galleon A heavy, square-rigged ship used between the 15th and 18th centuries. It was a vessel for war or trading.

Gallows A frame, usually made of wood, used to hang people.

Goldsmith A craftsperson who specializes in working with gold and other precious metals, usually to make jewelry, utensils, or ceremonial objects.

Heir The next in line to the throne.

Hierarchy The arrangement of people or objects into an order of ranking, such as from bottom to top or from worst to best.

Hinduism The main religion of India, which involves the worship of many gods, a belief in reincarnation (being born again in another life), and a caste system.

Hominy A food dish made of dried maize (corn) kernels that have been treated with an alkali of some type. First made by Native Americans in present-day Guatemala at least 1500 years ago.

Indigenous Something that lives naturally in a particular region of the world.

Ingot A bar of metal, often gold.

Ivory The teeth of certain mammals. Elephant ivory is the most abundant form, from the long, external upper incisors of the animal, called tusks.

Jacobites Followers of the late-17th century movement dedicated to the return of the Stuart kings to the thrones of England and Scotland.

Jainism An ancient Indian religion, with its own scriptures.

Jesuits Members of the Society of Jesus. Founded by Ignatius de Loyola in 1540.

Kasbah A kind of medina, Islamic city, or fortress.

Latitude The distance of a point from the equator, measured in a North–South direction.

Limelight A type of stage lighting once used in theatres and music halls. Long since replaced by electric lighting, the term survives to describe someone in the public eye.

Longitude The distance of a point from the equator, measured in a East–West direction.

Loom A machine or device used to weave thread into fabric.

Luddites A social movement of British artisans who protested against changes brought about by the Industrial Revolution.

Missionary Someone who campaigns to increase membership of the Christian church.

Monarchist A person who believes in the monarchy (rule by a king or queen).

Morse code A way of encoding information into sequences of short or long sounds, pulses, or marks so that it can be sent by telegraph.

Mortgage The transfer of property to a lender (usually a bank) as security for a debt.

Mother-of-pearl The hard, shiny substance found inside the shells of certain mollusks, such as the oyster.

Muslims Followers of the religion of Islam who worship one God and honor the Prophet Muhammad.

Nationalism The idea or feeling of belonging to the same culture by sharing language, history, literature, customs and traditions.

Native American A person whose ancestors lived in the Americas before the European conquerors and settlers arrived.

No Theater A form of classic Japanese musical drama performed since the 14th century.

Nomadic A person who wanders and does not settle down in any particular place.

Obsolete Something that is out of date or old fashioned and has been replaced by something better and more advanced.

Orrery A mechanical device that shows the relative positions and motions of the planets and moons in the solar system.

Patriotism Devotion to and love of one's own country.

Peasant A farm worker who survives by working a small plot of land

Periodical A publication, such as a newspaper or magazine, that appears in a new edition on a regular schedule.

Philosophy The study of human thought about the meaning of life and the correct way to live.

Physicist A scientist who studies physics including basic concepts such as force, energy, and mass.

Pilgrim A person who makes a journey to a sacred place to show their devotion to God.

Pilgrim Fathers (or Mothers) The Puritan settlers at Plymouth colony in Massachusetts.

Pirate A robber operating at sea.

Plantation A large farm or estate where valuable agricultural products such as cotton, tobacco, or sugar are cultivated, usually by slaves or resident laborers.

Policy The course of action decided by a ruler, minister, government, or parliament.

Poorhouse Also known as a workhouse, where poor people were housed and had to work hard in harsh conditions to earn their keep.

Privateer A privately owned ship that can be commissioned by a government to fight against the enemy in wartime. Also the name for the captain or crew of this kind of ship.

Proletariat A class of society that doesn't own property or the means of production but works in exchange for wages.

Puritans Protestants in 16th and 17th century England who wanted greater reform of the church than what was carried out under the Reformation.

Quakers The Religious Society of Friends, established in England in the 17th century by people who were unhappy with existing Christian churches.

Reform To change an organization or system to make it work better or more efficiently.

Regent Someone who governs on behalf of a young prince or princess before they are old enough to become the next king or queen.

Republic A country in which the ruler is elected and is not a monarch who rules by birthright.

Revolution A change in power or government which occurs in a short period of time, often as a result of violents protests and struggle.

Rigging The ropes used for controlling sails and supporting the mast on board a ship.

Risorgimento An Italian term, meaning "revival," used to describe the period of Italian unification.

Romanticism A movement in Europe beginning in the late 17th century, with emphasis placed on feelings, passion, and creativity.

Rudder A flat piece attached to the base of a ship, at the stern. It allows it to change course.

Sanitation Ways of preventing humans from having contact with wastes, such as sewage, that can cause disease.

Sawmill A place where trees and logs are cut into boards.

Secular Something that is not religious, for example a government, country, organization, festival or building.

Serf A farm laborer who works on the land but does not own it.

Shareholders A person or company that owns shares in a joint stock company.

Shinto The name of the native religion of Japan. Believers worship a number of gods, from whom the emperor is thought to be descended.

Shipwright Someone who builds ships.

Shogun A Japanese hereditary military dictator who had greater power than the emperor.

Siege The surrounding of a city or fort by the army of their enemy in an attempt to capture it.

Sikhism A religious philosophy founded on the teachings of Nanak and nine successive gurus in 15th century northern India.

Slave A person who is treated as the property of another and who is forced to work.

Smallpox An infectious human disease that killed millions of people until it was eradicated (wiped out) at the end of the 20th century.

Smelting A process of heating ores (rock) so that they release metals, such as iron.

Sultan A royal ruler of a Muslim country.

Taoism A popular Chinese philosophy that argues for a simple, honest life and the noninterference in the course of natural events.

Terra-cotta Hard, unglazed earthenware, made from clay. Early cultures made pottery and sculpture from terra-cotta.

Textile A flexible material, usually made by weaving, knitting, or knotting fibers.

Trade Union An organization of workers who have banded together to achieve common goals such as better wages, or working conditions.

Treaty A written agreement between two or more countries, often drawn up to end a war.

Tricolor A flag or banner more-or-less equally divided into three bands of differing colors.

Typhus A group of diseases caused by bacteria that is carried by lice.

Viceroy A governor of a province or colony who rules in place of a king or queen.

Warlord A person with military power over a given territory that has no central authority. Warlords enforce their power by threatening or actually making war.

Zionism An international political movement that supported the establishment of a homeland for the Jewish people in Palestine.

Index

PICTURE CREDITS

All efforts have been made to obtain and provide compensation for the copyright to the photos and illustrations in this book in accordance with legal provisions. Persons who may nevertheless still have claims are requested to contact the copyright owners.

MAIN ILLUSTRATIONS: Giorgio Albertini pp. 156–157; Sergio Bacchin 170–171; Lorenzo Cecchi p. 65, 96–97; Francesca d'Ottavi pp. 74–75, 76–77, 79, 205, 216–217, 232–233; M. Gaudenzi pp. 12–13, 22–23, 26–27, 48-49b, 50–51b, 52–53b, 60–61, 92–93, 114–115, 134–135, 136, 140–141, 148–149, 220–221, 224–225, 226–227; Inklink p. 154, 166–167, 178–179; Alessandro Menchi pp. 10–11; MM comunicazione (M. Cappon, M. Favilli, G. Sbragi, C. Scutti) pp. 14–15, 16–17, 20–21, 56–57, 62–63, 66–67, 84–85, 94–95, 102–103, 112–113, 128–129, 146–147, 174–175, 188–189, 218–219; Claudia Saraceni 172–173, 187; Sergio pp. 70–71, 86–87, 152–153;

OTHER ILLUSTRATIONS: Studio Stalio (Alessandro Cantucci, Fabiano Fabbrucci, Andrea Morandi, Ivan Stalio), Lorenzo Cecchi, Paola Ravaglia

MAPS: M. Paola Baldanzi

PHOTOS: Bridgeman Art Library, London: pp. 28–29c, 30–31c, 32–33, 34–35, 40–41b, 42–43c, 46–47b, 54–55, 59, 88–89, 90–91, 99, 100–101, 104–105, 106–107, 110–111, 116–117, 118–119, 123, 124–125, 126, 131, 133, 139t, 145, 151b, 160t, 161, 162b, 163b, 164tl, 165c, 168, 169br, 171tl, 173t, 173br, 174c, 177, 180b, 182tr, 182cl, 183, 186b, 190c, 190b, 191br, 191c, 191tr, 193tc, 193c, 195, 198tl, 201b, 206cl, 209tr, 216b, 220t, 227t, 228–229, 230c; Getty Images: 223t; Granger: p. 9b; Hulton Archive / Getty Images: pp. 185c, 193br; Imagno / Getty Images: p. 174cr; Lonely Planet Images pp. 72–73b (Brent Winebrenner); ©Photo RMN pp. 68–69b (Michel Urtado); The Art Archive: 203b, 204b, 206–207b, 207t, 207cr, 212c, 215b, 216b, 221t, 222b, 228c, 230t, 231t;